THE
BRITISH EMPIRE
A STUDY IN COLONIAL GEOGRAPHY

BY

ALBERT DEMANGEON
PROFESSOR OF GEOGRAPHY AT THE SORBONNE

TRANSLATED BY

ERNEST F. ROW B.Sc. (Econ.) L.C.P.
AUTHOR OF "WORK WEALTH AND WAGES"
"ELEMENTS OF ECONOMICS" ETC.
TRANSLATOR OF GIDE'S "PRINCIPLES OF
POLITICAL ECONOMY"

NEW YORK
HARCOURT, BRACE AND COMPANY
1925

Printed in Great Britain by Turnbull & Spears, Edinburgh

THE BRITISH EMPIRE

TRANSLATOR'S NOTE

THE translator has endeavoured to provide an exact English version of Professor Demangeon's *L'Empire britannique*, which was published in 1923. No changes have been made in the text, except the turning of metric measures into their English equivalents and the occasional correction of an obvious slip or misprint.

In the footnote references the number in black type following the author's name is the number of the book in the Bibliography at the end of this volume, where details as to title and publisher will be found.

E. F. R.

CONTENTS

7

THE BRITISH EMPIRE

BOOK II

BRITISH COLONIZATION AND CIVILIZATION

BOOK III

IMPERIAL PROBLEMS

8

CONTENTS

.

THE BRITISH EMPIRE

INTRODUCTION

THE best way to obtain a real understanding of European colonization—one of the most impressive of modern migratory movements and commercial enterprises—is to study the British Empire. From the enormous number of its colonists settled beyond the seas, the vast trade to which it has given rise, and the changes it has effected in native customs and civilizations, we may obtain a picture, on a huge scale, of the colonizing spirit in action. The contrast, moreover, between the smallness of the mother country and the enormous extent of the lands she has gathered round her is so strong that this phenomenon seems the more unique and unprecedented.

No other subject yields richer or fuller material for the study of colonial geography, properly understood as an independent branch of knowledge. It is no part of our business to tell the story of colonial conquests, which is the affair of the historian ; or to describe the countries themselves, which is a matter of regional geography. Our main object is to study the effects arising from the contact between the two types of peoples who are called upon to associate with each other in a colony : the one civilized, well provided with capital and material goods, in search of new wealth, thoroughly mobile, and alive to the spirit of enterprise and adventure, the strange and the unknown ; the other isolated and self-centred, faithful to its ancient modes of living, with a limited outlook, and ill equipped with weapons and tools. Our task is to explain how the colonizing race has gone to work to exploit its new territory, to create wealth, and to rule and employ the natives, and how the colony has reacted, in virtue of its physical formation and the degree of civilization attained by its inhabitants, to the breath of the new spirit. We propose to show, therefore, within the broad framework, as it were, of human geography, how a group of men has succeeded in setting to work its faculties of invention, adaptation, acclimatization, and propagation in a very peculiar and very varied sphere of action.

British colonization as a national phenomenon has reacted profoundly on conditions of life in Great Britain itself ; but it is also a world-phenomenon, inseparable from the life of other nations. We may well ask what Great Britain would be like without her Empire, and also what the world would be like without it.

Of all the countries in this Europe of ours, which has done so much in the way of exploring, exploiting, and populating the earth, it is Great Britain whose colonizing instinct has contributed most toward giving it form and life. There is no British family but has a son beyond the seas ; no newspaper but keeps its readers informed of events in the far-off lands of the Empire ; no household that does not consume Imperial products ; no career for which the colonies can offer no outlet ; no industry that does not work for a colonial market ; no great seaport that does not trade with one or other of His Majesty's possessions ; no capitalist or *rentier* without colonial stocks and shares in his portfolio ; no security for the homeland unless the way to the colonies is open and free to the British Navy ; no war that has not extended the Empire or defended it from attack. The conception of the Empire is familiar to every Englishman, while to the British Government it is the supreme national interest—an interest of literally world-wide extent. Without its overseas possessions the United

INTRODUCTION

Kingdom is merely a small group of islands off the coast of Europe ; with them, it has become one of the poles of the human race. The Englishman has property everywhere, and everywhere the English tongue is spoken. The Englishman never feels alone in a foreign land, and no journey can take him far from the sight of his own flag. When he thinks of his country, he sees her wherever her ships are sailing. He is hurt if he feels that Continental affairs are checking her or absorbing her ; he is at ease if her outlook is upon the ocean. No other land has a greater portion of her body and her soul beyond the seas. Business houses, factories, merchant shipping, banks, and bookshops —what would Great Britain be without her Empire ?

And now what would the world be without the British Empire ? There is no ocean without a British coast-line ; no continent without some inhabitants of British race ; no coming and going without British means of communication. In every settlement of British colonists there are the same forms of civilization, the same domesticated animals, the same cultivated crops, the same kind of material existence, the same methods of exploiting the soil, and the same spiritual needs. Without the British Empire we should have a different distribution of the races of the earth, for it has altered the field of expansion of negroes, Indians, and whites. Europe faces the other peoples of the world with an Anglo-Saxon front : the yellow races in Oceania, in North America, and in the monsoon region of Asia ; the blacks in North America and South Africa. Without the British Empire the political map of the world would be differently drawn ; it is a fact of world-wide import that Anglo-Saxon races dwell in both continents of the Northern Hemisphere and in two of the three continents of the Southern. The Empire supplies the whole world with goods whose production has been created, developed, or organized by its planters, colonists, engineers, and

13

merchants : the gold and diamonds of South Africa ; the wool, wheat, butter, and meat of Australia ; the wheat, fish, and timber of Canada ; the sugar of the West Indies ; the rubber and tin of Malaysia ; the wheat, cotton, jute, rice, and tea of India. Few nations contribute so largely to the maintenance and increase of the inheritance of the human race.

Other nations are but ill acquainted with the extent and vigour of these centres of British activity. Occasionally, however, they do perceive them, and measure them in the light of the great events that are agitating humanity. It was not without astonishment that the people of France saw squadrons of Hindu cavalry and Anzac and Canadian battalions marching through their villages—advancing right into the heart of our old Europe, to the rescue of the British Empire. And, when peace had come, it was with surprise and some measure of embarrassment that the French diplomatists found seated in the council chamber of the Allies the representatives of those far-off dominions which they were accustomed to regard as lying at the uttermost ends of the earth, and which now seemed close at hand, watching over the restoration of the civilized world. This widening of the circle of the nations is a British achievement whose origin, development, and structure we have to study. We have to see how Great Britain, after remaining for so long an agricultural country, with no other outside ambitions than her French provinces, at length settled down in her island, turned her back on the Continent, sought fortune beyond the seas, founded a province in the tropical zone, settled multitudes of her children on new lands in the temperate zone, added to her possessions from generation to generation, and ended by assembling beneath her flag the largest, the richest, and the most populous colonial empire that the world has ever seen.

BOOK I

FORMATION OF
THE BRITISH EMPIRE

CHAPTER I

BIRTH AND DEVELOPMENT OF THE COLONIAL
SPIRIT IN GREAT BRITAIN

THE colonizing instinct is a daughter of the commercial spirit. It is born in a community of merchants when the whole world, and not only their native land, is looked upon as a place of trade. This extended outlook is hard to achieve; it implies an already advanced stage of civilization, and can be attempted only by a nation that has created at home the very conditions of this outside life, namely, a homogeneous territory, secure frontiers, and some available capital. For a country with no acquired fortune, no security, and no cohesion all expansion is hazardous and even perilous. It was not until fairly late that Great Britain found herself in possession of these three elements of strength. She entered the colonial lists later than Spain and Portugal, and later even than France. But, once launched upon the waters of the outer seas, she quickly outstripped her rivals. To-day she shows us the most perfect type of a colonizing country. European expansion, which has transformed the world, finds its most original and complete expression in British colonization.

Influence of the Great Discoveries.—The British horizon, so long confined to the lands and seas of Europe, broadened out to an infinite extent after the great discoveries. Great Britain was more profoundly affected than the rest of Western Europe by this geographical revolution. The British archipelago—*Ultima Thule*—had hitherto lain apart from the world, at the western extremity of the known universe,[1] far from the centres of Mediterranean civilization, while away toward the setting sun lay the unknown and mysterious realms of Ocean. The Vikings, to be sure, had in the Middle Ages discovered the way to America by Iceland and Greenland, but the world had forgotten the practical bearing of their adventurous expeditions. When once the New World became known through the voyages of Christopher Columbus Great Britain ceased to be on the edge of the world. She found herself transported, along with Spain, Portugal, France, and the Netherlands, to the middle of the earth, for the Southern Atlantic had become, and was to remain for several centuries, the link between the old continent and the new, and the theatre of the world's traffic. On the eastern edge of this theatre Great Britain occupies a unique position. Posted in front of Europe in the midst of the waves, in a higher latitude than the Iberian peninsula, she lies right in the track of the south-west winds, on the route of the sailing ships from America, while behind her, beyond the North Sea, lie the straits that lead into the Baltic—the Mediterranean of the Germanic races.

Influence of Great Britain's Insular Position.—Now when did Great Britain reap the full benefit of this geographical situation ? Just at the moment when she realized all the political advantages arising from her insular position, and became a single unitary state. British expansion, indeed, could not begin until the national unity of the country was consolidated. It was by the same process of internal consolidation, or welding together, that Spain and France prepared themselves for the part that they were to play abroad—Spain after

[1] Mackinder, *The British Isles*, pp. 1-12.

the union of Leon and Castile with Aragon and the expulsion of the Moors, and France after the bringing of Burgundy and Brittany under the royal sceptre. Since the Norman Conquest no foreign invader had set foot in the British Isles, and almost all the human elements in the country had gradually become fused together into an Anglo-Saxon unity. Certain relics of the past, such as old customs and ancient tongues, had not disappeared in Scotland, Wales, or Ireland, but the same political sway extended everywhere, and at the beginning of the seventeenth century the Scottish crown was placed on the head of the sovereign who ruled in London. Throughout the British Isles, therefore, there was a single political authority, a preponderating language, a dominating civilization, a single organized nation.

England had no longer any Continental possessions; she had no interests in Europe but commercial ones. She had replaced that Continental colonization which had made the Channel 'English' by an insular colonization which was to result in the assimilation of Scotland and the occupation of Ireland. Mistress of her own island and of naught beside, she dwelt there impregnable, as in a fortress protected by the waves. France, on the other hand, with her long-drawn landward boundaries, had to spend her strength against her Continental neighbours in order to conquer her natural frontiers. Thus, just at the time when the horizon of commerce was broadening out to the ends of the earth, and when the peoples of the North were preparing to follow the trail of the Iberians across the seas, the people of Britain were gathered together in a strongly constructed state, protected by its insular position, freed from all Continental ambitions, and able to put all its strength at the service of the commercial instinct.

The sea, the only route to the outer world, has dominated British national life to an increasing extent, and

B

the Government has therefore kept a watchful eye on it. At a very early date we find it striving to obtain the freedom of the seas for English vessels, when English commerce was in the hands of foreign fleets. At the end of the fourteenth century, in the reign of Richard II, Parliament passed a Navigation Act compelling English merchants to import and export only in English ships.[1] This measure was premature, for the English possessed hardly any merchant shipping, but the principle of the Act made headway. The conception of mastery of the seas was already permeating English opinion. In *The Libel of English Policy*, attributed to Adam de Moleyns, Bishop of Chichester (1436–37),[2] we read that England's true policy should be to rule the narrow seas, so as to control the trade-routes that skirt her coasts—the routes of the Hanseatic League and the Italians. By a new Act of 1485 the right of importing Bordeaux wines and Toulouse dye-stuffs was withdrawn from foreigners and confined to English ships manned by English crews ; but it was not yet possible to enforce this measure.[3] At the end of the sixteenth century, however, these protective Acts began to take effect. Elizabeth forbade the importation of Gascony wines except in English ships, and also of salt fish prepared abroad. In the seventeenth century the policy of Navigation Acts, combined with naval support, protected British shipping from its foreign competitors, and guaranteed State aid to British merchants and seamen. The State was now full-grown, and the birth of the Empire was possible.

Influence of the Ancient Centres of Commercial Activity.[4]—There were already centres of commercial

---

[1] Lucas, 49, p. 3. [2] Williamson, 68, p. 29.
[3] Williamson, 68, p. 41.

[4] On this subject see Williamson, 68 ; Cunningham, 22a ; G. Schanz, *Englische Handelspolitik gegen Ende des Mittelalters*, Leipzig, Duncker, 1881, 8vo, 2 vols. ; W. J. Ashley, *An Introduction to English Economic History and Theory*, Longmans, 1913, 8vo, 2nd edition.

activity in Great Britain, all ready to take the chances of a new fortune and to equip the pioneers of distant enterprises. Currents of the general life of the world had long been penetrating the country.

In the Middle Ages two great trade-routes extended from the shores of the North Sea across the Continent. One went to the Baltic and the Black Sea, and then to the Levant by way of the plains of the Danube or else by Novgorod and Kiev; on this road were founded the fortunes of the Low German towns, such as Cologne, Lübeck, and Hamburg. The other road started from the Netherlands, and, passing by way of the Rhine or the Rhone, reached those *entrepôts* on the shores of the Mediterranean where the riches of the East were collected; from this route arose the prosperity of the Flemish towns, Bruges and its rivals. By these two routes, the Eastern and the Southern, the waves of world commerce advanced up to the doors of Great Britain. It was through them, and the German, Flemish, and Italian *entrepôts* which they served, that England received the very essentials of her commercial system.

It was by the Southern road that English wool passed to the workrooms of Florence and Lucca, and by the same route—the valley of the Po and the Alpine passes—did Venice and Amalfi speed the produce of the East to the lands bordering on the North Sea. Bruges was the staple town, the place where all these goods were unloaded. At the beginning of the thirteenth century the towns of France and Flanders that were served by this great stream of traffic combined to form a confederation which called itself the London Hanse, simply because it dictated the commercial affairs of England. Along this road Italian influence travelled as far as London, where, as financiers and papal tax-collectors, the Italians held a predominant place in the business community. Their influence increased yet further when the towns of Italy, in order to meet the needs of their manufacturing industry, resolved to fetch the English wool direct by sea. The land-route lost some of its traffic, to the benefit of the sea-route by way of Gibraltar. Italian merchants monopolized almost all the foreign trade of England; in the fifteenth century the galleys of Venice and Genoa came to load up with wool at London, Southampton, and Boston, bringing with them spices, drugs, alum, and dyes. Italians held in their hands the money trade of London, and became the bankers of kings: Lombard Street was one of the busiest quarters of the City. From contact with these foreigners England awoke to commercial activity.

Deeper and more lasting was the influence of the Germans. As early as the twelfth century branch establishments had been set up in London by those who called themselves the " Men of the Emperor." In the thirteenth century the Baltic towns Lübeck and Hamburg, already masters of the trade with Russia and the East, obtained complete control of all the commerce of the North. They founded a confederation —the famous Teutonic Hanse—whose power extended from Bruges to Novgorod, from the Scheldt to the land of Muscovy. Merchants affiliated to the Hanse and established in London were granted privileges by Edward IV, and installed themselves at the beginning of the thirteenth century in their famous house, the Steelyard. For more than three hundred years they dominated British trade, until the English, having acquired from them the business instinct, claimed it for themselves. Under the Tudor kings threats were already being muttered against German merchants; they burst out openly under Elizabeth; foreigners had to give place to natives, and the Steelyard was deserted.

Business relations in other quarters had also prepared

England for the rise of large-scale commerce. It is well known that Great Britain was subject for a time to the Scandinavian kingdom of Canute; she thus became a sort of commercial colony of the Vikings. Norwegian mariners came as far as the Irish Sea, by way of the Shetlands, the Orkneys, and the Hebrides, bringing with them the salt fish which was a popular article of consumption throughout all Christendom. The English, seeing them enriched by this lucrative traffic, conceived the idea of practising it themselves: the men of Bristol set out to obtain fish from Bergen, and then pushed on as far as Iceland to catch it. Thus in the fourteenth century began the commercial relations of Bristol with the Mediterranean lands, the chief markets for salt fish.

Ever since the Normans had introduced a taste for wine into English households, close trading relations had existed between our island and the vineyards of France. The transport of the wine was for a long time the business of Gascon and Hanseatic vessels, but their trade was concentrated in the hands of the London merchants. The guild of the wine merchants—the " Wine Tonners of Gascoyne "—contained families of French origin : Henri le Galeys was Lord Mayor of London one year and Mayor of Bordeaux the next. The wine trade with Bordeaux and Libourne was the source of huge fortunes in the City : like the cloth trade, it laid the foundation of the capital which was to render possible the great commercial undertakings of London. Thus there were centres of commercial activity in London which were turning already toward foreign trade, and for them the opening of a colonial sphere of action was merely an extension of their existing sphere.

Influence of the Spirit of National Independence.[1]— The germs of commercial independence had grown from contact with foreigners : foreign trade was transferred

[1] On this subject see p. 18, note 1.

very slowly and gradually from the hands of foreigners to those of the English. About the middle of the thirteenth century the wool merchants formed a corporation which was called, a little later on, the " Merchants of the Staple." It endeavoured to monopolize the transport of wool in the Flemish market, and Edward III was successful in securing this trade for them. By a similar effort directed toward the exportation of cloth the English were liberated from the hands of the foreign middleman. A group of eager spirits, keen on business, had drawn together among the cloth merchants of the eastern towns—York, Ipswich, Newcastle, Hull, and especially London. They joined forces, organized themselves, and in 1404 obtained a collective charter under the name of the " Company of Merchant Adventurers "—travelling merchants, anxious to escape from the tyranny of the great emporium of Bruges. They gradually became the mobile and enterprising element in English trade, entering freely into business relations, and setting up branch establishments in Prussia, Spain, Holland, and Brabant. In 1444 they settled at Antwerp, thus opening up a new route for English fabrics and dealing a fatal blow at Bruges. From Antwerp English cloths were distributed over the Continent, threatening the Flemish cloth markets. Driven out of Antwerp in 1582 by the ruler of the Netherlands, they transferred their headquarters to Middelburg. Later on, in the sixteenth century, they penetrated the Hanseatic area, and arrived at Danzig and Riga to shake the supremacy of Hamburg. Powerful enough by this time to attack the Hanse strongholds in London, they obtained commercial equality for all in 1551, and the closing of the Steelyard in 1598. With the coming of the Merchant Adventurers London trade was carried on in the North Sea, and the City merchants became masters of their own business. With experience of large-scale commerce the spirit of enterprise developed. At the time when new worlds were coming into view there were men in England who were capable of judging these prospects and forces ready to come into action. But the Englishman's field of action was limited, because other nations had been before him.

More than a hundred years after the discovery of America and the Cape route the English had not yet founded any colony. Colonial fortune was the property at that time of the direct heirs of the trading peoples of the Mediterranean—of the Spaniards, who owned vast territories in America, and of the Portuguese, who were exploiting the coasts of Brazil, Africa, and India. Everywhere, therefore, the English found the places they went to already occupied. But still all the spirit of adventure that was fermenting in English bosoms turned toward those distant horizons where fortune beckoned. Merchants and mariners wanted their share in the exploitation of 'the Islands,' 'the Indies.' The Government supported them and urged them on, for a new source of national wealth was the prize to be won. In America, in Africa, and in Asia English stations were set up on the coast, at the doorways of the new lands. In America there was the colony of Virginia with its tobacco plantations, and the Antilles with their fields of sugar-cane. In Africa there were trading-stations on the Guinea coast, reservoirs of black labour for the Antilles. In Asia there were the 'factories' of India, the land of spices and cotton cloth. For nearly two hundred years British commercial ambitions were confined almost entirely to these hot countries, with their wealth of valuable products, colonial goods, articles of native manufacture, and slaves. These splendid cargoes were conveyed in English ships. From the middle of the seventeenth century the English Government intended its subjects to be masters of their own transport.

All the trade of England with the plantations, the Levant, and India passed through English hands; foreign merchandise came to the warehouses of London, Bristol, Liverpool, and Glasgow, and enormous wealth was accumulated in these ports. All this capital, the produce of the plantations, of trade, and of naval power, formed henceforth an essential element in the national organization of Great Britain : it supplied the energy which was to build her factories and to bring about the Industrial Revolution. That revolution itself, the child of international trade, was destined in its turn to give birth to new business relations and new colonies.

Influence of the Industrial Revolution.[1]—It was under the impelling pressure of the world market that England became the land of inventions. The Industrial Revolution began in an industry that arose out of colonial trade. Through trade with the Levant the English public had long been acquainted with the cotton fabrics of the East. English weavers had copied them, and they were being made at Manchester, perhaps as early as the end of the sixteenth century, and certainly in the year 1641. The raw cotton, imported from Cyprus and Smyrna, was unloaded at London, whither the Lancashire weavers came to buy it. But as soon as direct relations were established with India by English ships the English market was invaded by the fine and beautiful fabrics made by the Hindu workmen. Fashion soon came to prefer these to the coarse produce of Lancashire, whose workers had neither the experience nor the taste of the Oriental. So, too, in the markets of Europe, Asia, and America, whither these cottons were conveyed in British vessels, the British fabrics were deserted for the Hindu. British manufacturers were driven at all costs to produce more and to turn

[1] See P. Mantoux, *La révolution industrielle au XVIIIe siècle*, Paris, 1905, 8vo, pp. 190–95; Cunningham, 22a, vol. ii.

out better work if they were to sell their goods and make a living, and this necessity was the mother of the technical inventions which they made. No raw material was more suitable than cotton for the new machines, for it is a light and pliable fibre; and it was cotton, the newcomer, the child of the Tropics, that henceforth held the first place among manufactures, driving out wool, the ancient product of the British moorlands. In 1802 the export of cotton fabrics exceeded that of woollen cloths; in 1822 they penetrated into India, and that was the beginning of the marvellous fortune that was in store for British cotton goods in the warm countries of the earth.

Henceforth there was an intimate connexion between industrial production, demanding ever wider and wider outlets, and commercial expansion, requiring ever a more and more extensive scale of manufacture. In this fact we should recognize not only the cause of British expansion overseas, but also the mighty driving force of the British industrial system. Everything was bound up with the conditions of existence of this organism, and everything tended ultimately to turn it in the direction of trade. In order that manufactured goods might be sold new markets had to be obtained and exports increased. In order that the factories might be kept supplied great quantities of raw material had to be acquired and imports increased. The fields of Britain no longer sufficed to feed the workers of the towns, so wheat and meat had to be purchased abroad. The food of the worker, like his work, depended upon foreign trade, and therefore it was necessary to acquire food-producing lands. When machinery killed the crafts of the countryside thousands of peasants were driven into exile, and made their homes beyond the seas, on shores where traders had already settled. Thus British communities were born, and grew, and became new customers for the mother country. The capital saved in the course of all these operations did not remain idle; the British trader, always on the look-out for a good investment, sought for some way to use it. By degrees the commercial orbit of Great Britain reached out to embrace the whole world: where there was no English trader there was no trade. Thus without the colonies the commercial edifice would collapse. Despite the ties of sentiment, trade remains ever the mainstay and binding force of the Empire, as it was the prime motive of those who founded it.

Influence of the Commercial Spirit.—It was the commercial spirit that inspired the first attempts at colonization and directed its progress. From the very beginning we find England's customers being fed with the produce of the fisheries of Newfoundland, whose salted fish was sold in Spain in exchange for wine, salt, and sugar. We can see mercantile motives at work in the founding of the colonies of Virginia and Maryland— such motives as the hope of finding spices, or gold and silver mines; the determination to get from these countries the timber, hemp, and pitch that were required in shipbuilding and that had hitherto come from the Baltic lands; and even the secret desire to set up bases of operations on the sea-routes by which the Spanish vessels sailed from the West Indies to Europe.[1] The maximum advantage of colonial trade was taken by ingenious combinations of routes, such as those triangular voyages which obviated the waste involved in making return journeys without a cargo. For instance, English ships conveyed articles of British manufacture to the Guinea coast, then embarked negro slaves for the Antilles, and loaded up in the West Indies with colonial merchandise for conveyance to England. At the beginning of the eighteenth century another and equally

[1] Williamson, 68, pp. 157, 341.

profitable triangular voyage linked up Europe, the North American colonies, and the West Indies : England thus disposed of her manufactured goods, the American colonies of their timber, fish, and agricultural produce, and the West Indies of their sugar. For a long time no distinction was made for administrative purposes between colonial and commercial affairs : both were under the same office, the Board of Trade and Plantations. The conception of the colonies as portions of the mother country, with the same rights, appeared somewhat late. They were regarded during the seventeenth and the greater part of the eighteenth centuries merely as parts of a commercial system that operated for the profit of the parent state. And now that the colonies have become free nations commerce appears still as the cement of empire, despite the bonds of sentiment.

It has been the traditional policy of Great Britain in every age that colonial trade should reflect the national interest, to which everything was subordinated, whether in peace or war. The series of wars in the eighteenth century, which made England the mistress of the seas, is described by the historian Seeley [1] as a second Hundred Years War, with the possession of the New World as the prize. While France was dividing her attention between the Continent and the ocean, Great Britain from the end of the seventeenth century turned her eyes and her rule upon the seas : there is no other instance of a policy pursued with such tenacity for so many generations. England was driven to take up arms in the War of the Spanish Succession because she was afraid of seeing French influence penetrating Spain and thereby winning the trade of America. When the war was over the English obtained, by the Asiento Treaty, the monopoly of the slave trade in the Spanish colonies. Throughout the eighteenth century, and down

[1] Seeley, 60.

to the fall of Napoleon, England was waging war
to enlarge her empire. Even when she was fighting on
the Continent she was still conquering colonies or else
defending some trade-route. She has never allowed the
shores of Europe that face her to be united under a
single rule, in order that the Continental balance of
power should secure to her alone the mastery of the
narrow seas : she has always regarded the presence of
the French on the Lower Scheldt or the Lower Rhine as
a danger, and her hatred of Napoleon arose because
Antwerp was at that time a French port. The control
of the sea-routes leading to the sources of her trade was
a matter of necessity to her. She held that the business
of the British Government was above all else to obtain
free markets for British traders, and so long as this
freedom was not threatened she abstained from taking
up arms. She made no great wars during the nineteenth
century : her equanimity was unshaken by the War of
Secession, by the Austro-Prussian War, and by the
Franco-Prussian War : never was British trade more
prosperous than in the years following 1870. And to
drive Great Britain into the war of 1914 it was needful
for Antwerp to be threatened by a power whose merchants
and mariners were already to be met with on every sea.
Trade is the greatest of the political interests of Great
Britain.

Trade appears also as the original form of British
civilization. There is no part of the world of commerce
from which British merchants are absent. In British
colonies where there are also other European colonists
the chief business is in the hands of the English. In
Canada the French Canadians are outstripped by the
Anglo-Saxons in the realm of commerce and industry :
it is the latter who control the trades that lead to wealth.
" The principal banks," says Siegfried,[1] " the chief rail-

[1] Siegfried, 61, p. 307.

way companies, the great business undertakings, commercial and maritime, all belong to the English. English is the business language, and as a business town Montreal is a satellite of London or New York—an Anglo-Saxon centre *par excellence*, where the presence of more than a hundred thousand French is actually a matter of minor importance." The same kind of superiority attaches to the Anglo-Saxon element in South Africa. There the Britishers are scarcely the rural, agricultural class : the influential party in the country districts are the descendants of the Dutch settlers. The British element plays the leading part in industry, mining, banking, and commerce ; by its control of capital it dominates the exchanges and the circulation of money ; it holds the mastery in the towns, where roads meet and business affairs are negotiated. Wherever the Englishman appears he gets to business. Even when he makes a home for himself in the country he remains a trader : as soon as his farm is cleared and put into cultivation he sells it and starts a larger one, which is destined in its turn to become an object of exchange.

This passion for trade is a mark of civilization that is deeply impressed upon the British community. To traffic is the individual occupation of everybody. The constitution of England's colonial empire advances step by step with the extension of her business relations. The trader is the pioneer of colonization. He it is who confers value upon all that makes up the wealth of the colonies—objects of luxury, precious metals, articles of everyday consumption, virgin forests, and new lands. He directs the movements of fleets upon the ocean, and attracts settlers to his estates, to become the progenitors of new customers. Commercial exploitation leads him on by degrees to territorial appropriation, and so, one branch establishment being followed by another, and colony being added to colony, he founds an empire.

THE BRITISH EMPIRE

Some nations, like the Phœnicians and the Dutch, have practised hardly any but commercial exploitation. But Great Britain, like Athens of old, has transformed her markets into possessions, and this political edifice, the work of her traders, is the greatest known to history.

CHAPTER II

THE BEGINNINGS OF THE EMPIRE

BEFORE the English set foot in the new lands more than a century had passed since the great discoveries of the Portuguese and the Spaniards ; the Iberian peoples controlled the sea-routes and divided the earth between them. But the idea of seeking for a route to the Indies which should not be the property of the seamen of Lisbon and Cadiz took hold of adventurous spirits, and found support among business men. This was the quest with which Great Britain began the era of her great overseas voyages, and which gave the first indication of a colonial spirit.

The North-west Passage and Newfoundland.[1]—It was Bristol that sounded the call to action. An ancient seat of the fishing industry, whose sailors were well acquainted with Icelandic waters, and a centre of trade with that Scandinavian world which had first foreseen and revealed the existence of the distant islands of the West, Bristol lay on the Atlantic route, face to face with the New World. Her merchants were stirred by the news of the marvellous voyages of Columbus. No one knew the shape of the new continent, or the fact that it stretched beyond the Arctic Circle, but it was thought possible to discover a North-west Passage to India. Such was the opinion of John Cabot, an Italian navigator who had come to England to seek his fortune. He had formerly made the spice voyage to the Levant, and the

[1] Williamson, **68**, pp. 69–76 ; *British Empire*, **11**, pp. 285–293 and 390 ; Lucas, **49**, pp. 22–25 and 53–54.

Arab traders whom he had met in the Red Sea had spoken to him of the Far East. Perhaps he thought that Bristol, the home of bold mariners, would form an admirable base for a voyage into the West. Henry VII granted him letters-patent charging him to discover unknown lands. Setting out from Bristol in June 1497 he reached North America, either in Newfoundland or at Cape Breton. A second voyage in the following year proved to him that he was not on the road to Asia. But now the English had broken the spell of the ocean, and from short voyages in European waters they passed to the great Atlantic crossing. Moreover, the Bristol folk knew of fishing-grounds in the vicinity of Newfoundland richer than those of Iceland, and this was the beginning of regular expeditions to those waters, with their wealth of cod and whales. In an Act of Parliament of 1540 we find mention of Newfoundland, under the name of ' Newland,' as a fishing centre ; the Bristol fishermen carried off cargoes of fish from the island, and sold it salted in Spain and Portugal, and by the end of the sixteenth century they controlled the fish trade of the Latin countries. This distant fishing-ground was a rough school of seamanship, and in it the mariners of Bristol and Devon learned their craft. They did not find the way to India, but they acquired a knowledge of the sea. About the year 1630 the Newfoundland fishing fleet was manned by upward of 10,000 sailors, from whom were drawn the crews of the English Navy. Such was the practical outcome of the Englishman's first overseas adventures. For the rest, the idea of a Northwest Passage died but slowly. In 1576 it drove Frobisher into the icy waters of Labrador ; in 1583 it determined the merchants of London to finance Davis's expedition to the western waters of Greenland ; and it inspired Hudson in 1610. Other explorers also sought in vain for an opening toward the West : Button in 1613, Bylot and Baffin in 1616, Fox and James in 1631, and still others in the following centuries. But, though fruitless, these attempts were not altogether useless. They trained the whale-fishers of Hull and the northern ports, and they also threw light upon the region in which after 1670 the Hudson's Bay Company was to work.

The North-east Passage and the Eastern Route to the Indies.[1]—The spice countries might still be reached by a northern route, however, if a North-east passage could be discovered. In this search the initiative was taken by the merchants of London. They brought over from Spain Sebastian, the son of John Cabot, who was considered an authority on nautical matters, and he strongly advised them to undertake the business. Besides being styled " Grand Pilot of England," Cabot received also the imposing title of " Governor of the Mystery and Company of the Merchant Adventurers for the discovery of Regions, Dominions, Islands, and Places Unknown." In May 1553 he published some information concerning a projected voyage to Cathay (Japan). In the same year an expedition set sail from Harwich toward the North-east of Europe, under the leadership of Richard Chancellor and Hugh Willoughby. The latter died on the way, but Chancellor discovered the entrance to the White Sea, and succeeded in reaching Archangel. Instead of opening a route to the Indies, this discovery was the beginning of regular intercourse with Russia and the origin of the Muscovy Company (1554). These new trading relations made England a market for the timber, hemp, furs, and tallow of Russia, but they also set her on the road to the whale fisheries of Spitzbergen, while beyond Moscow she could catch a glimpse of the Caspian and Black Sea lands. A little later on an agent of the Muscovy Company named Jenkinson set out from Russia to find raw silk

---

[1] Cunningham, *22a*, vol. i, p. 449 ; Williamson, *68*, pp. 26 and 90–91 ; Lucas, *49*, pp. 26–27.

C

markets in Persia. The East exerted an irresistible attraction upon the West. In 1581 was founded the Levant Company, which opened up direct relations with Constantinople, without the employment of Venice as an intermediary. The members of this company reached the Persian Gulf and pushed on as far as Goa, and they also aimed at controlling the spice trade by way of Bagdad. Thus, whether by Arctic seas or Continental deserts, English traders were striving to reach the spice-growing countries.

Winning the Mastery of the Seas.[1]—Nothing lasting could be accomplished until direct contact was set up with the lands of the Tropics. To reach these it was necessary to capture the sea-routes, and to open a passage, by force if need be, through the Spaniards and Portuguese. Off the Atlantic coast of America lay the West Indies, whence Spanish vessels returned every year laden with riches. The owners of these islands guarded the approaches to them fiercely; only by force or fraud could an entry be effected, and every foreign ship was looked upon as a pirate. If trade was to be carried on with these places the door would have to be forced, and this solution was out of the question for English traders without Government backing. Now it was during the sixteenth century that the English Government became conscious of its strength, and, being an island power, concentrated that strength in its navy. For the first time the English grasped the idea that the future of their country lay upon the sea, and that commercial expansion was entirely dependent upon naval power. It was then, indeed, in the Elizabethan age, that England's maritime career really began.

Before founding any colonies England wrested from Spain the mastery of the sea. The struggle did not take

[1] J. Bridge, *British Imperialism*; Williamson, 68, pp. 105–106 and 134–147; Lucas, 49, pp. 25–31.

the form of pitched battles, but was essentially an affair of raids by privateers. With the exception of Martin Frobisher, a native of Yorkshire, and Thomas Cavendish, who was born in Suffolk, these famous seamen belonged to West of England families, and especially to Devonshire. Their early years were spent on the shores of the great ocean that led to the Spanish seas, and there a school of mariners grew up that was as remarkable for its nautical knowledge as for its bravery, from William Hawkins to Francis Drake, Sir Humphrey Gilbert, and Sir Walter Raleigh.

The Spaniards had organized in a methodical manner their trade with their American empire. Every year two fleets set out from the New World for Spain, one laden with the gold of Mexico and the other with the silver of Peru, sailing by way of Porto Bello. They met at Havana, and then journeyed to Spain by way of the Azores, escorted by ships of war. This regular traffic followed the routes necessitated by the direction of the prevailing winds, and the ships were a prey easy to ambush, attack, and capture. Long before they were officially recognized by the Government, English corsairs had commenced their forays. Already on several occasions between 1562 and 1569 John Hawkins had forced his way into some of the ports of the Caribbean Sea. In the same region Drake played the pirate for a long time with impunity, giving chase to Spanish galleons. In the course of one of these raids, in the year 1573, he saw displayed from the heights of the isthmus of Panama the wide expanse of the Pacific Ocean, and prayed, it is said, that God would grant him life, and allow him one day to sail across that ocean in an English ship. Among his most valuable prizes was a Spanish vessel whose papers revealed to the merchants of the City more than one secret concerning the trade of the Indies and China. If this fact is true it is certainly not unconnected with

Drake's great voyage round the world. Starting from Plymouth in 1577, he boldly crossed the Atlantic, rounded Cape Horn, entered the Pacific, captured off Panama a Spanish vessel laden with Peruvian ore, and returned to England by the Cape of Good Hope (1580), the first Englishman to sail round the world. By these lessons and these experimental ventures English seamen were being prepared for the rulership of the seas. In 1587 Drake entered the port of Cadiz and set fire to the transports that were assembled there. In the following year the great Spanish Armada was destroyed by the English fleet in the Channel. But the struggle did not end with this victory. On the routes to America, though they were now more free, the raids of English sailors increased. They cruised among the Antilles, always in search of plunder, but more and more eager to find strategic points for the security of their next moves; thus arose the idea, quickly followed by the opportunity, of founding a settlement in the West Indies. In this struggle with the greatest colonial power of that period England had been preparing herself to become a colonial power.

How far had British Expansion gone at the Beginning of the Seventeenth Century? [1]—We have now reached the end of the sixteenth century and the beginning of the seventeenth. What acquisitions had the English made so far in lands beyond the seas? It is not correct to say, as it is often said, that the period just ended saw nothing but the exploits of adventurers and filibusters. As a matter of fact, all these ' irregulars ' were maintained, equipped, and financed by English merchants : they were, after their fashion, the pioneers of trade. What they gave to their country was primarily a profound sense of her maritime calling. They had sought

---

[1] Caldecott, 15, *passim*; Lucas, 49, pp. 32–54 and 93–95; Cunningham, 22a, vol. ii, pp. 26–30; Mantoux, *La révolution industrielle*, pp. 75–80; Mondaini, 54, vol. i, pp. 32–33, vol. ii, pp. 208–209.

for a North-west Passage and for a North-east Passage ; they had scoured the seas of tropical America ; and they had sailed round the world. Voyages of adventure, exploring expeditions, piratical raids—none of these things had brought forth any immediate fruit ; but they had led the English toward those Western and Eastern lands whither their colonists were soon to follow the seamen and the traders.

The English had got into direct touch with the New World by way of the Antilles and Newfoundland. No settlement had yet been made in tropical America. But our sailors had taken stock of the Spanish possessions : they knew how to reach them, and they sailed freely among them. Near the mainland there existed but a single colony—Newfoundland, the first of all the British colonies. Thither every year went a multitude of fishermen from all countries : in 1578 there were 50 English vessels, 100 Spanish, 50 Portuguese, and 150 French, without counting the Basque whalers. The interests of the men of Bristol led them to set foot on the island in order to keep an eye on the fishing-ground, and in 1583 Gilbert arrived with five ships and solemnly took possession of Newfoundland in the name of the Crown. The settlement was entrusted to the people of Bristol, and in 1610 the island received a band of colonists who installed themselves at Cuper's Cove, on the shores of Conception Bay. This was the beginning of the permanent colonization by the English of the coast of Canada.

Contact had also been made with the East, where commercial relations were organized by the merchants of London. The whole of the latter part of the sixteenth century is remarkable for the astounding series of trading companies that were set up to deal with Eastern lands : the Muscovy Company (1554), which reached Persia by way of Moscow ; the Levant Company (1581), which traded with Syria and Bagdad through Constantinople ;

and the East India Company (1600), which reached the spice countries by way of the Cape of Good Hope. On their way to the Indies merchants of Exeter and London traded with Senegambia, and in 1588 they founded the African Company. For the moment there was no fixed settlement on the African coast ; it was not till the end of the seventeenth century that England took up a position there in spite of the Portuguese ; at the same period she established herself in the East Indies, in despite of the Dutch.

British expansion, whose first tentative beginnings we have been watching, was to be accomplished in two great periods, whose characteristics were determined by the development of the economic condition of Great Britain. They may be called respectively the era of plantations and the era of settlement. Up to about the close of the eighteenth century British colonization took place primarily in the hot countries of the Tropics. When once the routes to America and Asia were known all the efforts of commerce were directed toward those favoured lands, made known to the world by the Iberian peoples, whence came the precious metals and certain other rare commodities. The problem was how to convey these goods to the centres of consumption in Europe, to sell them there, and thus to play the part of a broker making a great fortune. Men were seeking not for unoccupied lands in which to settle, but for products that they could sell at a high price, such as tobacco, sugar, cotton, spices, and silk : they were founding plantations rather than colonies. Beside the tropical lands exploited by troops of slaves the English colonies—the new Englands—held at first only a very modest place in the commercial system.

But from the middle of the eighteenth century, and especially from the beginning of the nineteenth, the growth of industry and of world commerce introduced into British society profound changes, such as the establishment of great agricultural schemes, the disappearance of the small cultivator, the enclosure of the commons, the decay of domestic crafts, and the extension of pasture land at the expense of arable. Everywhere were being loosened the ancient bonds which had bound to the soil most of the inhabitants of the country districts, and from this floating population there went crowds of emigrants, especially to those temperate oversea regions where it was possible for Europeans to set up homes and make a living by their labour. Thus were formed those new Englands, those colonies of Anglo-Saxon settlement, which, alike in the Northern and the Southern Hemispheres, have made British colonization the most progressive and representative type of European civilization.

CHAPTER III

COLONIES OF EXPLOITATION

I. GEOGRAPHICAL DISTRIBUTION OF THE COLONIES OF EXPLOITATION

THE first efforts of British colonization were directed toward the Atlantic lands. This natural westward tendency resulted from the geographical position of Great Britain. Her first settlements were made in North America, in the West Indies, and on the west coast of Africa. It was not until later that she turned to the East, where she was at first held at bay by the Portuguese and the Dutch.

In North America.[1]—In the territory which is now the United States the merchants of London established their first colony in 1607. This was at Jamestown in Virginia, a country with a warm climate, on the shores of Chesapeake Bay. In 1612 began the cultivation of tobacco, which was afterward to make the fortune of the country; in 1619 the first negro slaves arrived. Thus we have here already the plantation system, which soon spread to Maryland, the Carolinas, and Georgia. We must not forget that throughout the seventeenth century these Southern regions, owing to their trade and population, were the most active centre of the area that was to become British America. In them were harvested the cargoes of tobacco that were to enrich the warehouses of Glasgow and Liverpool, and in them, about the year

---

[1] Zimmermann, 69, vol. i, *passim*; Lucas, 49, pp. 95–100; Williamson, 68, pp. 125 ff.; Besant, 8, pp. 40–45; Higham, 42.

1700, the colonial population was most thickly concentrated. Farther north lay the colonies of New Plymouth, founded in 1620, New Hampshire (1622), Massachusetts (1626), Rhode Island (1636), and Connecticut (1637). These were situated in a cold climate, and had no other resources at the outset than their fisheries, forests, and a small amount of agriculture. New York in 1664 had only 1500 inhabitants, and was nothing like as large as the towns of Virginia and Carolina. Later on, in the eighteenth century, when the Northern colonies had grown up round Boston and New York, it needed a fierce war to convince the merchants of Britain that they were faced by a real nation and not a colony of tobacco-planters and slaves.

In the West Indies.[1]—The Virginia undertaking led the English to the very gateway of the Antilles. The occupation of the Bermudas in 1610 was entirely natural, as these islands were on the direct route to Virginia. Moreover, the decay of the Spanish power opened up to English adventurers a wide field of action in these tropical archipelagos. All these islands held an exceptional place in the British Empire, out of all proportion to their meagre extent. Not for a long time did British commerce know a more abundant source of wealth. They were islands of sugar, rum, cotton, indigo, and tobacco, and some of them yielded so much that they became exhausted. The Spaniards occupied the largest of the Antilles—namely, Cuba, Haiti, Porto Rico, and Jamaica. They had neglected the smaller islands, and it was on these that the latest arrivals among European colonists settled. The Lesser Antilles served

---

[1] Zimmermann, 69, vol. i; Caldecott, 15, pp. 89–92; Lucas, 49, pp. 55–58; Mondaini, 54, vol. ii, pp. 172–173; Cunningham, 22a, vol. ii, pp. 543–544; Williamson, 68, pp. 155–156, 261–288, and *passim*.

at first as naval bases for the corsairs who raided the ports of Spanish America ; by degrees they were turned into trading-stations. In 1605 the English appeared in Barbados, and they settled there permanently after 1625. A few years later it was the turn of St Christopher, Nevis, Antigua, and Montserrat. All these virgin lands were quickly given over to intensive exploitation : they were transformed into veritable sugar factories, and became human ant-hills. In the middle of the seventeenth century more than a hundred ships came every year to Barbados to load up with sugar, molasses, and rum. In 1656 this island, the same size as the Isle of Wight, supported 25,000 whites and more than 35,000 negroes. From this crowded mass of men streams of emigrants set out to people South Carolina : between 1640 and 1668 Barbados poured into other colonies more than 12,000 of its inhabitants. In Jamaica, " the pearl of the English Antilles," captured from Spain in 1660, there were 50,000 inhabitants in 1698, and 210,000, including 192,000 slaves, in 1775, though the island produced and sold nothing but sugar. The whole of the American archipelago—St Christopher, the Bermudas, Grenada, St Vincent, Tobago, Antigua, Dominica, St Lucia—was dominated by the same intensive system, based upon tropical plantations and slave labour. But the Antilles were not valuable to the English only as a field to be exploited : they were used also as an *entrepôt* for the trade with Latin America. Through Cartagena and Porto Bello the English extended their operations to cover all the Spanish possessions, and when open trade did not suffice it was supplemented by contraband.

From the Caribbean Sea a stream of wealth flowed over to Great Britain. It might even be said that the centre of British colonial interests lay for a long time in the West Indies, for the temperate colonies were still only feeble undertakings in comparison with the tropical ones. After the emancipation of the United States the trade of the West Indies remained the most substantial element in the colonial fortune of London and Bristol. Froude speaks feelingly of the part these islands have played in the building up of the Empire. " They had been regarded," he says,[1] " as precious jewels, which hundreds of thousands of English lives had been sacrificed to tear from France and Spain. The Caribbean Sea was the cradle of the Naval Empire of Great Britain. There Drake and Hawkins intercepted the golden stream which flowed from Panama into the exchequer at Madrid. . . . In those waters, in the centuries which followed, France and England fought for the ocean empire, and England won it." To-day the West Indies have fallen from their high estate, and have become impoverished by economic crises. But they still retain a special value in the eyes of the English, for they link up the British Empire to the great era of heroic voyages and adventures; they recall to them their first steps in tropical colonization.

In Africa.[2]—Without negro slaves the Antilles would have been nothing but a desert, so a close bond was speedily formed between the West Indies and Africa: the West African colonies were born of the slave trade. Until about 1600 the Portuguese, masters of the Guinea coast, were the only people who transported slaves to the American plantations. In the seventeenth century this monopoly was taken from them by the Dutch. The English took little part in the slave trade before 1660, and did not follow the example set by John Hawkins, who carried three shiploads of negroes from Guinea to Haiti in 1562. In the seventeenth century,

---

[1] Froude, *The English in the West Indies*, pp. 9–10.
[2] Zimmermann, **69**, vol. i; Lucas, **49**, pp. 58–60; *British Empire*, **12**, pp. 140–142; Cunningham, **22a**, pp. 314 ff.; Williamson, **68**, pp. 75–85; Muir, *A History of Liverpool*, London, 1907, pp. 180–195.

however, the African trade aroused interest in London. Companies were formed, and trading-stations, which soon developed into bases for the traffic in slaves, were set up on the Gambia in 1631 and at Cape Coast Castle in 1661. The lucrative trade in ' ebony ' increased in volume, until between 1680 and 1688 no less than 46,400 negroes were transported to America in English ships. In the eighteenth century the slave trade passed almost entirely into the hands of the English : in 1713, by the Asiento Treaty, they obtained from Spain the privilege of supplying the Spanish colonies with slaves. It was the shipowners of London and Bristol who first took the lead, but after 1730 the chief place was taken by those of Liverpool, whose vessels conveyed 303,737 slaves, valued at £15,186,850, from Africa to America between the years 1783 and 1793. This huge transport business was carried on over a triangular route : the slave ships left Liverpool with cheap manufactured goods from Lancashire, such as guns, glass beads, spirits, hardware, and woven fabrics, which they exchanged on the Guinea coast for slaves, whom they conveyed to the West Indies by the trade-wind route, returning to Europe with cargoes of sugar, rum, tobacco, and cotton. This traffic reached its height about the year 1770, when it employed 197 English ships. Of these 107 were from Liverpool, 57 from London, and 33 from Bristol. Through this trade enormous wealth was accumulated in Lancashire, and the employment of this capital facilitated the progress of large-scale industry. Thus the whole course of Great Britain's development was determined by her extensive commerce. It had yet another consequence, whose influence is felt to-day beyond the borders of the British Empire : entire regions of the New World became peopled by negroes, while vast areas of Africa were bereft of men, and America was faced by the negro problem.

COLONIES OF EXPLOITATION

In the East Indies.[1]—The road to India and the Far East, the ancient spice countries, was not as easy for the British trader as the route to America. It involved a long voyage round Africa ; the Indian Ocean was but little known ; and Portuguese fleets were to be met with on the way, while the lands themselves were occupied by Portuguese garrisons. But, with the prospect of fortune before them, the merchants of London could not hesitate. In 1599 some City traders combined to send a fleet of ships to the Sunda Islands. The royal letters patent were granted to them in 1600, and thus was founded the " Company of the Merchants of London trading into the East Indies." The name ' Indies ' meant in those days the spice islands, and the first voyages were to the Malay Archipelago. In 1601 a squadron of five ships under James Lancaster visited Sumatra and Java, and set up a ' factory ' at Bantam in the latter island. The vessels returned to England in 1603 with a wonderful cargo of pepper and spices. English traders made further expeditions into the same parts, and pushed on even as far as the Moluccas. By these voyages and this trade they became acquainted with India. On their way to the islands they had noticed in Malaysia the craze for Indian cotton fabrics, and they conceived the idea of becoming agents for them themselves. So in 1612 they set up a branch establishment at Surat. Before long necessity compelled them to settle permanently in India. In 1623 all the members of an English factory had been massacred at Amboyna by the Dutch. It was evident that the Dutch intended at any cost to destroy all their rivals in the Asiatic archipelago, and the English were thereby driven to change their tactics. Other English trading-stations

---

[1] Zimmermann, 69, vol. i ; Lucas, 49, pp. 64–66 ; *British Empire*, 11, p. 393 ; Mondaini, 54, vol. ii, pp. 3–15 ; Cunningham, 22a, vol. ii, pp. 125, 267–282, 337, 593 ; Williamson, 68, pp. 162, 215–220.

were set up in India, at Masulipatam and in Orissa in 1631–32 ; in 1639 Fort George, the first British fortress in India, was built near Madras. Little by little the network of English interests extended : it embraced Bombay in 1661, and Calcutta (Fort William) in 1696, reaching also to Siam, and even as far as Japan. The East India Company became a colossal business : upon it was built the fortune of the City of London, in the same way that Liverpool grew by the slave trade and Glasgow by the tobacco trade. The Company's vessels conveyed to India the precious metals, lead, and woollen cloth, bringing back to England cotton fabrics, silk, diamonds, tea, porcelain, and spices. From 1744 to 1772 it transacted business to the value of between two and three million pounds a year, and in the latter year it had at its disposal a fleet of 61,680 tons. This Indian trade was fraught with marked consequences for England— alike for her material prosperity and for her spiritual development. It penetrated the whole country like a new force ; it concentrated in London the *entrepôt* trade which was slipping away from Amsterdam ; it introduced to the English such Eastern products as calicoes, muslins, and prints, whose competition stimulated home manufactures ; it made more general and popular every day that colonial outlook which was taking possession of the intellectual part of England and familiarizing her people with countries and matters that lay beyond the seas.

At the end of the eighteenth century, after Great Britain had lost the United States, the majority of her colonies were situated in hot countries. It was there above all that her merchants and shipowners went in search of fortune, and it was there that her soldiers and sailors strove to ruin her competitors and to extend her frontiers. In 1763 she annexed the French Antilles (Dominica, St Vincent, the Grenadines, Grenada, and

COLONIES OF EXPLOITATION

Tobago), and in 1803 St Lucia. From Spain she took Trinidad in 1797. She occupied Honduras in 1783, Sierra Leone in 1787, Penang, in Malaysia, in 1786, and Guiana in 1803. Some of her acquisitions show her desire to hold the lines of communication between the mother country and all the colonies; such are Gibraltar, 1704, Malta, 1800, Mauritius, 1810, Ceylon, 1795, and the Cape, 1806. This tropical empire did not extend to the interior of the continents; it resembled the mother country in being made up of islands and coasts stretched out along the sea.

II. TERRITORIAL EXTENSION OF THE COLONIES OF EXPLOITATION

There came a time when the tropical settlements were no longer able to remain content with their boundaries. Defence of their commercial position made it necessary that they should dominate the hinterland, and instead of merely advancing into the interior the settlers began by degrees to take actual possession. This territorial extension did not proceed according to a plan laid down beforehand : it depended upon circumstances. But the British merchant was not the man to neglect circumstances; he knew how to utilize them as forces to be applied methodically to the consolidation, and aggrandizement of his tropical domain. In proportion as the modern organization of industry developed, based on the mass production of manufactured goods, the search for extensive markets, and the exploitation of the native races, so this territory became increasingly valuable to Great Britain as a source of raw materials and as an outlet for manufactured articles. In America she retained, without adding much to them, the possessions that the eighteenth century had bequeathed to her. In Oceania, in the west of the tropical Pacific,

47

she acquired some scattered possessions, separated sometimes by wide stretches of sea : Fiji, New Guinea, the
Bismarck Archipelago, the Solomon Islands, the Tonga
Islands, and Samoa. But in Africa and Asia there
were two empires covering enormous areas. One was
the Asiatic empire, mainly in India, already an ancient
structure, provided with a complete system of dependencies, ramparts, and approaches ; the other was the
African empire, newer, less homogeneous, and still at
the stage of arrangement and organization.

**Extension of the African Colonies : Chartered
Companies.**[1]—For long years the British colonies in
tropical Africa were merely commercial agencies established on the coast. Many of them, like the Gambia,
Sierra Leone, the Gold Coast, and Lagos, were descendants of the old slave trading-stations. From the point
of view of internal trade, the African continent, solid,
impenetrable, and hostile, remained for a long time
inaccessible ; it was not opened to world trade until
after the time of the great explorers of the nineteenth
century. At each decisive stage in our knowledge of
Africa we meet with British names : Mungo Park,
Clapperton, Denham, Lander, and Richardson in the
Niger district ; Stanley in the Congo basin ; Burton
and Speke in the region of the Upper Nile ; Livingstone
on the Zambezi. Up to about 1880 these expeditions
threw rays of light, little by little, upon the ' Dark
Continent,' but they provoked no territorial acquisitions.
Even in England some political parties were in favour
of putting an end to all extension, and went so far as
to demand the abandonment of certain colonies. But
after 1880 there broke out a veritable fever of colonization among the industrial nations of Europe. Those,
like Germany, that were less well provided reached out
their hands over Africa ; the grabbing of lands began ;

[1] Lucas, 49, *passim* ; Zimmermann, 70 ; Carton de Wiart, 16.

then commenced that partition of Africa from which Great Britain emerged not empty-handed, nor with the least attractive morsels.

The forward march of the English bore the mark of their mercantile spirit, for it was accomplished by the method of chartered companies. Although they had fallen into discredit after the winding up of the East India Company, these companies soon recovered and became a powerful and flexible instrument for preparing the way for occupation. At a trifling expense they civilized the new lands and made them ready for commercial exploitation. These companies—associations of capitalists and merchants, invested with political powers —carried on the work of trade and organization at the same time. They supervised the first contact between white men and natives, established the first business relations, and prepared the first outlines of a regular system of administration ; in a word, they laid out the ground in preparation for colonization. Three of them played a preponderating part in the building up of British Africa : the Royal Niger Company (1886), the Imperial British East Africa Company (1888), and the British South Africa Company (1889).

During the nineteenth century English traders had settled in the delta of the Niger, on the various branches of the main stream known as Oil Rivers. Fearing the competition of the French and Germans, they combined in 1879 to form the United African Company. In 1884 the Berlin Conference recognized the Lower Niger as a British zone of influence, and in 1886 the English Government granted a charter to the Niger Company. Developing its 'factories' and extending its operations, the Company made a continuous advance into the interior, well beyond the limits of the delta, and reached the shores of Lake Chad after concluding more than four hundred treaties with native chiefs. But there came a

D

time when the State had to intervene to keep order in these vast territories; the Crown did not renew the Company's charter, but resumed its own rights. Two protectorates were created in 1900, called Northern and Southern Nigeria. In 1914 all these lands on the Niger were combined into the Colony and Protectorate of Nigeria, which now, including the districts annexed from the German Cameroon, covers an area of about 365,000 square miles, or more than three times the area of the United Kingdom.

On the east coast of Africa the island of Zanzibar stood sentinel over one of the oldest entrances to the heart of the continent—the gateway through which the Arab traders had passed when they made their raids as far as the basins of the Congo and the Nile. On this threshold the merchants of India had long since established their stations, while British traders in their turn had installed themselves on this passageway leading from Muscat and India into the negro hinterland. In 1886, fearing the setting up of a German station, Great Britain, who was already mistress of the island, resolved to set foot on the mainland. The position was a valuable one from the point of view of British interests, and since 1872 it had been a calling-place for certain regular lines of steamships of the British India Steam Navigation Company between India and Europe. In 1888 it was entrusted to the Imperial British East Africa Company —the celebrated I.B.E.A. As soon as it was founded this company turned toward the interior. It sent expeditions from Mombasa to reconnoitre the country and sign treaties with the chiefs, and in 1890 it reached Uganda, on the shores of Victoria Nyanza. But the Company had spent so much without thinking sufficiently of dividends that it had to give up its rights to the English Government in 1895, just when it was about to build the railway which was a necessary instrument of colonization. It had lived only six years, but it left ready prepared the plans which had been drawn up by Governor Macdonald for this purpose. The Government, having thus become direct rulers of the country, began in 1896 the construction of the railway, which in 1901 reached Victoria Nyanza at Port Florence, 584 miles from Mombasa. This line established communication between the Indian Ocean and Uganda, a fertile and populous district in the region of the great lakes, and enabled British power to penetrate to the Upper Nile by a shorter route than the valley of the great river itself. If we include the enormous slice of German East Africa annexed after the Great War, British East Africa has an area of about 740,000 square miles—say six times that of the United Kingdom.

The youngest, the most celebrated, and the most fortunate of the chartered companies, the British South Africa Company, was founded in 1889, and dates, therefore, from the time when British trade, disquieted by German and Portuguese designs on the interior of South Africa, decided to thrust forth its agents to the north of the Limpopo. This was the task of a syndicate of capitalists under the leadership of Cecil Rhodes. Their intention was to reach the Zambezi country, and they had to engage in terrible warfare against the native Matabele tribes. But they were working in a climate that was favourable to Europeans, for on these lofty tablelands the tropical climate was kind to the white man. Once the Zambezi was crossed the men of the ' Chartered ' carried British influence through the heart of a tropical country right up to the borders of the Belgian Congo. By the might of its capital and its arms the Company had made almost the whole of South Africa into a British land. If we add together Rhodesia and Nyassaland, we get a great land-mass of about 480,000 square miles, four times as large as the United

Kingdom. This region adjoins East Africa, and is thereby linked up with the Sudan and Egypt, so that one can now traverse Africa from Alexandria to Cape Town without leaving territories that are either British or under British influence.

The last few years of the nineteenth century, therefore, saw three British colonies mapped out on the coast of Africa, created by private companies and born of the enterprising spirit of British merchants and capitalists. The Empire owes it to her business men that she acquired in Africa, at the end of the nineteenth century, a territory of nearly 1,600,000 square miles, four times as big as her African possessions twenty years earlier. Nigeria, British East Africa, Rhodesia—all these new provinces belong, in their origin and development, to the pure type of British colonies. In their foundation the great financiers who supplied the capital were associated with members of the aristocracy who did not regard it as degrading to take part in business affairs, and who always knew how to make them further the interests of their country. Thus these colonies have been the theatre of action of such men, eminently representative of the British temperament in their bold and practical common sense, as Goldie in Nigeria, Mackinnon in British East Africa, and Cecil Rhodes in Rhodesia.

Extension of India.[1]—Among all the marvels of political architecture there is none more wonderful than that which the English have constructed in India, round India, and for India. In this country Great Britain possesses not only the stronghold of her Asiatic power, but also the commercial storehouse from which her merchants have drawn wealth for hundreds of years— the ideal tropical estate, as it were. To defend these

[1] Zimmermann, 69, vols. i and ii; Mondaini, 54, vol. ii; Bowman, 9; Carton de Wiart, 16; *Empire and Century*, 34; *Journal of the Royal United Services Institution*, May 1922.

material interests and to ensure the safety of this huge territory and its communications has always been a fundamental principle of British policy. India's natural frontiers had first to be won, and then she had to be made secure beyond these frontiers, on every side, by land and sea, in Africa, in Asia, in Malaysia, with such an array of advanced positions, defensive works, and lines of communication that she became a veritable empire surrounded by vassals and satellites. This building up was a slow process, but every day it grew more perfect and complete.

Up to the beginning of the nineteenth century Great Britain regarded the Deccan and Bengal as the most essential parts of her Indian empire. Peninsula and delta alike looked forth upon the sea, and by sea alone they seemed likely to be threatened. Was it not by naval warfare especially that the English had saved them from the French peril? But the safety of India was before long to be menaced from the land side. The might of Russia had arisen in Central Asia, and Great Britain turned her attention toward those passes on the north-west frontier whereby India had in every age been open to invasion. This region was inhabited by a war-like population who could not possibly be entrusted with the keys of India. Similarly on the eastern side the rich plains of Bengal lay at the mercy of the plundering Burmese highlanders. On every side, north-west, north, and east, it was necessary to strengthen the continental frontiers of India by a ring of possessions, fortified positions, dependencies, and alliances. This task was tenaciously carried out, not in accordance with any preconceived plan, but by taking advantage of circumstances as they arose.

This spirit of offensive defence led the British power to overflow, as it were, into Burma. By way of reprisal for the incursions of Burmese robber bands on the confines of Bengal a British expedition entered Burma (1825–26), and before long a treaty was made which ceded to Great Britain Assam and the coastal regions of Arakan and Tenasserim. In 1852, some traders having suffered at the hands of the Burmese, a short campaign of repression led to the annexation of Pegu in Lower Burma, with the port of Rangoon. Finally, in 1885–86, after yet another expedition, Upper Burma passed under British rule, and the whole country became a dependency of India.

In the north Great Britain succeeded by force or diplomacy in making peace among the mountain peoples of the Himalayas. She launched expeditions against Bhutan (1863–69) and against Chitral (1895). Little by little after 1890 the small Himalaya states of Nepal, Sikkim, and Bhutan, which had hitherto been faithful to the suzerainty of the Chinese, came under the protection of Great Britain.

British pressure was exerted longest and most strenuously toward the north-west. The English had to advance as far as the natural boundaries of India, and even into the land of the Afghans, beyond the passes which command the entrance to the peninsula. This advance was made in several stages. Scinde, the country of the Lower Indus, was conquered in 1843, while in 1849, after two campaigns against the Sikhs, the Punjab was annexed and a beginning was made with the building of the great road to Peshawar, the frontier town at the gates of Afghanistan. The natural frontiers of India were thus reached, but it remained to defend them against dangers from without. It was thought best not to await these foes at the foot of the mountains, on the line of the Indus, but to forestall them by advancing westward over the mountains into Afghanistan itself. This meant constructing defensive works on the farther side of the frontiers, and so the

English were led to leave India and set foot in Afghanistan, on the road to India.

The safety of her communications with India is the cardinal principle of the policy of Great Britain. Lines of fortified posts or centres of British influence radiate in all directions round India, and every point is guarded by British soldiers or agents. This defensive network, combining military and political methods, has been stretched slowly and patiently over land and sea in front of India, and often at a great distance from her. It covered first the old sea-route to India by way of the Atlantic, and then the new Suez route, while it also reached out as far as the threshold of the Chinese world.

Along the old Cape route to the Indies lies a series of calling-places, harbours, and fortified posts. Such are Gibraltar (1704), which prevents the French Mediterranean fleet from joining the Atlantic fleet; the island of St Helena (1651), for a long time a regular port of call for sailing ships going eastward; the Cape (1795 and 1815), a position that commands both oceans, and a resting-place for Indian officials in the days of long voyages; the island of Mauritius (1810), an ancient base of the French seamen who raided the English settlements in India and gave chase to British shipping in the Indian Ocean; and Zanzibar, whose trade was largely in the hands of Hindu merchants. Now that most ships have abandoned this old route, the new one is no less well provided. Gibraltar still commands it, and the rest of the chain contains these strong links: Malta (1800); Cyprus (1878); Egypt (1883), the mistress of the Suez Canal and the entrance to the Red Sea; the little island of Perim, in the middle of the Straits of Bab-el-Mandeb (1855); Aden, occupied in 1839 by the East India Company and joined administratively to the Indian Empire; Somaliland (1884); the island of Socotra; and the Kuria Muria Islands (1876), which guard the outlet of the Gulf of Aden. The principality of Oman remains independent, but the trade of Muscat is in Indian hands.

In the opposite direction the route to the Far East is marked out by British possessions. Some of them date from the time when the vessels of the old East India Company used to trade with China; others are more recent creations; almost all of them have the double character of being at the same time commercial *entrepôts* and naval bases, and they are closely attached to the Indian economic and strategic system. Thus we find in succession Ceylon, which was conquered in 1795; the Straits Settlements, Malacca (1824), Penang (1786), and Singapore (1819), which guard the ocean-route from the Indian seas to the China seas; and the Malay states, protected since 1874 and federated under British control since 1895. On the southern shores of the China Sea the coast of Borneo is occupied by a group of British settlements: the protectorate of Sarawak (1841), the protectorate of Brunei (1888), the island of Labuan (1845), joined administratively to Singapore since 1906, and the territory of the North Borneo Company (1881). The charter of incorporation of this latter company makes no secret of the imperial reasons determining its foundation: it was to prevent that part of Borneo from falling into the hands of any other country, since in case of war Great Britain possessed no port of refuge on the 1400 miles of coast between Singapore and Hong Kong. Farther north, at the gates of the Chinese world, Hong Kong was acquired in 1842 after a war waged to secure a Chinese market for the opium of India. On the way to Pekin, at the entrance to the Gulf of Chihli, Great Britain also obtained a lease of Wei-hai-wei to serve as a naval base (1898).

For a long time the approaches to India were held by sea. But toward the end of the nineteenth century the continental routes across the deserts of Asia seemed to rise out of oblivion. By means of modern methods of transport these inhospitable regions were opened up anew to the currents of world traffic. That great overland road by which the Eastern Mediterranean was linked up with the Persian Gulf, and the Persian Gulf with the delta of the Indus, was brought under British control. From Beluchistan and Afghanistan to Palestine and Arabia, by way of Persia and Mesopotamia, the influence of Britain was unceasingly pushed forward, in furtherance of her Indian policy. Even if the *pax Britannica* did not everywhere hold sway, and if everything did not fit in with Great Britain's schemes, she was yet watchful and vigilant everywhere.

As soon as the might of Britain had reached the natural frontiers of India it was faced by the lofty tablelands of Iran, the region of the age-old routes between West and East, the abode of Moslem peoples in a frequently disturbed state, and a region of weak and precarious governments. This area appeared to the English as a covering land where a curtain of defence might be drawn in front of India. Two great roads descended from Iran to India : one led from Kandahar and Quetta to Scinde, over the Bolan Pass and through Beluchistan ; the other from Kabul in Afghanistan, over the Khyber Pass to Peshawar and the Punjab. Both these routes are now under British control. Since 1879 the greater part of Beluchistan has formed an Anglo-Indian province having Quetta for its capital and divided into six districts— Quetta-Pishin, Sibi, Zhob, Loralai, Bolan Pass, and Chagai—while British agents keep a watchful eye upon Kelat and Las Bela, the two remaining native states.

On the Khyber route British influence was established with difficulty, and is not always peacefully maintained. The Afghans have never desired contact with Christian peoples : they prefer to remain isolated. Fearing a

Russian advance into Afghanistan, Great Britain tried to impose her suzerainty upon Kabul, but the expedition of 1839-42 broke down before the resistance of those fierce mountain warriors. After forty years of peaceful but not cordial relations the fear of Russian expansion again had its effect on British policy, and in 1878 an expedition succeeded in reaching Kabul and Kandahar, though only after a hard and bloody march. But diplomacy obtained what arms alone had been unable to achieve : it succeeded in placing upon the throne of Afghanistan an Amir who was favourably disposed toward Great Britain and sensible of the benefits she could bestow. This official friendship has always remained in force between the two countries, but it has not served to keep peace on their borders. The common frontier established by the agreement of 1893 was drawn to the west of the Khyber Pass, over difficult mountains inhabited by warlike tribes. In 1901 the Anglo-Indian Government had to create the North-West Frontier Province between the Punjab and Afghanistan, divided into five political agencies : Northern Waziristan ; Southern Waziristan ; Kurram, Khyber, and Dir ; Swat ; and Chitral. This province has no regular administration, but is simply under military occupation, and it is never tranquil. In 1914 a violent native revolt, adopting the methods of European warfare, necessitated the presence in this region of an Anglo-Indian army of 200,000 men. More recently still, in 1918 and 1919, the British troops have had to engage in fierce warfare, and at the present time, despite the official alliance of the Amir, the Waziris are still in arms. Great Britain holds the keys of the gate, but she has to be continually on guard.

Beyond Beluchistan and Afghanistan Persia has been drawn, willingly or unwillingly, into the circle of Anglo-Indian interests. She has long held a place in the continental system of communications between Europe and India. In virtue of various agreements, the first one dating back to 1863, a great line of telegraph, under British management, crosses the whole of Persia from Bender-Bushire to beyond Tabriz, passing through Ispahan and Teheran, and thus joining the Persian Gulf cable to the Russian telegraphic system. Another and more direct line was constructed by the Indian Government and completed in 1904; this reaches Beluchistan by way of Yezd, Kerman, and Bam, and joins the first line in Persian territory at Kashan. But British influence clashed in Persia with Russian influence. Russia, driven from the Pacific by Japan, was looking to the Persian Gulf for an outlet toward the seas of the Tropics, and this constituted a menace to the landward communications of India. The Anglo-Russian agreement of 1907 averted this fear by adjusting the respective interests of the two Powers; it gave Northern Persia to Russia and Southern Persia to Great Britain as spheres of influence, with a neutral zone between the two, recognized by Persia, and extending from Beluchistan to the mouth of the Persian Gulf. The collapse of the Russian power after the Great War left Great Britain by herself, and she began to organize the defence of India in Persia, both economically and politically, for she saw an opportunity to throw across Western Asia the last stage of the great bridge that was to join the Eastern Mediterranean with the Indian seas. The political edifice is tottering; by the Anglo-Persian treaty of August 9, 1919, Persia actually handed over to England the control of her army and her finances, but the British protectorate, condemned by national feeling, has not succeeded in taking root. The Persians, anxious to save their country from the fate of India, have not permitted the agents of the British mission to exercise the functions allocated to them by the treaty, and in 1922 Great

Britain's political plans were relegated to the background, awaiting, maybe, a more favourable opportunity. The economic edifice, however, stands firm. Since 1914 and 1917 the Anglo-Persian Oil Company, a British undertaking officially supported by the English Government, has held a large concession, covering three-quarters of the country, in order to search for and exploit oil in Persia. Oil springs are already gushing from the earth, and Persian oil extracted at Maidan-i-Naftun, some 200 miles from the Persian Gulf, travels by pipe-line to Abadan, on the Shat-el-Arab River. It is owing to these oil-fields, accessible as they are to the shipping of the Indian Ocean, that Persia is becoming drawn into the imperial system of Great Britain.

The lofty, mountainous, and arid tableland of Iran provides no roadways except along its lines of oases and through the openings in its mountain chains. But the alluvial plain of Mesopotamia forms a wide pathway between the Mediterranean and the Indian Ocean, and Great Britain has striven for many years to approach it. Her earliest intervention was aimed especially at defending her commerce against the pirates of the Persian Gulf; at the beginning of the nineteenth century rough police operations cleared out the bays that sheltered these rovers of the sea. Soon Great Britain concluded treaties with the native chiefs of the Arabian coast, and the Bahrein Islands became a protectorate under the Resident at Bushire, with reference, in the last resort, to the Indian Government. On the Lower Euphrates British commerce for a long time dominated the navigation of the river as far as Bagdad. Beyond this city the horizon seemed to close in on the unchanging desert. But this region was suddenly thrown, as it were, into international life by the construction of the railway from Constantinople to Bagdad, a German undertaking after 1888 and particularly after 1902. The new route led toward India, but its control slipped from Great Britain. She succeeded, however, in keeping for herself the immediate approaches to the Persian Gulf. She established herself at Koweit, the proposed terminus of the railway, and took this town under her protection ; and she managed to ensure that the Bagdad line should not be pushed farther than Bassorah, and that no extension of it beyond that point should be made without her consent (1914). All opposition disappeared before her, however, during the Great War. Having occupied Bassorah in 1914 and Bagdad in 1917, she received a mandate for Mesopotamia by the Treaty of Versailles. She is still seeking for a political formula that will allow her to rule the country, and she seems to incline to the setting up of an independent Arab kingdom behind which she can take shelter for her actions. On the economic side, however, the Empire has scored. The whole plain of Iraq as far as Mosul and Mejadin has passed under British influence, and, whoever may be the nominal sovereign, its exploitation depends on British capital and British engineers ; the fruitfulness of bygone ages will be born anew on these fertile fields, and the riches of the Arab world will flow into British warehouses. The oil-fields of Mesopotamia belong to the Anglo-Persian Oil Company ; joined to the Persian fields they will secure for the Empire the control, on the shores of the Indian Ocean, of this new fuel, the future rival of coal itself. Moreover, the control of Mesopotamia secures for imperial communications a continuous land-route between the valley of the Nile and that of the Indus, for a string of British dependencies extends from East to West, from the kingdom of Iraq to the confederation of petty Arab states established on the borders of Syria, and to Palestine, which, under a British mandate, widens the zone of defence of Egypt and the Suez Canal. New routes are already being mapped out. An air line is in operation between Cairo and Bagdad; it skirts the coast of Palestine, crosses the Judean hills to the north of Jerusalem, and then passes over the desert. This journey is performed in two days, as against the three weeks occupied by the sea voyage by way of the Persian Gulf. Before long there will be a regular air service also from Bagdad to Bassorah, and thence to Karachi. The great air-route between London and Delhi, however, does not pass through Cairo; its course remains to be traced. Some think that it should follow the Bagdad railway after leaving Europe at Constantinople, while others would like to see it entirely British—all red—at all events in Asia. Hence arises the plan for a railway from the Persian Gulf to the Mediterranean, for purposes of commercial transport, and at the same time to serve as a guide and land base for the air line across these desert regions. We see, then, how the political edifice for the protection of India has been completed in Western Asia : both the sea-route and the land-route from West to East are dominated by Great Britain.

CHAPTER IV

COLONIES OF SETTLEMENT

THROUGHOUT the whole of the seventeenth century and a large part of the eighteenth British colonization was almost entirely a traders' affair—a matter of commercial exploitation. But through the growth of settlements in temperate lands and the exodus of the rural populations it was destined to become a colonists' affair, and a matter of territorial occupation. The distinguishing feature of the British as compared with other empires was soon to appear—namely, the crowd of emigrants it has received from the mother country, building up new Englands in the vast unoccupied spaces of the new continents.

I. BRITISH EMIGRATION

British emigration is one of the mightiest movements of population that history has to show us. It began when the first effects of commercial enterprise on the agricultural production of the country made themselves felt and certain classes of British society were profoundly affected by the unstable condition of things. At the end of the sixteenth century a first wave of emigration was caused by the increase of enclosures and the resulting substitution of pasture-land for arable. At the end of the eighteenth century and throughout the whole of the nineteenth the people were stirred by another movement, deeper and stronger than the first, which gave

63

expression to the economic changes which were affecting the country ; and a stream of humanity, of extraordinary volume, force, and continuity, set out from the British Isles.

British Emigration before the Nineteenth Century.[1]—The first great exodus took place in the sixteenth century, when the growth of the woollen industry led to the conversion of plough-land into pasture, the enclosure of the commons, and the setting up of large farms at the expense of the small holdings of the villagers. A multitude of the smaller folk thus lost all connexion with the land, and were driven to seek homes elsewhere. The literature of that period bears witness to this depopulation. " These enclosures and these pasturelands," says a writer of the year 1581,[2] " are bringing us all to ruin. We can no longer have lands to till, for all is taken for pasturage, either for sheep or cattle—so much so that I have seen around me during the last seven years and within a distance of about six miles, a dozen ploughs abandoned. Where thirty people used once to find a living, there is nothing to be seen now but a shepherd and his flock. . . . These flocks of sheep have driven husbandry out of the land ; now it is everywhere sheep, sheep, sheep." At every extension of pasture-land the beast drove out the man. We shall see the same phenomenon repeated at the close of the eighteenth century and the beginning of the nineteenth in Scotland and Ireland. To harbour these uprooted families it was necessary to seek for thinly peopled lands, and these were found, some at the very gates of Great Britain and others in the new worlds beyond the sea. Thus grew all those ' plantations ' which were fostered by the Governments of Elizabeth

---

[1] Duval, 30 ; Johnson, 44 ; Cunningham, 22a, vol. ii ; Leroy-Beaulieu, 47a ; Caldecott, 15 ; Besant, 8 ; Lucas, 49 ; Williamson, 68.
[2] Quoted by Leroy-Beaulieu, 47a, pp. 89–90.

and the Stuarts. The Irish expeditions were to some extent the political and military side of the problem, while the economic side is seen in the thousands of Anglo-Saxons who went to settle on the lands of the dispossessed Irish clans and replaced Celtic forms of ownership and methods of cultivation by Anglo-Saxon ones. From this period dates the Anglo-Saxon settlement of Ireland, accomplished by the first wave of British emigration : Ireland was the first British colony of settlement.

The earliest attempts at 'plantation' in the New World date from the time of Elizabeth. It is interesting to note that the thinkers and politicians of that period had views on colonial settlement. Thus Bacon argued against the search for the precious metals, and would rather have the colonists engage in work of a less hazardous kind which would yield more useful and more permanent wealth. Later on, when Frobisher was leaving England on his search for the North-west Passage, the members of his expedition received instructions from Richard Hakluyt for the setting up of colonies. They were advised to select a good maritime position, capable of being at once a fortress and a market, and to choose a temperate climate and a site provided with fresh water, food, fuel, and building materials. The first enduring settlements, however, date only from the beginning of the seventeenth century. Then, in the year 1606, were founded two companies : the Plymouth Company, formed to exploit the district now known as New England, and the London Company, whose sphere was to extend southward as far as Virginia. At their birth these companies had at their disposal the human material necessary for colonization. An important section, especially in the matter of quality, was formed by the religious Dissenters, who were driven from England by persecution ; these people formed the nucleus of these little new-born communities. It appears, however, that the part played by religious sects has been exaggerated: the sources of emigration were in reality all places where economic conditions made life too hard for the people of the country districts.

The first permanent centre of colonization owed its origin to the London Company, which in 1607 installed some 150 emigrants at Jamestown, on the shores of Chesapeake Bay. In 1620 a hundred English Dissenters who had taken refuge in Holland obtained leave to come over and embark at the English Plymouth on the *Mayflower*; and they landed in midwinter at the American Plymouth. By the year 1625 the little colony was growing enough maize to support itself, and in 1642 it had already 3000 inhabitants. Close by was founded in 1629 the colony of Massachusetts, which was afterward to absorb Plymouth. So quickly did colonization advance that in 1643 the four provinces of Massachusetts, New Plymouth, Connecticut, and Newhaven formed a union, under the name of the New England Confederation, for common defence " against French, Dutch, and Indians," the dread of the foreigner giving birth already to a kind of national solidarity. Other colonies were set up successively in Maryland, New Jersey, and Pennsylvania, and fed by a continuous stream of emigrants. Without speaking of the tropical island of Barbados, which in 1656 contained 25,000 white colonists, we may refer to Maryland, which contained more than 12,000 in 1652. In 1688 the British settlements on the Atlantic coast contained more than 200,000 colonists. Like the Anglo-Saxon settlement of Ireland, the British settlement of North America derived its vital force from the troops of emigrants who were driven from Great Britain by the economic condition of the countryside.

COLONIES OF SETTLEMENT

British Emigration at the End of the Eighteenth Century and during the Nineteenth.[1]—Emigration slackened between the middle of the seventeenth century and the middle of the eighteenth; the same thing was noticeable in the enclosure movement. There was no regular exodus during that period, though emigration took place in exceptional circumstances, as at the time of the severe winter of the year 1709, when the Government offered free passages to the poverty-stricken, and nearly 30,000 of them went to London to embark for America. But until the Industrial Revolution drew near the springs of emigration seemed to dry up. Moreover, it was prohibited by the Government on several occasions. When the modern economic system came to upset the conditions of life of the peasants, however, the migratory movement recommenced. It would be wrong to think that the beginning of this new wave of emigration coincided with the end of the Napoleonic wars. The movement was apparent much earlier than that, when the old system of rotation of crops suffered its first checks, and the small farms began to be swallowed up by the big ones, and it became more intense whenever an agricultural crisis severed the bonds that bound to the land a new generation of peasants. At the end of the eighteenth century began the departure of the Scottish Highlanders, when the landlords took their ancient holdings away from the small cultivators in order to set up large sheep-farms, and all their little

[1] Same references as for the preceding section, and also the following: R. Gonnard, *L'émigration européenne au XIXᵉ siècle*, Paris, Colin, 1906; *British Empire*, II, pp. 275–280; R. Gonnard, "L'émigration britannique depuis trente ans," in *Questions diplomatiques et coloniales*, March 1, 1909, pp. 336–343 (see also *Revue économique internationale*, 1913, p. 40); H. Bunle and F. Leurence, "Les migrations internationales de 1901 à 1920," in *Bull. statistique générale de France*, October, 1921, pp. 70–108; and, finally, many articles in *The Times*, *United Empire*, and *The Round Table*.

fields were merged into huge 'sheep-walks.' Every one who had lived in the mountains on a scrap of a field and common pasture-ground had to find a new source of livelihood or else go into exile. In 1771 we find the Scots of Cantyre arriving in Prince Edward Island. Year after year emigration to Canada increased, taking away the inhabitants of the poor and wild lands of the Highlands, the Shetlands, and the Hebrides. Everywhere that the sheep advanced man went back, and the stream never ceased to flow toward America and Australia. When men were wanted for a colony it was from Scotland that they were drawn. When the discovery of the gold-mines in 1851 threatened to deplete the country districts of Australia of their inhabitants the manufacturers of Yorkshire, fearing lest the rush to the 'placers' should endanger the production of Australian wool, turned to Scotland and asked for 'squatter' colonists, and a society was even formed to preach Australian emigration among the small folk of the island of Skye. The path, once followed, was not forgotten, and many Scots are still setting out to-day for the Antipodes. During the half-century between 1853 and 1913 Scotland provided more than a million and a half emigrants.

In Ireland the mass of the peasants were affected by the same disturbing influence, and thousands of country-folk were driven into exile by the extension of the pastures. During the first part of the nineteenth century, down to 1840, some twenty thousand Irishmen set out every year for the United States. When the great famine of 1846 occurred it brought misery to the whole of a humble class whose existence was already a precarious one, and a swarm of people left the island— upward of four millions between 1850 and 1900. If emigration is on a smaller scale nowadays, it is because the country has been drained of its life-blood. Moreover, the conditions of agriculture have become better for those who have remained. At the time of the crisis, however, emigration degenerated into depopulation; the people set off in crowds, whole families together, with no intention of returning, at their own expense, and at their own risk; they went out in search of a home, a scrap of land where they could live in safety.

The peasants of England have also emigrated at different periods, but from the same causes. There was an exodus about 1820, following on the peace settlement, which led to a fall in the price of corn and a fresh enclosure movement. Another wave of emigration began about 1870, when the cultivation of cereal crops was ruined by the competition of the new lands. A fresh extension of pasturage became necessary, and farm workers no longer found employment for the harvest. This crisis reached its highest point between 1880 and 1890.

Other causes have contributed to the instability of rural existence, especially in England. Thus home industries used formerly to keep a numerous population in the villages and small towns, until the coming of machinery took away their livelihood. Each advance in mechanical invention caused an exodus. About 1830 the use of steam-driven spinning-machines drove millions of workers out of employment, and such was their distress that emigration had to be officially organized and directed. About 1840 the growth of the weaving industry led to a terrible crisis in domestic weaving. Emigration seemed the only remedy, and the Commission of 1841 that inquired into the matter came to the conclusion that the weavers must be assisted to emigrate, provided that they were farmers as well, and would find no difficulty in working on the land in a new country. This stream of men was divided by public departments and private societies between the different colonies: one agency interested itself in the

Cape, another in Canada, and a third in Australia, and thus they all strove to assist in cultivating the virgin lands of the colonies.

While generations of men were thus torn from their native soil and driven into exile by a new industrial system, that same system was opening up to them vast habitable areas beyond the seas, for Great Britain, driven onward by her commercial expansion, had extended her network of interests over the whole earth. Apart from North America, where in 1760 two millions of Anglo-Saxons were already dwelling, the temperate lands of the Southern Hemisphere had become British. To emigrants they offered a prospect of an assured future : freedom, facilities for acquiring land, and, above all, the possibility of living the same kind of life as in the mother country, with the same cereals and the same domestic animals. During the nineteenth century out of 100 British emigrants 65 went to the United States, 15 to Canada, 11 to Australia, and 5 to South Africa. Nor were freedom and property the only attractions that drew these emigrants to the new lands : at certain periods the lure of the gold-mines provoked great rushes —to California in 1848, to Australia in 1851, to New Zealand in 1861, and to South Africa (Witwatersrand) in 1888. So, too, in 1870 the Kimberley district was peopled by the influx of the diamond-seekers. Not all these newcomers were wandering adventurers : many of them, when the gold-fields were exhausted and the fever had subsided, settled down permanently to till the soil, the investment that depreciates least. For Australia in particular the gold rush marked the decisive stage in the peopling of the country : in a single month 82 vessels entered Melbourne carrying 12,000 emigrants, and in the ten years from 1851 to 1861 508,802 British emigrants were disembarked. The population of the state of Victoria rose from 76,200 in 1850 to 541,800 in 1861, and that of the whole of Australia from 430,600 in 1850 to 1,203,000 in 1861.

British emigration is the greatest of all the human streams that have ever crossed the seas. In the absence of statistics it is difficult to measure it before the year 1815, though we have figures relating to subsequent years. Taking only rough estimates, it is said that between 1815 and 1920 the huge number of more than seventeen million persons left the United Kingdom. It is important, however, to deduct from this total first of all those foreigners who emigrated by way of Great Britain, and of whom we have no documentary information until after 1856, and secondly the number of emigrants who returned, and who are not mentioned until 1870. Perhaps we should not be far from the truth in saying that six or seven millions of these emigrants have not returned, including 800,000 for the period 1910-20 and nearly two millions for the period 1880-1910. We can trace in the figures the influence of the crises which have swelled the number of departures during certain periods, as, for instance, the Irish crisis of 1840-60 and the agricultural crisis of 1880-90. The movement was strongest in the middle of the nineteenth century : the number of departures rose from 60,000 in 1843 to 260,000 in 1847, 300,000 in 1849, and 370,000 in 1851 ; in this latter year, therefore, more than a thousand persons set out every day.

It is a remarkable thing that, notwithstanding this exodus, the population of the country did not diminish, save only in Ireland ; the excess of births repaired the breaches made by emigration in the store of human capital. Between 1841 and 1861 the population of the United Kingdom increased by more than two millions, and between 1853 and 1900 it rose from $27\frac{1}{2}$ to $40\frac{1}{2}$ millions. In this case, therefore, emigration and increase of population are not conflicting phenomena ; they are, rather, the outcome of a state of civilization that is favourable to human vitality. Since this outpouring of men began it has sometimes slackened, but never stopped ; it even appears to be a law of the British community. So far this exportation of human material has always been regarded as a blessing both to the mother country with too many children and to the colony waiting for men. In the minds of economists who studied the subject as early as the beginning of the nineteenth century emigration was not a form of impoverishment, for it widened the field of the national economy by giving birth to communities which produced raw materials and purchased manufactured articles.

Emigration has always persisted as a natural function of the British organism. There were 44 emigrants per 10,000 inhabitants in 1841, 120 in 1851, 44 in 1861, 64 in 1871, 57 in 1891, 41 in 1901, and 60 in 1911. The Great War put an end to it all ; it did not eliminate the causes of emigration, but the struggle demanded soldiers, and maritime transport worked badly. With the coming of peace the departures were resumed ; a terrible industrial crisis threw thousands of workmen out of employment. During the War there had been an excess of returning emigrants ; after 1918 the departures were again in excess—27,000 in 1919, and 173,000 in 1920 (excluding the number of returns).

It may be said, indeed, that emigration has not ceased for a century and a half to be a British habit. The foreigner travelling in Great Britain comes across it everywhere as an idea familiar to the people of the country. At the railway stations, even far away from large towns, attention is drawn by coloured posters to the overseas regions that are asking for colonists, and information is given about fares and the advantages accruing to emigrants, while there are agencies engaged in organizing the exportation of men. The British mentality has been formed on this tradition. In every family the child very soon regards himself as personally free. He goes away, generally with no intention of returning, and knowing that he will get to an Anglo-Saxon country where he will find men of the same tongue, the same customs, the same civilization—fellow-country-men, in short. The colonies, on their side, need these men in order to cultivate their soil, and they know the benefit they derive from receiving them ready-made. An Englishman coldly estimates the cost of bringing up a man to the age of twenty-one at £175, and considers that, at this rate, Australia has received from the mother country in thirty years a gift of £175,000,000.

Since the end of the Great War this need for men has become more urgent. Emigration is regarded as an imperial necessity and a means of strengthening the British overseas communities. The man who goes out to the Dominions is not lost to his native land, but serves her far better at a distance than if he remained in the old country. In Australasia especially great estates have been divided up, monetary advances have been made to emigrants, and schools of agricultural training have been instituted for them. Unfortunately, neither in Australasia nor in Canada is the right kind of man always obtained. It is not a matter of giving shelter to the dregs of the town populations, and increasing still further the urban congestion of the colonies. It is rural emigrants who are particularly needed—those, that is to say, whom the mother country is most anxious to retain ; and hence arises the necessity of so organizing emigration that it benefits equally the mother country and the colonies. Besides, the emigrants need to be directed toward those parts of the Empire which require them : far too many of them go to the United States when they would be warmly welcomed in Canada. Among the institutions working to support and direct emigration the Oversea Settlement Committee has devoted its efforts particularly to demobilized soldiers. At the end of 1920 it had directed 38,700 persons to the Dominions, of whom 14,658 went to Canada, 11,983 to Australia, 7417 to New Zealand, and 3068 to South Africa. Thus the flow of sap still continues which gave rise in earlier days to the overseas Anglo-Saxon communities. It still feeds them, and they go on continually growing, more, indeed, through these imports from the mother country than through the internal growth of their own populations.

II. DISTRIBUTION OF THE COLONIES OF SETTLEMENT [1]

There are three great countries to which British emigrants go : North America, which was the first to receive them at the beginning of the seventeenth century ; Australasia, which was discovered by English sailors in the South Seas at the end of the eighteenth ; and South Africa, which the English captured from the Dutch to defend the road to India at the beginning of the nineteenth. These three countries are offshoots of British stock. The earliest to be established and the most powerful no longer entirely belongs to the British Empire, for the greater part of it split off to form the United States of America. It remained for a long time the chief destination of British emigrants, owing to the start it had obtained in colonization. Between 1815 and 1906 it absorbed 65 per cent., Canada 15 per cent., Australasia 11 per cent., and the remaining colonies 7 per cent. Sir Charles Dilke remarked in 1864 that

[1] Same references as for the last two sections. Numerous monographs or geographical studies are available for consultation dealing with each of the Dominions, and most of them contain very useful information, but these regional bibliographies would be outside the scope of this work.

out of 20 emigrants from the United Kingdom 16 went to the United States, 2 to Australia, and 1 to Canada. But these proportions have changed since that time. Since the early years of the twentieth century there is to be observed an increasingly marked preference for the Dominions. The United States still headed the list in 1901, in 1902, and in 1904; but the Dominions beat it in 1910 (62 per cent.), in 1912 (70 per cent.), in 1919 (75 per cent.), and in 1920 (71 per cent.). A very simple table will show how the situation has altered between 1901 and 1920.

DESTINATIONS OF BRITISH EMIGRANTS

(*Percentages of the number of departures minus the number of returns*)

Period	U.S.A.	Canada	Australasia	S. Africa
1901–1903	51	21	5	19
1913	21	53	24	0.2
1920	29	44	17	6

United States.—When the first British exodus took place at the commencement of the seventeenth century it was on the Atlantic coast of North America that the earliest nucleus of a colony was set up. In 1688 all the colonies, ranged along the coast from Maine to Carolina, contained 200,000 white inhabitants. At the beginning the centre of gravity of this British community lay in the Southern states, enriched as they were by the labour of the negroes on the plantations. But gradually there grew up in the Northern states a European type of organization, based on the exploitation of the forests, the cultivation of cereal crops, and sea-fishing. It was the English colonists of this region who took Nova Scotia from the French in 1713, as well as that part of

75

Newfoundland which was not already English, and who conquered Canada and the banks of the St Lawrence in 1763. About the year 1770 the population of the English colonies as a whole was already 2,312,000, and Boston was a town of 20,000 souls. But the war against nature made slow progress on those rocky and timber-covered uplands; access to the interior was barred by forests and mountains. If a burst of emigration were to come, however, it would be powerful enough to open the gates of the West. In the nineteenth century, thanks to British emigrants, it did come, though it was not due to the political action of Great Britain, who even at the end of the eighteenth century still looked upon the colonies as economic dependencies whose destiny it was to produce raw materials and foodstuffs and to consume the manufactured goods of the mother country. She forbade them to have any manufactures, to weave cloth, to work in iron or steel, and to refine sugar. She sorely tried her colonies of settlement, and lost the first of those she had reared. But the political independence of the United States did not destroy their affinity with Britain. Delivered over to their own resources, they were unable to grow without the infusion of British blood. A good half of the American people are sprung from the British inhabitants who settled in the country at the beginning of the nineteenth century. Furthermore, between the years 1820 and 1870 more than half the immigrants who landed in the United States were of British origin, while between 1870 and 1900 the proportion still reached one-third. At the present time more than two-thirds of the population of the Union is of British descent: the physical basis of the American nation is Anglo-Saxon.

This Anglo-Saxon element, however, tends to lose its purity. The country is like a huge melting-pot into which other elements have been continually thrown ever since the later years of the nineteenth century. Italians, Slavs, and Hungarians arrive in serried masses. The composition of the industrial workers of Massachusetts, as determined by their country of origin, was completely transformed between the years 1890 and 1913. The proportion of those who had come from Great Britain fell from 19 per cent. to 11 per cent., of the Irish from 30 per cent. to 13 per cent., of British Canadians from 16 per cent. to 3 per cent., and of French Canadians from 21 per cent. to 17 per cent. The Poles, on the other hand, who do not appear in the statistics for 1890, have a proportion of 14 per cent. in the figures for 1913, while there also appear Portuguese, Greeks, Lithuanians, Armenians, and Syrians. The physical type of the American diverges from the British type in proportion to the progress made by the infiltration of these elements from Eastern and Southern Europe. This tendency is further accentuated by the fact that the birth-rate is falling in the old Yankee states where the British blood still remains fairly pure ; births are most numerous among recent immigrants of Slavonic and Latin race and among the negroes. It may be that, if they are not careful, the Anglo-Saxons will be submerged.

But nothing threatens American civilization, which is Anglo-Saxon to the backbone. It has a marvellous power of assimilation. Immigration has never taken place after the fashion of an avalanche, with risk of injury to the social equilibrium. American society seems to digest and assimilate the foreign elements. It imposes its own tongue upon them to such an extent that this mass of more than a hundred million men remains an Anglo-Saxon community *par excellence*, and in studying the British Empire this fact must never be forgotten.

Canada.—The settlement of Canada went on more slowly than that of the United States, because the exploitation of the country was retarded by the coldness of the climate. The population was still only 240,000 in 1801 and 582,000 in 1825. In the middle of the nineteenth century there was a marked rise : to 1,843,000 in 1851, and 3,635,000 in 1871. Progress then slackened (the number in 1891 was 4,833,000), only to pick up again with the coming of the twentieth century : the population was 7,207,000 in 1911 and 8,400,000 in 1920. This increase was largely due to immigration from Great Britain. The Scottish element played a great part in it from the end of the eighteenth century and the beginning of the nineteenth. Scottish settlers founded Perth in the district of Johnstown in 1815, Beckwith in 1818, and Lanark and Dalhousie in 1820. Many Scots were to be found among the employees of the Hudson's Bay Company, and, as in the case of the squatters of Australia, they were to be met with here among the pioneers of colonization, with the advance-guard of the discoverers of the North-west. Many Irishmen too settled in Newfoundland. But the peopling of the country progressed slowly as compared with that of the United States. From 1829 to 1833 Canada received on an average only 33,000 emigrants per year ; from 1834 to 1844 the number was 22,000 ; from 1844 to 1854 38,000 ; and from 1854 to 1859 15,000. Moreover, out of this number many landed in Canada only in order to pass on to the United States ; only one-third remained in Canada. There was a spurt, however, at the close of the nineteenth century, owing to the development of steamship lines and railways and in consequence of the cultivation of the corn-lands of the West. In spite of its long winters Canada attracts more colonists than Australia with its magnificent climate. This is because the voyage out is shorter, the grants of land are more generous, and legislation is less vexatious. In 1881–82 60,000 emigrants settled in Canada ; in 1885 the number was 80,000 ; in 1909–10 it was 210,000 ; and in 1912–13 it was 402,400. Among these newcomers the British element far exceeds the rest. The annual average number of British emigrants for the years 1902 to 1912 was 110,000, and it rose to 150,000 in 1913. If we deduct the number of returned emigrants we may say that during those ten years Canada received more than 600,000 British subjects, who settled for the most part in the Far West. The movement, though retarded by the War, has been since resumed : there were 8600 British immigrants in 1915, 8200 in 1916, 3200 in 1917, 9900 in 1918, 10,000 in 1919, and 75,000 in 1920. The British element, moreover, is reinforced by the American farmers who cmoe to the corn-lands of Alberta, Assiniboia, and Manitoba ; between 1900 and 1910 this influx yielded nearly 500,000 colonists, if not all of British stock yet at least all Americanized. It continued during the War : the numbers were 37,000 in 1915, 61,000 in 1916, 71,000 in 1917, 40,000 in 1918, and 50,000 in 1920. Despite the higher birth-rate of the French Canadians this human tide is every day extending the rule of Anglo-Saxon civilization over the country. Canada remains a Promised Land for British settlers.

Australasia. — It was not until the close of the eighteenth century that prospects of British colonization were opened up in the Southern Hemisphere, in Australasia. Australia, visited by Bougainville in 1766–1769 and by Captain Cook in 1769–74, received its first English settlement in 1787. This event was one result of the loss of the United States, for the English, in search of a new convict station, landed their first batch of criminals in 1787 at Botany Bay, on the coast of New South Wales. To colonize those vast solitudes, peopled only by nomadic tribes, would have required a regular influx of free men. But Australia was avoided by emigrants for a long time, on account both of its distance and of the presence of the convicts. During the first part of the nineteenth century it was the United States that attracted them most. Until the discovery of the gold-mines in 1851 many of the European inhabitants of Australia were convicts: between 1787 and 1836 New South Wales received 75,200 and Tasmania 27,760. Deportation was abolished, however, in 1853. As for the free emigrants, they arrived but slowly: a few hundreds between 1820 and 1830, 5300 per year from 1830 to 1839, and a total of 12,700 between 1840 and 1849. After 1851, however, there was a rush of gold-seekers, and between 1851 and 1861 there landed 510,000 colonists from the United Kingdom. Then the movement was retarded by the deliberate action of the Australians themselves. Despite the extent of their unoccupied lands, despite the scantiness of their population, and despite their low birth-rate, they closed their country to newcomers. Their object was to improve the condition of the working classes by preventing congestion in the towns. In no country in the world is so large a proportion of the population urban. Nearly half the inhabitants of Australia live in the six state capitals ; these cities, already overgrown, absorbed the greater number of the immigrants, and each newcomer made the conditions of life harder for the rest. Unfortunately, by thus putting a stop to immigration, the Australians were condemning the whole of their country to solitude : the towns were relieved, but the nation was left to decay. So since 1905 Australia has sent out appeals for colonists. After deducting the number of departures there have remained in the country the following : 2100 in 1904–6, 18,000 in 1907–9, 70,000 in 1910–12, 65,000 in 1913, and 17,000 in 1914. During the War the departures exceeded the arrivals, but after the Peace the movement was resumed, and the net gain for 1920 was about 8000 colonists. These modest figures reveal the slowness of British settlement. We find the same thing even in New Zealand, where 14,200 permanent settlements were made in 1913 and 11,100 in 1920. It is true that these Southern lands are far away from Europe, and that the journey thither is an expensive one. But they have one inestimable advantage from the imperial point of view: out of a total of rather over a million immigrants Australasia has received practically none but Anglo-Saxons, and that is its leading characteristic among British colonies. The United States has her medley of races, Canada her French province, and South Africa her Dutch settlers. But Australia and New Zealand can claim purely British descent for almost all their inhabitants : next to Great Britain herself they are the most British countries in the world.

South Africa.—There are certain obstacles in the way of Anglo-Saxon settlement in South Africa. It is true that the country has vast territories to offer to the European to live and labour in. But the English are faced by a large black population and a compact colony of Boer peasants. From the beginning they have wanted to plant British colonists in order to balance the Kaffirs and the Dutch. In 1814 a subscription list was opened in London for assisting emigration, and in 1820 some thousands of emigrants landed on the shores of Algoa Bay, and set up a purely British colony, which has grown and prospered. Throughout the country as a whole, however, Anglo-Saxon settlement has never made much progress. The land attracts many workmen, employees, engineers, technicists, and traders, but very few rural colonists. Statistics often reveal an excess of departures over arrivals, and the British element increases but slightly through immigration. In the Union of South Africa there is only one white man to

F

four blacks. The Boers make up about half the white population and, among the whites, almost the whole of the rural population, while the Anglo-Saxons dwell for the most part in the towns.

The colonizing movement that has sprung from British emigration has founded four Anglo-Saxon communities, which have arrived at different stages of power and are made up of British material in differing proportions. The greatest of these, the United States, with 110 millions of inhabitants, does not belong to the Empire. The three others—Canada with 8,400,000 inhabitants, Australasia with 6,300,000, and South Africa with 1,300,000 whites—are Dominions, or nations that are quasi-independent, but always closely associated with the mother country.

III. TERRITORIAL EXTENSION OF THE COLONIES OF SETTLEMENT [1]

In the matter of population Canada, Australasia, and South Africa form only a small part of the overseas Anglo-Saxon communities. They are small collections of men, with scarcely twenty millions of inhabitants to set against the one hundred and ten millions of the United States. But, on the other hand, they are enormous masses of land. Their territorial grouping was accomplished long before they were completely settled. Too poor, in fact, in living material to people their land, they were able to command means of communication sufficiently powerful to dominate the whole area. By the building of roads and railways they accomplished their territorial development long before they completed their demographic growth. In their formation they went through the same phases. Originally they were

---

[1] Same references as for the two preceding sections.

little independent nuclei, which germinated and grew, even though they were separated sometimes by great distances. Then these isolated colonies joined their branches together across space by a kind of natural radiation. Finally we see them becoming fused into a single state as soon as the development of their circulatory system enabled them to live as members of the same body.

Canada.—In the middle of the nineteenth century British America consisted of several groups of colonies, separated from each other by great distances. On the shores of the Great Lakes and the banks of the St Lawrence lay Lower Canada and Upper Canada, and on the Atlantic coast were the maritime provinces of New Brunswick and Nova Scotia, cut off from the interior by dense forests and a projecting portion of the state of Maine. Far away on the shores of the Pacific, behind the Rocky Mountains, British Columbia dwelt alone. It was by way of the Pacific that she had received her first colonists, as well as the later ones who were attracted by her gold-mines in 1856. In 1858 she ranked as a Crown Colony. Between British Columbia and Canada, from the Rockies to the Great Lakes, there stretched a vast and almost empty region under the control of the Hudson's Bay Company. It had practically only one important centre of colonization, which lay near the Red River, on the site of the present city of Winnipeg. Between all these British communities there existed a real feeling of solidarity which through fear of the powerful American republic impelled them to unite. Thus was accomplished in 1867 the federation of the two groups of eastern provinces : Canada (Ontario and Quebec) on the one hand and the maritime provinces (New Brunswick and Nova Scotia) on the other. A condition of this federation was the construction of an intercolonial railway between the Atlantic provinces and the Great Lakes. To this group of eastern provinces the remaining ones were to be joined one after the other. The decisive stage in this amalgamation was reached in 1871, when British Columbia entered the federation, making it a condition that a railway should be built to unite Vancouver with Canada. This railway, the Canadian Pacific, was completed in 1886, and may be regarded as the ligament of Canadian unity. By joining the east and the west together, and by opening up the prairies to colonization, it has established a living continuity from one end of the continent to the other. More recently the construction of the Grand Trunk Pacific and the Canadian Northern Railway has broadened the ligament, as it were, and thus strengthened the territorial unity of the Canadian Federation. By uniting the two oceans these transcontinental railroads have given Canada a place on one of the most important routes in the Northern Hemisphere. On the Atlantic she commands the shortest route to Europe, and on the Pacific the shortest route to China and Japan. Great Britain can communicate with the Far East by way of Canada as well as and more quickly than by way of Asia. Canada is the half-way house of the Empire.

Australasia.—In Australasia during the first half of the nineteenth century fresh colonies grew up on the coast, alongside of the mother colony of New South Wales : Tasmania in 1803, Western Australia in 1829, and South Australia in 1834. New Zealand appeared in 1840. By a natural process of partition Victoria split off from New South Wales in 1850, and Queensland in 1859. Little by little the extension of the sheep-grazing lands into the interior diminished the area that was free and unoccupied, and since 1860 the whole of Australia has been divided into six colonies, sharing the entire continent between them. Here again territorial extension preceded human occupation. The continent was not, and is not yet, settled except on the south-eastern edge and at isolated points on the west, north-west, and north. For a long time each colony lived isolated from its neighbours, and Western Australia long remained more closely connected with England than with New South Wales. The country still suffers from this old spirit of individualism, for the railways of each colony have been built on a different gauge. Since 1885, however, the feeling of isolation in those distant seas and the fear of having to defend their interests in the Pacific have led these colonies to realize the necessity for union, and this movement resulted in 1901 in Australian federation. Broadly speaking, this union still remains to some extent an external one, resting partly on maritime relations, such as the services of the British India Steam Navigation Company to the west and those of the P. and O. and the Orient lines to the east. But it is tending to become internal, through a system of continental circulation. Despite the differences of gauge the railways are gradually joining Queensland to New South Wales, Victoria, and South Australia. In 1917 the transcontinental railway was opened, uniting the western part of Australia with the eastern states of the Commonwealth, and preparations are being made for the unification of the whole Australian system, with the same gauge. Since 1872 a line of telegraph has crossed the whole continent, from Port Darwin to Adelaide.

South Africa.—Territorial extension has been accomplished much less easily in South Africa than in the empty spaces of North America and Australia. The country originally contained inhabitants who were fixed in the soil and difficult of absorption. Then later on British expansion had but one single and distant base of operations—the coast of Cape Colony. To advance northward the British had to travel along the table-lands of the Orange and the Vaal, avoiding alike the deserts of the west and the mountains of the east. The first advance was the annexation in 1843 of Natal, the little Boer republic on the east coast; but this was not an advance into the interior: the English had merely widened their coastal base. There was no real continental extension until 1902, the date of the annexation of the Boer countries. Between 1843 and 1902 Great Britain did nothing but acquire or clip off portions of native territory: Griqualand West in 1871, Basutoland in 1875, Griqualand East in 1885, and Zululand in 1887. Every attempted advance toward the north meant a collision with the Boer states which occupied the habitable and healthy zone of the lofty tablelands.

This extension was prepared for by the slow penetration of British capital and commerce. The signal was given by the discovery of the diamond-mines of Kimberley (1869–70), to the north of the Orange River, on the western border of the Orange Free State. The mining district was purchased from the Free State and annexed to Cape Colony, and a town of adventurers, business men, and British colonists was quickly set up, in the midst of the veldt, at the very gateway of the Boer states. Henceforth the Anglo-Saxons, settled there, no longer allowed the northern horizon to close down in front of them. Germany having annexed South-west Africa in 1883, they had British authority proclaimed over Bechuanaland in 1885. At the same time (1884–85) gold was discovered in the Transvaal. In the course of a few years the mining country (Witwatersrand) received a swarm of foreigners, coming for the most part from Cape Colony and England. Powerful companies were formed to exploit the mines, almost all of them with British capital, and a centre of Anglo-Saxon civilization was set up in the midst of the Boer country. And while British influence was thus penetrating into the heart of the Dutch republics it was also overflowing in a northerly direction, and, with the support of the South African Company, was spreading over all the South African tablelands from the Limpopo to Lake Nyassa.

This British ' push ' was dependent upon the railway. In 1885 the railway starting from the Cape reached Kimberley, in 1894 it reached Mafeking, and in 1897 Bulawayo. At the same time another line, leaving Port Elizabeth, penetrated the Free State, and between 1890 and 1895 reached in succession Bloemfontein, Pretoria, and Lourenço Marques. Thus the whole of South Africa was connected by rail with the sea-ports, and traversed by streams of British traffic, even before Great Britain had established a unified political sway by the war of 1899–1902. The result of the Great War of 1914–18 was the extension of British hegemony to German South-west Africa as well as to German East Africa. From the Cape to the Upper Nile, from Southern to equatorial latitudes, there is now no need to leave British territory. The great railway from the Cape crosses the Zambezi and goes as far as the Belgian Congo, 2300 miles from its starting-point. It is a part of the great transcontinental or trans-African railway which for so long a time was merely a dream and is now becoming a reality. On this great arterial line are grafted, as it were, the side lines that reach the sea in different latitudes : the line from Prieska to South-west Africa by which Cape Town has been joined since 1915 to Walfish Bay ; the lines from Pretoria to Durban and Lourenço Marques ; and the line from Beira to Fort Salisbury. It is by means of railways that the Anglo-Saxons take possession of their colonial domains. In every continent the railroad is their most powerful instrument of colonization, and the spread of their civilization cannot be understood without reference to the development of the general circulatory system of the world.

CHAPTER V

GEOGRAPHICAL STRUCTURE OF THE BRITISH EMPIRE

I. EXTENT AND POPULATION OF THE EMPIRE

THE British Empire, the outcome of the labours of three centuries, has attained a size that no other empire in history has ever rivalled. The Roman Empire was no more than one-seventh as large, and the empires of the Arabs, the Mongols, the Spaniards, and the Chinese only a third.[1] The empire of the Tsars alone was rather more than half its size. We can properly grasp this unique feature only through the concrete conception of the space covered by the Empire. With its 13,800,000 square miles it embraces nearly a quarter of the land area of the earth, and is more than three times as large as Europe, and twice the size of South America. Some portions of it are enormous continental masses : Canada alone is almost as big as Europe, and Australasia is bigger than Canada, while the Indian Empire is half the size of Europe. And what still further increases the impression of immensity is the fact that these territories are out of all proportion to the small area of the mother country : the Empire is a hundred times as large as the United Kingdom.

This disproportion may be said to have been a characteristic of the Empire from the very beginning. At the close of the eighteenth century this little group

[1] Wagner, *Allgemeine Erdkunde*, p. 700.

of European islands was already ruling over vast areas in North America and India. But this peculiarity has gone on continually increasing. From 8½ million square miles in 1841, the Empire grew to 11 millions in 1901, and 13.8 in 1921. During the active colonizing period from 1880 to 1900 it increased by over two million square miles—that is to say, by an area twenty times the size of the United Kingdom.[1] After the War of 1914–18 British acquisitions amounted to nearly a million square miles, or an area eight times as large as the United Kingdom.

Area, however, is only a rough criterion for estimating the geographical value of a phenomenon : we must add to it the distribution of these lands on the surface of the globe. Almost the whole of the Empire lies outside Europe : 16 per cent. in Asia, 24 per cent. in Australasia, 27 per cent. in Africa, 32 per cent. in America, and only 1 per cent. in Europe. In its territorial constitution the Empire is an extra-European organization. Its spatial foundations lie outside Europe, in all parts of the world, and herein it differs from the Roman Empire, which lay around the Mediterranean, and from the Russian Empire, whose constituent portions lay next to each other in a compact mass to the north of the Euro-Asiatic continent.

These territories, which appear on the map to be scattered over the various continents, are divided almost equally between the temperate and the tropical zones, between the regions where the European can live and labour and those in which he can only supervise native industries. In the temperate zone the men, the plants, and the animals of Europe have been able to settle down and multiply ; in the tropical zone there is room only for traders and business directors from Europe. These two systems are largely represented in the Empire

[1] According to Baines, quoted by Mondaini, 54, vol. i, pp. 70–73.

GEOGRAPHICAL STRUCTURE

in virtue of the general distribution of the British colonies, and by their co-existence they create an element of solidarity among its different parts, since they are able to combine and supplement each other. This solidarity is not a natural phenomenon, but arises rather from commercial relations than from geographical proximity. At the same time, this proximity does exist in the case of an important block of imperial lands—those, namely, which lie together round the Indian Ocean and whose continuity has been established by Great Britain. Round this ocean, a veritable British Mediterranean, it is possible to travel without leaving British territory, either actual possessions or spheres of influence. From Cape Colony to Egypt along the whole length of Africa, from Egypt to the East Indies by way of Arabia, Mesopotamia, Persia, India, and the Malay Peninsula, and from the East Indies to Tasmania by way of Australia, one never leaves the British Empire : the Indian Ocean is its geographical centre of gravity.

There are 450,000,000 people in the British Empire. This is a quarter of the population of the world, about the same population as that of Europe, and ten times that of the United Kingdom. This disproportion between the mother country and the Empire, though less marked than in the case of area, has none the less been a fundamental characteristic of the Empire since the conquest of India : it dates from the time when Britain annexed the human ant-hills of the valley of the Ganges. India alone accounts for 71 per cent. of the population of the Empire, and through this fact the lands around the Indian Ocean take a preponderating place in the whole structure. Though the physical mass of the Empire is divided between all the continents its human mass is concentrated especially in tropical Asia. Moreover, the whole of the hot countries have far more weight than the rest, because they possess 85 per cent. of the inhabitants of the Empire.

These swarms of natives belong to different races, to differently organized societies, and to civilizations in every stage of maturity. Apart from India, which is a world in itself, we find that, out of every thousand inhabitants of the Empire, for every 300 white men dwelling mainly in temperate lands there are more than 500 blacks and 70 yellow men and Malays living for the most part in hot countries. In the whole of South and East Africa the negroes are far more numerous than the whites. The majority of the Moslems of the world are dwellers in the Empire. It is this very diversity which up to the present has enabled a minority of white men, living outside the Tropics, to rule over so many peoples of the hot countries. But the power exercised by this handful of men over so many lands and so many human beings proceeds from another cause, which is to some extent innate in the life of the Empire, because it is itself a natural law of the United Kingdom—the influence of the sea.

II. THE PART PLAYED BY THE SEA IN THE EMPIRE

The isolated position of Great Britain at the western extremity of Europe is more apparent than real, because the ocean which washes her shores is an ever-open route, conducting her vessels to every part of the world. In the sea the Empire possesses a principle of internal unity.

Sea-coast Positions.—All the seeds of the British colonies were conveyed by sea. The islander's instinct led the merchants and colonists of Great Britain to seek for islands, peninsulas, and coastal positions in which to settle. The continental expansion of the Empire is of recent date; for a long time it remained entirely a matter of the coast. The first conquest of the seventeenth century was that of an island—Jamaica —and the first of the eighteenth was that of a tiny peninsula—Gibraltar. In India for a hundred years the English avoided all penetration inland, and occupied only fortified positions along the coasts : Madras with Fort St George, Bombay on her island, and Calcutta with Fort William are classical types of commercial settlements. While all other conquerors of India entered by the north and advanced toward the sea, the British conquest started from the sea and progressed toward the mountains. In Africa British occupation was confined for the greater part of the nineteenth century to coast stations : Bathurst, Cape Coast Castle, Lagos. It was only during the last twenty years of the century that England turned to the hinterlands : Nigeria, East Africa, Egypt, and the Sudan. In Canada the earliest zone of occupation was along the St Lawrence, a great maritime highway ; expansion toward the prairies came much later. In Australia the British settlements were originally made on the shores of well-protected harbours : Botany Bay (Sydney), Port Philip (Melbourne), Port Arthur (Tasmania). British colonies rested on maritime bases, and their centres of population, their large towns, are still on the coast or on navigable rivers : Auckland, Melbourne, Sydney, Cape Town, Montreal, Calcutta, Bombay.

Naval Stations.—As in the case of the other great empires, unity depends upon a system of communications. In ancient times the Persian Empire owed its cohesion to its system of roads : thanks to relays of horses and riders news could be transmitted in less than a week from Susa to Sardis. Similarly the internal unity of the Roman Empire depended upon its fine highways, by which orders could be circulated at the rate of 112 miles a day. So, too, it is a system of communications,

93

the gift of nature and not a work of art, that provides the cement for the worldwide structure of the British Empire. Throughout the centuries the English have occupied in succession all the positions along the sea-routes necessary to the safety of their traffic. At the beginning they were places that were indispensable for supplying their ships with fresh water,[1] for in days when it was not yet possible to distil sea-water vessels could not carry enough water on board to last them during a long voyage. The need for water hampered their freedom of movement then, as did the need for coal at a later date. Watering-points were necessary along the sea-routes, and several British possessions originated in this way. Nowadays there is a limit to the distance a steamship can travel without coaling. For an ironclad steaming at a moderate speed this distance is estimated at 3000 miles. Hence arises the necessity for coaling-stations on the great ocean-routes and their crossings. Then the submarine telegraphic cables also require landing-places. For all these reasons there is a chain of naval stations along the sea-routes of this oceanic empire. Each ocean has its own, chosen with the practical good sense of a nation of sailors, and situated at the nodal points of world traffic.

In the Mediterranean the Empire has two great fortified naval bases : Gibraltar and Malta. Gibraltar is a rocky promontory three miles long, joined to the mainland by a low and sandy isthmus. This position is of no use for commerce or for colonization : it is simply a fortress commanding the trade-route from the East and the Far East, a coaling-station, a cable-station for England, South Africa, and the Eastern Mediterranean, and a deep-sea port, and its garrison constitutes a fifth of its population. Half-way between Gibraltar and Egypt, at the point where the Mediterranean narrows

[1] *British Empire*, ii, pp. 737 ff.

between Sicily and North Africa, Malta is the base of the Mediterranean fleet. Its port, Valetta, formed of two bays that pierce deeply into the island, can take ships of the largest size, but its accommodation is insufficient. The island of Cyprus has no fortifications, but it commands the coast of Asia Minor at 40 miles' distance, the coast of Syria at 60 miles, and the coast of Egypt at 220 miles. There are other useful positions in the Mediterranean, and Great Britain has never lost sight of them. It is well known that at one time she occupied the Ionian Islands at the mouth of the Adriatic Sea. On the island of Lemnos, close to the Dardanelles and the Black Sea, the Bay of Mudros served as a base for the operations of the British fleet against the Dardanelles during the Great War. Since the end of the War Great Britain has not become reconciled to leaving Constantinople. As for the Suez Canal, its safety is regarded as one of the conditions of existence of the Empire, and the independence of Egypt will therefore have to allow of the maintenance of a British military force in Egypt ; the British Prime Minister announced to the whole world on February 28, 1922, that " His Majesty's Government would regard as an unfriendly act any attempt at interference in the affairs of Egypt by another power, and they would consider any aggression against the territory of Egypt as an act to be repelled by all the means at their command." [1]

Naval stations and coal-depots are scattered over and around the Indian Ocean—the imperial sea. On the route from the Cape to India there are Cape Town, Port Elizabeth, Port Natal, Mauritius, Zanzibar, and the Seychelles. At the mouth of the Red Sea is the island of Perim, a bare rock, wanting in fresh water, but with a well-sheltered harbour from 24 to 48 feet deep. Then comes Aden, on the edge of a bay sprinkled

---

[1] Speech by Mr Lloyd George, February 28, 1922.

with sandy islets, with a burning hot soil, and provided with drinking water by means of distilling apparatus and its ancient tanks. This is succeeded by Point de Galle and Colombo, and then, on the way to the Far East and along the Malay Straits, come Port Blair, the island of Penang with Georgetown, the island of Singapore, the island of Labuan with Victoria, and farther on the island of Hong Kong with another Victoria. Finally, in the middle of the Indian Ocean there are the island of Diego Garcia and the Chagos Archipelago, at the crossing-place of the direct route from Aden to Australia and the route from the Cape to Colombo, and the Keeling or Cocos Islands on the route from Ceylon to Australia.

In the Atlantic Ocean other nations—France, Spain, Portugal, and America—have taken their precautions, but the English are not altogether unprovided. We find them on the coast of Africa at Freetown, Elmina, Walfish Bay, and Cape Town ; in the middle of the ocean at the islands of Ascension and St Helena, on the line of the direct cable from England to the Cape ; and in Southern waters at the Falkland Islands, on the route from Australia and from Chili to Europe by way of Cape Horn. To the north of the Antilles, on the line of communication between Canada and the West Indies, the Bermudas [1] offer an interesting example of a British station. These islands, or coral reefs, surround a little inland sea which is entered by difficult winding channels. On the shores of this central basin, far from the sea, stand the military buildings. As cultivation is difficult on this limestone soil almost without vegetable mould, practically all the food of the islands is imported. The springs are brackish, and fresh water is everywhere scarce, so that rain-water is collected in tanks. But this admirable position provides a strong base for the Navy, and during the winter season it harbours the

[1] Avalle, 5, p. 272.

North American and West Indian squadron. It is connected by submarine cable with Halifax (Nova Scotia) and with Jamaica. On the European side the Atlantic coast is guarded by long-standing friends of Britain. Lisbon, in the hands of her old Portuguese ally, is a calling-place for ships on the way to Africa, the West Indies, and South America, while in the open sea a similar reception is accorded them by the Azores, Madeira, and the Cape Verde Islands. Lisbon holds an important place in the British cable system, commanding the Eastern Telegraph Company's line (Mediterranean, Red Sea, Aden, the Far East, Australasia, and the east coast of Africa) and that of the West African Telegraph Company (Madeira, St Vincent, and the Cape).

In the Pacific Ocean the little island of Hong Kong guards the entrance to the Chinese world. But the Northern Pacific has no other British station in the Far East except Wei-hai-wei, for the Philippines and the Sandwich Islands belong to America, the Ladrone Islands, the Caroline Islands, and the Marshall Islands are in the hands of the Japanese, and the control of the Panama Canal has slipped from Great Britain. In the Southern Pacific, on the other hand, maritime communications among the islets of Oceania are flanked by British positions : Thursday Island, in Torres Strait, north of Australia, is a coaling-station for vessels heading for Eastern Australia, and the Fiji and Tonga Islands are on the line of the trans-Pacific cable between Canada and Australia.

Oceanic and Interoceanic Communications.—From station to station, from depot to depot, an almost continuous chain conducts British ships across the world by way of British lands. Straits, passages, isthmuses, islands, and capes are all made use of in the interests of imperial traffic. Everything that can assist this traffic binds closer the bonds of imperial

G

solidarity. Steam has shortened distances since olden days, and one can now travel from England to the Cape in seventeen days, instead of the sixty or seventy days taken by the sailing-ships of the early nineteenth century. The Suez Canal has brought England nearer to her Eastern and Southern possessions : cargoes can reach Zanzibar from Southampton in ten days less by way of the Canal than by the Cape route, while the saving of time is twenty-four days to Bombay, nineteen to Calcutta, eighteen to Singapore, and eighteen to Hong Kong. A great saving of time has also been effected by the knowledge and experience of the westerly winds—the ' Roaring Forties '—in Southern waters : these are utilized by sailing ships going from England to New Zealand by way of the Cape and on the return journey by Cape Horn. Telegraphic cables [1] likewise tend to eliminate geographical isolation : all the main portions of the British Empire are connected with each other by submarine lines. Of the sixteen cables that lie between Valentia and North America twelve terminate in Newfoundland and Canada. Canada is connected with the Bermudas, Jamaica, and the British Antilles, and since 1902 she has been in communication with Australia by the all-British line which goes from Vancouver to Brisbane in Queensland, and to New Zealand at Doubtless Bay, by way of the Fanning, Fiji, and Norfolk Islands. Down to the year 1901 the cable connecting England with the Cape touched numerous points on the African coast which were too near to foreign possessions, but since then a new and more independent line has been made to the Cape by way of Madeira, St Vincent, Ascension Island, and St Helena. And to communicate with the Indian Ocean a web has been cleverly woven which is as free as possible from all contact with non-British lands.

[1] Bright. 10; *British Empire*, 12; *Empire and Century*, 34, pp. 250–280.

GEOGRAPHICAL STRUCTURE

It is in the neighbourhood of India, in fact, that the most direct telegraphic routes from Europe cross the continent. Communication was effected for the first time in 1864 by the line from London to Constantinople, thence to Bagdad by a Turkish line, from there to Fao on the Shat-el-Arab, and from Fao to Karachi by a submarine cable. This connexion remained a precarious one, as it traversed Turkish territory. After 1869, however, another continental line was brought into use. This started from Lowestoft, and by way of Germany, Russia, Caucasia, and Teheran reached Bender-Bushire, on the Persian Gulf, whence it was continued to Karachi by submarine cable. This line, though well managed, was unfortunately at the mercy of Germany and Russia in time of war. Great Britain, therefore, in order to keep open her telegraphic communication with India, entrusted it to the sea by laying a submarine line, longer and very costly to run, but entirely British. This cable has since 1870 connected up London, Lisbon, Gibraltar, Malta, Alexandria, Port Said, Aden, and Bombay. The line is a triple one in the Mediterranean and the Indian Ocean, and a quadruple one in the Atlantic and the Red Sea. There has even been some desire to make it independent of Portugal, England's age-old ally, for since 1898 London has been connected with Gibraltar by a direct line.

Even this line, however, is not entirely free from danger, for in the Mediterranean it runs the risk of being cut. There are many Englishmen, therefore, who believe that communications between England and India will not be perfect until South India, which is linked up with the Cocos Islands (south of Sumatra), is joined up there to the cables from Mauritius and Australia—that is to say, to the Atlantic and Pacific systems of British cables. In the meantime India can communicate with England without making use of the

99

Mediterranean cables, for there is a line from Aden which passes along the east coast of Africa and reaches Durban by way of Zanzibar, the Seychelles, and Mauritius. As for Australasia, her telegraphic communications with the Old World passed through foreign territories until the year 1901 : a cable went from Port Darwin in the north of Australia, crossed Java from Banjuwangi to Batavia, and joined at Singapore the British cable from that island to Labuan and Hong Kong. But since 1901 a direct cable has united Australia with South Africa by way of Perth, the Cocos Islands, Mauritius, and Durban. Moreover, since 1902 another line has joined Australia to Canada by way of Brisbane, Fiji, Fanning Island, and Vancouver. A complete circuit of British wires thus girdles the earth, and the thoughts and commands of the British world can be freely exchanged and circulated everywhere.

The railways have themselves cemented British unity by joining the oceans together. By her geographical position Canada forms an immense bridge between the Atlantic and the Pacific. Her transcontinental railroads, connecting links between the young colony of British Columbia and the old St Lawrence region, end at each terminus in a great maritime highway, the one going eastward to Great Britain, and the other westward to Australasia. Thus between the west and the east of the Empire, as well as between its northern and southern parts, Canada acts as a great continental roadway.

In order rightly to understand the structure of the Empire, we must avoid comparing it with land empires. On land geographical dispersion is a weak point in a state, for it involves the risk of dissociation : a continental empire lives an uneasy life in separate fragments. The British Empire, on the contrary, being born of an island and founded upon commerce, draws its strength from the sea, the worldwide road which binds its dependencies together. The sea is the common bond, the essential principle, of everything that is British; without it the Empire would split up into fragments of land—a dust of islands, as it were. Just as in his private life the sea is the familiar horizon of every Englishman, so in public life it represents the national interest with which all other interests are co-ordinated. The thought that he may no longer be free upon the seas makes the British citizen angry; the thought that he may no longer be their master makes him anxious; for the ship is the carrier of all that lives in the Empire, and of all that supports its life.

BOOK II

BRITISH COLONIZATION AND CIVILIZATION

WHEN Great Britain founded her colonies she stamped them with the imprint of her own spirit. Just at the time when her rule was extending over the world she represented a state of high civilization, owing to the conquests she had made at home over her own soil. By harnessing natural forces, by making steam and water her slaves, by taming the strength of iron, by piercing tunnels and digging canals, by creating new varieties of domestic animals, by transforming the methods of agricultural production, by draining marshes, dredging estuaries, and building harbours, she had shown a type of progressive civilization, wrought out through a fierce struggle against nature : nature was subdued to the service of man's welfare. This spirit of initiative applied to the search for the means of earning a livelihood by the exploitation of nature will be met with again, in all its manifestations, in British colonization.

The habit of wealth has undoubtedly developed conservative tendencies among some Englishmen of the present day : their lack of curiosity and the decay of the spirit of adventure are occasionally commented upon. Other nations that are younger in industrial life have outstripped Great Britain in the applications of electricity, of motor transport, and of metallurgy, as well as in the popularization of technical knowledge. But a comfortable existence is not the characteristic of the whole community, and it has not broken down in the Briton that instinct of adaptation, of assimilation to physical conditions, of the struggle for existence, which has made him so long the pioneer of European civilization. The classic type of Anglo-Saxon still remains, eager for gain, energetic and enterprising, thoroughly master of himself, " an inaccessible island where peace holds sway," such as he has been made by centuries of business. We find specimens of him among all those younger nations in America and Australasia for whom we in Europe are the Old World. This type of man has only had to settle down at any point of the globe for it to be at once exploited and transformed.

CHAPTER I

WEAPONS OF BRITISH COLONIZATION

TO colonize a country is to increase its trading capacity, to link it up with the world system of communications, to make its soil bring forth crops by giving it or restoring to it its fertility, to exploit its resources in the matter of labour, to break down those forces of inertia which hold it bound, and to inoculate its organism with the vital ferments prepared in the hothouses of Europe.

I. MEANS OF TRANSPORT

The English have always realized that one of the first needs of new countries is the conquest of distances. The improvement of methods of getting about, the construction of roads, the creation of circulation—these have always been the first care of British settlers and almost an instinctive action on the part of their pioneers. To make roads, and to thrust them, as it were, into the desert, the prairie, the bush, or the forest, is to dominate space and to remove the prime obstacle to commerce. It is the engineer rather than the soldier who marks out the road for the colonist. The British South Africa Company began its occupation of the lands which its charter granted to it by constructing a road.[1] Two ex-officers, Selous and Johnson, who were well acquainted with the country and its inhabitants, undertook to lead an expedition of 200 Europeans and 150 natives into

[1] Carton de Wiart, 16, pp. 177–179.

the heart of Mashonaland, and on their way to build a road for transport purposes. The column set out in June 1890, and made a methodical advance, marking out the direction of the road, building bridges, laying out fords, and making forts, resting each evening in an entrenched camp. By the end of September it had reached its objective, Hampton Hill, and a road over 370 miles long, called the Selous Road, was thus opened up for the colonists.

The chief tool, however, was the railway, and no nation has better known how to utilize it than the English. The colonial railway, constructed rapidly and without any unnecessary expense, with few stations and none but the essential accessories, but destined to create life and to direct it across vast spaces, had its prototype already in the transcontinental railroads of the United States, which pierced the solitudes of the interior and drew men along in their wake. To overcome distance was one of the earliest objects of the Anglo-Saxon in the immensity of North America. California could not remain isolated on the shores of the Pacific, on the farther side of the Rocky Mountains ; so first of all there were established the overland mails, which carried dispatches from San Francisco to St Louis in three weeks, and then, in 1860, a service of horsemen, with numerous relays, carried the same mails in six days. But to unite the two oceans it was necessary to build a railroad more than 1850 miles long, which was a colossal undertaking. This was the Pacific Railway, begun in 1862 and finished in 1869, and executed with that breadth of outlook, boldness, and enthusiastic ardour which characterize the Anglo-Saxon spirit, leading the squads of workmen, fired by emulation, to lay in a single day as many as six, seven, and even $10\frac{1}{2}$ miles of rails. The connexion between British Columbia and the St Lawrence region was established in Canada by the same method : the Canadian Pacific Railway, begun in 1880 and completed in 1886, ran from Vancouver to Montreal, a distance of 2904 miles, and formed a main artery along which the forces of colonization advanced toward the virgin lands of the prairies and the Far West. The railway opened up the country to colonists and traders, and increased its capacity for settlement and production.

The railway, however, is not merely an instrument of economic exploitation. It is also an agent of imperial unification, and as such it effected the conquest of Canada with surprising swiftness. The British North America Act, the foundation of the unity of the Canadian Dominion, contains a declaration that the construction of an intercolonial railway, to unite the maritime provinces with Quebec, is essential to the consolidation of the Canadian Union. And later on, when British Columbia agreed to join the Dominion, she did so on condition that the Canadian Government built a railway joining the Pacific coast to the railway system of Canada. As Sir Charles Lucas has said,[1] the railway is a " nation-making factor."

There is only one British Dominion, Australia, whose railway system has not been planned in due proportion to the scale of the great continent that it has to serve. It would seem that originally the sense of space was lacking, for each colony was content to construct rail-roads for itself alone, and the gauge varied from 3 ft. 6 in. in Queensland, the Northern Territory, and Western Australia to 4 ft. 8½ in. in New South Wales and 5 ft. 3 in. in Victoria and South Australia. Owing to the trouble caused by these variations it is proposed soon to begin standardizing the entire Australian system on a uniform gauge of 4 ft. 8 in.[2]

Before Russia had constructed the Siberian Railway

---

[1] *British Empire*, 12, p. 25.   [2] Ashley, 2, p. 57.

or France had planned the Trans-Saharan Railway, Great Britain was already thrusting forth her colonial railways, the necessary pioneers of penetration. In South Africa in 1885 the great line from the Cape had reached no farther than Kimberley ; from that date all progress northward depended on the progress of the railroad. On December 3, 1890, the Chartered Company started to use the Kimberley-Vryburg section (124 miles), while at the same time it was constructing, by means of native labour, a telegraph line as far as Mafeking. The railway reached Mafeking in 1894, and Bulawayo in 1897. The work then had to stop, owing to the non-arrival for political reasons of material from the Cape. But this difficulty was circumvented ; the line from Beira to Salisbury was completed in 1899 ; from Salisbury it was pushed on to Bulawayo (1900–2) ; and by the end of 1902 there was a continuous line of railway, 2100 miles long, joining Cape Town to Beira by way of Salisbury. But the objective of the Chartered Company was the Zambezi, and, farther north, the tableland of the lakes. The railway reached the Zambezi in 1905, and crossed the river on a single-span bridge nearly 220 yards long. It reached Broken Hill in 1906, and the frontier of the Belgian Congo in 1909. Between Kalomo (93 miles north of the Zambezi) and Broken Hill, on a long section of 280 miles, the building of the railroad proceeded at an average rate of $5\frac{3}{4}$ miles a day.

In tropical Africa the English have always looked upon railway construction as a work of prime necessity, and one which is vital to commerce. Sir F. D. Lugard [1] notes this after describing an example. He points out the advantages arising from these railways, which are quickly built and used as soon as possible without waiting for the completion of works of secondary importance. These advantages are as follows : a reduction in the cost of

[1] Lugard, 52, pp. 461–465.

keeping the white men supplied with food ; less waste of time in the replacement of officials ; a reduction in the size of the police force, made possible by its increased mobility ; an increase in the yield of direct taxes, owing to the opening of a market for native products ; the transfer to more productive labour of natives employed in portage ; and an easy and rapid access for British goods to the markets of the interior. In West Africa five years (1898–1904) were sufficient for each colony to have its railroad as the first means of penetrating the forests : the lines from Lagos to Abeokuta in Nigeria, from Sekondi to Kumasi on the Gold Coast, and from Freetown to Bo in Sierra Leone. The improvement of the country advances with the railway system : from Lagos the railway reached in 1912 the town of Kano, in the middle of the Sudan, over 700 miles from the Guinea coast.

Among colonial railroads on a large scale must be placed the Uganda railway.[1] In view of the disturbed condition of the lands on the Upper Nile the problem was to connect the coast of the Indian Ocean as quickly as possible with the shores of Victoria Nyanza, across an almost uninhabited and almost waterless region. The metre gauge was temporarily adopted, in the interests of speed, and on certain sections a funicular railway had to be set up to overcome the difficulties of gradient. Everything had to be brought from outside —both food and building materials. The needs of transport were met at the beginning by caravans of camels, mules, and asses, and 1500 native carriers. More than 18,000 labourers were brought from India, and work was carried on unceasingly, despite the diseases that decimated the workmen, despite the tsetse-fly that worked havoc among the beasts of burden, and despite the rigours of the arid climate. In the six years from

[1] Baltzer, 6.

1896 to 1902 they built 584 miles of line. Ten years before, in 1893, the transport of a ton of goods between Mombasa and Uganda still cost £300, whereas to-day the produce of Uganda—cotton, hides, carbonate of soda, and coffee—can be carried down to the Indian Ocean in two days and at very moderate rates. The beds of carbonate of soda of Lake Magadi and the coffee plantations of Thika are served by branch lines, recently constructed. Thus the country has been opened up to the outside world and drawn into the stream of world circulation by means of the railway that penetrates deeply into it.

II. IRRIGATION WORKS

When the English had thus conquered the difficulties of distance they undertook a systematic warfare against the climate, in order to make the arid soil productive. Being natives of a humid land where there is no lack of water, they have learned the art of seeking for it, storing it, conveying it, and disposing of it in lands where the dryness of the climate makes irrigation necessary. They cause life to animate desert places and security to spread around the crops. In some countries, like South Africa and Australia, the supply of water, limited by the rain system and the absence of high mountains, scarcely permits of a complete scheme of irrigation works. But the matter is being undertaken locally, and certain efforts are already bearing fruit and opening up the way for further schemes. In South Africa [1] the flood water has long been collected, by means of barrages across the rivers, for distribution in time of drought. Thus have been formed the irrigated farms of the valleys of Oudtshoorn, the Sunday River, and the Nuy, and several great works are in course

[1] *The Times*, May 24, 1921.

of construction in the valley of the Great Fish River. Irrigation is necessary, however, on more than four-fifths of the lands of the South African Union, so it is regarded now as a great work of national utility. Since the enactment of a law of 1912 it has been possible for landowners to form themselves into associations for the construction of irrigation works, and the State is empowered to make advances of money to them. Already seventy of these districts have been organized, for providing irrigation for 250,000 acres of new lands.

In Australia [1] there is a desire to open up to colonization the plains of the interior, and in particular the basin of the Murray, and as no development is possible without water irrigation works are to be established. Irrigation colonies are already in a flourishing condition at Mildura in Victoria and Renmark in South Australia, on the Murray. But three great barrages are being erected which will give rise to three centres of cultivation. The first of these is the Hume Dam, on the Upper Murray above Albury, nearly 100 feet high. It was begun in 1919, and when finished will hold the waters of an immense lake covering over 37,000 acres. The second, the Burrinjuck Dam, on the Murrumbidgee, is expected to supply water to more than 250,000 acres of land, while the third, the Sugarloaf Dam, on the Goulburn River, a tributary of the Murray, will form a reservoir some 10,000 acres in extent. Following the example of the western Americans, who have created so many oases in their arid valleys, the Australians are preparing to develop the cultivation of fruit. The waters of the Murrumbidgee are already irrigating orchards of peaches, apricots, and plums; drying apparatus has been installed; and soon, no doubt, we shall see the produce

[1] *United Empire*, 1921, p. 53, and 1922, pp. 317, 360; *The Times*, May 24, 1922.

of the new plantations of the Southern Hemisphere arriving in the markets of Europe, like that of California.

It is in such ancient centres of irrigation as Egypt and India, however, that the great irrigation works of the English are particularly to be found. In these lands the practice of irrigation dates back to ancient times, and the English learned the art on the spot, from observation of the natives. But, as a matter of fact, by their understanding of the local economy, and by the application of modern scientific methods, they have turned it into a fine art whose creations are un-equalled throughout the world. Among these gigantic works the most remarkable is undoubtedly the Ganges Canal,[1] built by Cautley and opened in 1857. The waters of the river are held up by a barrage at Hurdwar, where they leave the mountains, and turned into an artificial channel, which has to cross several torrents in the first thirty miles of its course, sometimes above and sometimes below their bed. Two hundred miles downstream a second barrage collects the water brought into the bed of the Ganges by springs and tributaries, and this new supply is turned into a canal which joins the first one. This mass of water, nearly 10,000 cubic feet per second, is distributed by a multitude of small canals over the alluvial lands that form the Doab, between Allahabad and the Himalayas. What remains of the water rejoins the Ganges at Cawnpore after a journey of a thousand miles, the total length of the distributory canals being some 4000 miles. The waters

[1] Strachey, 65; Sir J. Douie, *The Panjab, North-west Frontier Province, and Kashmir*, Cambridge University Press, 1916; A. Normandin, "Les irrigations aux Indes britanniques," in *Bulletin économique de l'Indo-Chine*, 1913, pp. 618–756; Chailley-Bert, "L'irrigation dans les Indes anglaises," in *Revue générale des sciences*, 1903; H. M. Wilson, "Irrigation in India," in *U.S. Geological Survey*, Washington, 1903, 238 pp.

of the Jumna are distributed in a similar manner by three canals which are of smaller dimensions, but which would be marvelled at in other lands.

Irrigation is still more necessary in the west—in the Punjab, where the annual rains are insufficient to ensure the safety of the crops. The natives already knew how to utilize flood water for the purposes of cultivation at the moment when the snows melted, but in some years the overflow happened to be small, and insufficient to reach the fields. The English were anxious for permanent resources in place of these precarious and temporary ones, and, as in the Ganges basin, they have built canals that take all the water of the river as it leaves the mountains and lead it over the fields to fertilize them. These are the Ravi Canal, opened in 1859, which waters the plain between the Ravi and the Boas; the Sutlej Canal, which was completed in 1882; and the Chenab Canal, finished in 1892. The last of these is as powerful as a river, and discharges on an average fourteen times as much water as the Thames at Richmond. Before it was opened the British Government, following the example of the Americans, had prepared the irrigable districts for settlement, building villages, making roads, and organizing police: everything was ready for the arrival of the water. Then life burst forth from the earth; some three million acres of barren soil were converted into fields, whose crops were conveyed to Karachi, and in ten years' time nearly a million men were living on that piece of land which had but lately been a desert. This resurrection is to be continued by other works, for a canal is to carry the waters of the Sutlej over the desert region to the south of the river, watering some $3\frac{3}{4}$ millions of acres. So, too, in Scinde the Sukkur barrage on the Indus will enable the area under good-quality cotton to be increased to 500,000 acres.

H

THE BRITISH EMPIRE

In Egypt [1] British rule has started a new era for the irrigation works of the Nile. The object of these works is to store up the winter waters in order to use them in developing the summer cultivation of cotton and sugar-cane. The idea is an old one ; it was carried out by the ancients in Lake Mœris (Fayoum), which was made 5000 years ago to store up the excess of the flood water and deliver it over Lower Egypt during the months of low water. It was taken up again by Mehemet Ali, but he could find no capable workmen except among the English. The barrage of the Delta, below Cairo, was completed in 1883 by British engineers, and was definitely handed over for use in 1901. Between 1898 and 1902 they constructed the Assiut barrage, to regulate the height of the Nile at the entrance of the Ibrahimieh Canal, which waters 1060 acres in Middle Egypt and the Fayoum. But the Aswan barrage is the finest monument of British enterprise. In accordance with the plans made by the great engineer Willcocks in the years 1890–93, a barrage was constructed across the river, a mile and a quarter long and 130 feet high, pierced with 180 openings, the effect of which is to raise the level of the Nile for a distance of a hundred miles upstream. The reservoir thus obtained was enlarged in 1912, and contains over 70,000,000,000 cubic feet of water. This huge quantity, accumulated during the fall of the Nile, is distributed during the months of low water to the cotton and sugar fields of the valley. The gigantic task of building this barrage, which was financed by the bankers of London, required as many as 8550 workmen. Yet it is still inadequate to secure the existence of the Egyptians, whose number is continually increasing. Already, therefore, another

---

[1] J. Barois, *Les irrigations en Égypte*, Paris, 1904, 8vo, 386 pp.; Sir W. Willcocks and J. I. Craig, *Egyptian Irrigation*, Spon, 1913, 2 vols.; Sir W. Willcocks, *The Nile Projects*, Cairo, 1919.

reservoir is being projected on the White Nile, to the south of Khartoum, at Djebel Aulia; with a capacity of 350 milliards of cubic feet it would double the Egyptian reserve supply of water. While this would secure the waters of the White Nile for Egypt, the Blue Nile would be used to irrigate the Sudanese plain that lies between the two rivers (El Gezira), the water being raised by a barrage near Sennar in such a way that it could be conveyed by a canal 37 miles long to irrigate 375,000 acres of cotton fields. British engineers are thus preparing to tame the Nile completely, and to make it a permanent handmaid for cultivation over the waterless regions of the Sudan and the Sahara. They are also dreaming of the resuscitation of Mesopotamia by the same methods, for there, in the opinion of Sir W. Willcocks, some $3\frac{3}{4}$ million acres could be sown with cotton every summer. British genius is everywhere arousing lands from their slumber, bringing forth new wealth, and creating new homes for the human race.

In this warfare against nature the English rely upon two forces: one is the power of their capital, and the other is the knowledge they have borrowed from the common store of European civilization.

III. BRITISH CAPITAL

One essential element of Great Britain's material strength consists in her capitalist power, the fruit of the savings of several centuries of trade and industry. She distributes this reserve of energy throughout the Empire and the whole world, to feed the great undertakings from which new wealth is to be drawn. All these savings, all these surpluses of income over expenditure, were first invested at home for the execution of the great works of the modern age of machinery—canals, railways, docks, merchant shipping, steam-engines, viaducts, and tunnels through mountains and under estuaries. Then they were lent to all the young countries that were anxious to grow. The railways, telegraphs, and irrigation canals throughout the entire Empire were created by British capital. Without it the earth would remain in a state of inertia, and the native races in a state of infancy. According to the *Statist* of January 1, 1916, out of a total of £3,836,104,000 of British capital invested abroad the colonies received £1,935,740,000 : 570 millions were in Canada, 443 in Australasia, 390 in India, and 455 in Africa. Since the beginning of the nineteenth century there has been an increasingly marked tendency to prefer colonial to foreign investments. On grounds of security as well as through the sentiment of imperial solidarity capital shows an extreme willingness to remain in the Empire. Between 1907 and 1913 colonial investments rose from 30.2 million pounds to 99.8 millions, whereas foreign investments rose only from 59.2 to 97.7 million pounds,[1] and yet these figures take account only of investments publicly known. Since the War the same movement has continued, as the following table shows :

LOANS RAISED IN LONDON [2]
(*in millions sterling*)

—	1921	1920
United Kingdom	276.1	328
British possessions . . .	90.5	31.6
Foreign countries . . .	22.2	7.8
Total	388.8	367.4

[1] Grice, 40.　　　[2] *The Times*, May 24, 1922.

WEAPONS OF BRITISH COLONIZATION

In young countries capital is as necessary as colonists. From their relations with the London banks the colonies reap the great benefit of obtaining cheap money. London supplies money to the whole Empire. London, the world's banker, floats public loans and gathers funds for private undertakings. Many colonial banks have branch offices in London, and several of the biggest of them have their head offices there : such are the Bank of Africa, the Bank of Australasia, the Bank of New Zealand, the Bank of British Columbia, and many others. Apart from the public debts of the colonies, of which almost all the bonds are held in Britain, the capital of the mother country is to be found at the base of all big business and at the birth of all the colonies.

The occupation of West Africa was due to the initiative of the merchants of Liverpool,[1] who had formerly been enriched by the slave trade. In the year 1890 the Liverpool Chamber of Commerce energetically took up the exploitation of the country ; building a fleet of ships, maintaining a bank for West Africa, founding the British Cotton-growing Association, sending its mining prospectors to the Gold Coast, starting railway construction for the penetration of the country, and setting up the Liverpool School of Tropical Medicine. During the nineteenth century enormous supplies of capital flowed into India, carrying with it Western methods of economic exploitation. Railways, mines, factories, plantations, docks—almost all this modernization of India is of British origin. In Bengal alone there are 63 jute factories employing 252,000 hands, 300 tea plantations with 130,000, and 530 colliery companies with 135,000, working with almost entirely British capital. All the banks, three-quarters of the foreign trade, and the shipping companies are in British hands.

[1] E. Baillaud, *La politique indigène de l'Angleterre en Afrique occidentale*, Paris, 1912, pp. xxxii–xxxix.

It is the financiers of London who have made fortunes out of sugar in Egypt and the West Indies, wool in Australia, timber in Canada, and rubber in Malaysia, while but for them the gold-mines and diamond-mines of South Africa would simply have lain idle.

The diamond-mines of the Kimberley region suffered for a long time from defective organization. The Kimberley mine in particular had been divided and subdivided into a large number of portions, belonging to 1600 proprietors, the smallest of these portions being only five square yards. The result of this was that the mine was a confused medley of small enterprises, hindering each other and working at great expense, and it was British capital on a large scale that fused together all these fragmentary properties. The De Beers Company, under the leadership of Cecil Rhodes, succeeded in buying out the smaller companies, and then grouped the larger ones together in 1888 under the name of the De Beers Consolidated Mines Company. This company gathered all mining business into its hands, obtained control over the diamond production of the world, and even managed to bring all its weight to bear upon the political life of South Africa. We meet with these same capitalists again in connexion with the gold-mines of the Witwatersrand. It was only powerful companies that could exploit these fields. Gold is not found in veins or in 'placers,' but embedded in a quartzy conglomerate in a minutely divided state, and in very small quantities. To work this ore it was necessary to have huge factories, equipped with powerful plant, making use of elaborate processes, and working with large quantities of ore.[1] So the Rand companies were formed, with the aid of capital from the City, and in the midst of the pastoral veldt they established an industrial centre on European lines. Ardently imperialist

[1] Mondaini, 54, pp. 393 ff.

in their outlook, they pushed British influence so far as to destroy the independence of the Boers, and it was from among them that the Chartered Company recruited the financial means that carried British expansion beyond the Zambezi.

IV. SCIENTIFIC INVESTIGATION AND RESEARCH

The power of material resources is not sufficient in itself to endow a colony with life. In most cases material exploitation needs to be directed by a preliminary process of methodical inquiry and scientific research. The art of colonization does not consist merely in the crude appropriation of wealth. It presupposes also an intellectual appropriation of the colonial territory—a knowledge of the general conditions of relief, climate, flora, fauna, and inhabitants of the country in question. A man cannot live without a knowledge of his surroundings, and it is only when he has this knowledge that he can arrange and adapt them to his own use. Toward the end of the nineteenth century, when the economic condition of the West Indies was causing keen anxiety owing to a terrible crisis in the production of the sugar-cane, it was decided to create a service of agricultural study—the Imperial Department of Agriculture for the West Indies, established at Barbados [1] in 1898. The advantages arising from this plan were quickly discovered : it led to an improvement in the cultivation of the sugar-cane and the introduction of new varieties ; a study of the diseases of that plant and the cacao-tree ; favourable experiments with the cultivation of Sea Island cotton in 1903 ; and the setting up of agricultural schools in St Vincent, St Lucia, and Dominica. Similar services on the same model are in operation in certain tropical

[1] Ashley, 2, pp. 186 ff.

countries—India, Malaysia, Nigeria, and East Africa. They serve as nurseries for the officials who are sent to other colonies, and their pupils are to be found in India and as far away as the Fiji Islands.

Nowhere has scientific research met with more success than in the study of tropical diseases, which is trying to make it possible for the white man to reside in tropical lands. In British colonies much has been done in the struggle against malaria. In India, about the year 1898, Sir Ronald Ross studied the transmission of the microbe of malaria by the mosquito, and he was commissioned to defend the Suez Canal area of Egypt against this plague. He succeeded in reducing the number of admissions to hospital for malaria from 1842 to 214 per year. Measures of the same kind have been successful also at Khartoum and in the Malay States. Again, during the nineteenth century the Anglo-Indian troops were decimated by epidemics of cholera, arising from the contamination of water : in 1869 a British regiment lost a third of its effective strength from this cause. Now in 1911 the death-rate from cholera among these troops had fallen to 1 per 10,000, while taking the years from 1880 to 1911 as a whole the mortality among British soldiers fell from 25 to 5 per 1000, and among the Indian troops from 40 to 5 per 1000.[1] These triumphs of tropical hygiene are equalled only by those of the Americans in the Panama Canal zone. The Universities of London and Liverpool both maintain schools of tropical medicine, and in connexion with the Colonial Office there are several richly endowed services at work—the Advisory Medical Committee for Tropical Africa, the Tropical Diseases Bureau, the Tropical Diseases Research Fund, the Sleeping Sickness Bureau, and the Tropical Entomological Research Committee. Science is learning better

[1] *British Empire*, 12, pp. 191 and 280–283.

every day to understand the origin of tropical diseases, and especially the ways of the insects that carry the disease-germs. "It is the man of science, as Lord Robson said, who is to decide the fate of the tropics ; not the soldier, or the statesman with his programmes and perorations, but the quiet entomologist." [1]

The question, however, is not merely how to live in safety : it is also needful to organize the colony, to administer it methodically, and to know it thoroughly. Colonization has for a long time drawn much assistance from surveys and censuses. No country possesses such good information services in regard to the colonies as Great Britain. One of the first things to be done by every British colony as soon as it is officially constituted is to number its inhabitants and its goods. It was remarked by Sir Charles Dilke [2] that no British colony could compare with Minnesota, which had a State Historical Society in existence a week before the foundation of the state ; but he observed that the state of Victoria (Australia) was without doubt the only one to possess statistics from the date of its birth. The tradition of exactness has become a law in all the Dominions, and many pages would be required for the enumeration of the official services which take stock of the inhabitants and their activities in every great colony. To take the case of India alone, it is astonishing what masses of material have been accumulated by the English for the study of the country. Since 1871 India has had a systematic census, taken regularly every ten years. The reports of this Indian census form an invaluable collection of demographic documents, and by these methodical enumerations, making use of improved processes from decade to decade, the British administration keeps itself informed of all that concerns the life and habits of a multitude of three hundred

[1] Ashley, 2, p. 169.　　　　[2] Dilke, 28, p. 300.

millions of human beings. The quintessence of our knowledge of India is contained in such valuable collections as the *Statistical Atlas*, the *Climatological Atlas*, and the *Imperial Gazetteer of India* in twenty-six volumes, a veritable encyclopædia of the country. India is more advanced, also, than some European countries in possessing a large-scale topographical map. This map of India, which was finished at the end of the nineteenth century, was based on the triangulation work carried out during the century by such men as Colonel Lambton, Sir George Everest, and Colonel Colin Mackenzie. It is true that in such a vast work, covering a huge and difficult country, all the sheets are not of equal value, and many of them will require revision. But it is none the less true that at the end of the nineteenth century there existed an atlas of maps for the whole country on a scale of $1 : 253,440$ such as no other tropical region possessed for a similar area; in fact, there was even a $1 : 63,360$ map for all except the Presidency of Madras and certain native states. Since 1905 a new map on a scale of $1 : 63,360$ has been executed in five colours, and by 1914 there were already published over six hundred sheets, covering an area of 150,000 square miles.

CHAPTER II

TYPES OF BRITISH COLONIZATION

BRITISH colonization bears everywhere the imprint of the people by whom it has been conducted : energetic, enterprising, practical, and efficient, the race is visible everywhere in its works. But this colonization has not met everywhere with the same geographical conditions, the same problems to be solved, the same peoples to be ruled, or the same resources to be exploited. Sometimes it is applied to hot lands where the European finds it hard to live, and sometimes to temperate countries where he can settle. Colonies of exploitation and colonies of settlement are therefore two aspects of the colonial work of Great Britain ; they are also, as a matter of fact, two original types of civilization.

I. COLONIZATION IN HOT COUNTRIES

Since the very earliest days of colonization the factor that has given value to colonies in hot countries has been the quantity of costly products that they provide for trade—spices, cotton, tobacco, coffee, tea, cocoa, sugar, rice, oil-seeds, and rubber. Colonial activity takes the form of organizing the production of these commodities under white supervision. But there is another advantage that accrues to the mother country from the possession of these colonies : ever since the day when industrialism took possession of Great Britain she has looked upon her colonies as outlets for her manufactured goods, and it was by seeking for new customers that she enlarged her territorial possessions. It has been truly said that the English pioneer is the trader, or the missionary, who is almost always a trader as well, and that the engineer comes next. As producer and consumer the tropical world holds an important place in British commerce. Of the total amount of goods exported by the United Kingdom to imperial lands the tropical colonies receive (in value) 57 per cent., and of the total exports of the Empire, excluding the United Kingdom, they are responsible for 51 per cent., while the tonnage of the tropical ports is 62 per cent. of the total traffic of non-European British ports.

Different Kinds of Tropical Settlements.—In seeking to analyse the characteristics of this tropical empire we notice an amazing variety of types of colonial settlement, unequal in extent, different in development, and exploited with varying aims. At the opposite extreme from India, a continent and a world in itself, stand the scattered isles of the Caribbean Sea and the Pacific Ocean, while over against the Antilles, fertile and over-peopled lands, enriched by plantation cultivation, we have the colonies of tropical Africa, living mainly on extensive native cultivation, and in some cases remaining still at the fruit-picking stage of development. Similarly we find on the one hand vast areas of settled life and on the other such thoroughfares as Hong Kong—minute points in space which are nevertheless centres of eager activity, focusing in themselves all the trade and traffic of an extensive area.

India.—India is the most remarkable monument of tropical colonization, combining on a huge scale its original features, namely, a very scanty white population compared with the vast multitude of natives, and enormous quantities of commercial products provided by peasant labour. There are some nations, like the Dutch in Java, who have less space at their disposal, and can cultivate their plot more intensively; but none of them penetrates the tropical world more extensively than the English. In India there is only one Englishman to every 2000 natives. It is impossible for the European to become completely acclimatized in the country, no matter what hygienic precautions he may adopt, and in the hot season he is compelled to leave the unhealthy plains and 'winter' in the hills. Once upon a time, before the coming of the steamship, the great sailing-ships which rounded the Cape of Good Hope used to carry cargoes of babies every year to England to spend the whole of their childhood there. It is not by their numbers, therefore, that the English have succeeded in conquering and retaining their hold over this populous country, but by the superiority of a method which has enabled them to develop the commercial output of the country without breaking down its social system. This domination of 300 millions of men by 120,000 English is the finest triumph of native policy, and it will continue as long as the essential principle remains unshaken by any internal force.

The English conquered India in spite of their numerical weakness. It is remarked by Seeley that they do not owe this conquest to their military superiority, that it was effected at times when the mother country was faced by terrible wars in America and Europe, that it did not require the levying of a strong expeditionary army, that the English army in India in 1773 contained only 9000 Europeans as against 45,000 natives, that this proportion is still less to-day, and even that the army was recruited in quite early times almost entirely from among the natives—in short, that it is not right to say that the English conquered India, but

rather that she conquered herself. This employment of
the natives to aid in the subduing of their own country
was based upon a knowledge of its social condition ;
India had never constituted a political whole, conscious
of its unity ; it was really only a geographical expression, owing to its diversity of races, of tongues, and of
religions, and supremacy was bound to attach to the
greatest organizing power.

Hence is derived the time-honoured principle of
the native policy of the English in India,[1] namely,
to leave untouched the fundamental conditions of the
life of the natives, letting the framework of their
civilization remain. The English hold themselves soci-
ally aloof from the natives, and in India we do not,
as in Java, see white colonists living in the villages and
tilling their land themselves with the help of local
labour. There are no British colonists in the villages,
and no mingling or joining of the two elements.
English city and native city are far away from each
other. This attitude, originally adopted for the maintenance of British prestige, has hardened into a tradition,
or even a law. The aim is to interfere as little as possible
with the life of the natives, so as to show respect
for their customs and their beliefs. It is held that
the failure of the irrigation works and the paralysis
of the railway system would be catastrophes less
dangerous to the exploitation of the country than the
downfall of the native civilization, of those ancient
relations, that is to say, by which men are bound to
each other. The English try not to upset the habits
of the natives as ordered by their religion and caste
and not to disturb their moral life, which is so closely
associated with their material existence. Colonization
has not broken down the traditional framework of
this society of village cultivators. It has adapted itself

[1] Chailley, 17.

to it, and gradually, without any violent revolution, it has turned this community toward the newer forms of production. Ever since ancient times the peasant had cultivated for himself his rice, wheat, millet, and cotton. He has now been led to produce not only for his family, but for the market also—to grow things for sale. This development, which has made India one of the greatest reservoirs of raw materials in the world, has been effected within the very framework of the village life of the country. The Englishman, almost always at a distance, plays the part of banker in the towns and exporter at the seaports; he turns to the native shopkeeper, the local man of business, or the *banian*, when he wants to recommend to the peasant the kind of cultivation that will yield the most profit, and in general to shake the vast agricultural world out of its torpor. In this ancient colony, which was only lately exporting spices and muslins, he has built up a great market for wheat, cotton, jute, opium, tea, and oil-seeds.

Commercial entrepôts.—It is possible to exploit tropical colonies without exercising political domination over them. It is possible to settle at their gates without entering them. It is possible to select an island, a bay, or an estuary near by, and there to trade in perfect security and attract other merchants thither. These trading-stations, or *entrepôts*, in distant waters are perhaps the most original type of British settlement. They are, as it were, suction pumps, gathering to themselves the commerce of vast regions. Such are Aden, on the threshold of the Arab world; Singapore, in the centre of the Malay world; and Hong Kong, at the gateway of the Chinese world—places which recall to us the Phœnician establishments on the shores of the Mediterranean, or those of the Genoese on the Black Sea. Being crossing-places and meeting-places on the ocean highways, they are cosmopolitan towns, and their population is recruited in part from among the wanderers whose business it is to exploit the road-ways of the sea.

Inhabited by a motley colony of Europeans, Parsees, Indians, Arabs, Somalis, and Jews, Aden [1] lives in a sunburnt solitude. Her function is that of a port of transhipment for goods proceeding from, or consigned to, the numerous little ports of the Red Sea, Southern Arabia, Somaliland, and even the east coast of Africa. They leave there or come there to join the great stream of traffic that flows between Europe and the Far East. There can be seen in transit at Aden the cotton fabrics and the coal of Great Britain, the coffee of Arabia, the gums and hides of Somaliland, the mother-of-pearl of the Red Sea, the spices of Zanzibar, the sugar of Mauritius, and the tobacco of India. In the year 1919 the amount of traffic entering the port amounted to nearly a million tons.

At the entrance to Far Eastern waters, on the Straits of Malacca, Singapore on her island occupies an essentially British site. Since her foundation in 1819 she has triumphed over the competition of Malacca and Penang, both of them far less favourably situated, and her port has become the commercial *entrepôt* of the Malay archipelago. An obvious calling-place for vessels sailing from Europe or India to the Far East, she distributes European goods throughout the Malay world, and receives local goods intended for a wider commercial sphere. For the years 1907–11 her traffic amounted to nearly 14,500,000 tons, a figure exceeded in the Empire by Hong Kong and London alone. Here are collected for re-export to Europe and America such commodities as tin, rubber, copra, spices, hides, tapi-oca, coconut oil, and sago, and here are unloaded, for

[1] Avalle, 5, p. 111.

redistribution among the smaller ports of the China Sea, textiles, rice, flour, oil, tobacco, hardware, machinery, and matches. With her population of Malays, Chinese, and Indians, Singapore belongs to the class of cosmopolitan establishments maintained by British commerce on the best maritime highways. Their function is a double one : on the one hand they attract trade and transport for the benefit of British firms and ships ; on the other they open up markets for British goods in the countries they serve. A British trader used to quote the amusing example of a village in North Borneo that had quite recently sprung up in a forest clearing, and whose inhabitants, but lately risen out of savagery, were now buying Huntley and Palmer's biscuits and Crosse and Blackwell's pickles.

Not one of these ports comes up to Hong Kong,[1] the *entrepôt* of Southern China, at the mouth of the Canton River, British territory since 1841, and the proudest monument of England's commercial genius. Its task is to collect the produce of the Far East destined for European and other markets, and to distribute the merchandise of European and other markets destined for the Far East. Here Great Britain practises on a large scale that transhipping and forwarding trade in which she excels and in which she still holds the foremost place, despite the progress of her rivals. In the waters of Hong Kong are brought, transhipped, and carried away enormous cargoes of sugar, flour, rice, cotton and cotton goods, silk, hemp, hides, tin, petroleum and other oils, fish, tea, coal, cement, condensed milk, opium, and matches. The greater part of the tea and silk trade of China is in the hands of Hong Kong firms.

Hong Kong offers us an arresting picture, on its

[1] *Bulletin économique de l'Indo-Chine*, 1921, pp. 336–339 ; Smith, 63, *passim* ; *The Times*, May 24, 1921.

I

meagre site of 400 square miles, of what can be created by mercantile genius : a wonderful position facing a great river and a great city ; a rocky islet so small that it has had to be artificially enlarged to allow of the building of the harbour and the laying out of the town of Victoria ; an extraordinary growth of urban population, rising from 2000 in 1841 to 370,000 in 1911 ; a well-sheltered roadstead, surrounded by islets, and so deep that ships can sail day and night without troubling about tides ; a port of transit for the whole of the Far East, and a banking, telegraphic, and passenger steamship centre ; a seat of industry on modern lines, with spinning and weaving mills, sugar refineries, paper mills, rope works, cement works, and shipbuilding yards ; a waterside railway station for Chinese emigrants ; and a total movement of ships, entered and cleared, of nearly 40 million tons in 1920, placing it in the front rank of the ports of the world, before London, New York, and Liverpool.

Out of a total steamship tonnage of 8.7 millions (entering) in 1920 the British flag covered 4.2 millions. In the same year out of a total importation of 89.2 millions sterling (excluding China) 30.3 millions came from the British Empire, and out of 55.1 millions of exports 14.2 were destined for the Empire. These latter figures do not indicate any British preponderance, and there is nothing strange in this, since much of the trade of Hong Kong is done with the Far East and the United States. It is an essential fact, however, that this trade is always assisted by British equipment and British business. The largest bank in the Far East, the Hong Kong and Shanghai Banking Corporation, is of British origin ; it is this bank which fixes the rate of exchange, while other banks merely follow its lead. The success of British banks is easily explained. To begin with, they work in concert with the mercantile marine : commerce follows the flag. Then in the second place the English obtained experience of the East in India ; among the British merchants in Hong Kong are Parsees, members of that wealthy Bombay community which has served as a bond of union between East and West. Finally, the English merchant in China has long had a reputation for honesty. There are British firms, as Mr Middleton Smith says, whose word is accepted for millions of dollars, and whose paper is as good as that of the Bank of England. There are other great British firms established in Hong Kong. Such are Jardine, Matheson and Co., who settled at Macao at the beginning of the nineteenth century, then at Canton, and since 1842 have been at Hong Kong, a huge importing and exporting house, owning cotton factories at Shanghai, with an interest in the railways of China and building works in Shanghai, and owning also a fleet of merchant ships. Such, too, is the firm of Butterfield and Swire, Ltd., whose employees are almost all Scottish, and which does a large business in maritime transport, shipbuilding, and sugar-refining. Then there is the Union Insurance Society of Canton, which has been established at Hong Kong since 1841. It is through these old and powerful corporations, concentrated in Hong Kong, that the whole of China is penetrated by British influence. A whole fleet of British ships, based on Hong Kong, is engaged in what might be called the coasting trade of the China seas ; they touch at the Philippines, at Java, and at the Chinese ports ; they ascend the Yangtse as far as Hankau ; and they serve Canton and Tientsin. Two-fifths of the traffic of the Chinese ports, even after the War, is carried on under the British flag ; though pressed and menaced by others, it maintains its lead. Everywhere, therefore, British interests are on a solid foundation. There were sixteen British chambers of commerce in China in 1920. It was an Englishman, Sir Robert Hart, who organized the maritime customs service, and it is Englishmen who direct the lighthouses, the Post Office, and other services. All this expansion of power, of wealth, and of influence has radiated from Hong Kong.

Despite the enormous preponderance of the Chinese element, which numbers 300,000 inhabitants out of 310,000 in the town of Victoria, the British stamp is impressed everywhere, in the style of the buildings, the comfortable hotels, the electric tramway system, the development of motor roads, the organization of sea-borne traffic and the money market, and in the order and peace that hold sway under the protection of the sea and the fleet. In times of trouble the inhabitants of the mainland come and take refuge in this British spot : many wealthy Chinese have sheltered here with their wealth. Though merely a port of entry for Southern China, Hong Kong remains, in the midst of a tropical clime, the masterpiece of a mercantile civilization whose other original creation stands upon the banks of the Thames.

Except in the matter of political sovereignty Shanghai is almost as British a town as Hong Kong or Singapore. Alongside the Chinese city and the French settlement lies the true Shanghai, the foreign settlement, which is a miniature commercial republic, a third of whose citizens are British, where the quays, the docks, and the factories have been built with British capital, and where the Anglo-Saxon imprint is visible in the banks, the houses, the churches, the clubs, and the race-courses. By this route British commerce penetrates into the heart of China—into those lands of the Yangtse whence it imports silk, tea, and cotton, and to which it sends cotton goods, machinery, and timber. Here, too, in a narrow space, is concentrated the business of an immense hinterland. The soul, as it were, of the commercial city resides mainly in the British colony, for out of 12,500 whites 4465 are English. This 'settlement' type of colony completes the series of forms in which British colonization adapts itself to the tropical world of Asia, and it is here that Great Britain has her richest possessions and her most individual achievements.

The West Indies, Africa, and the Pacific.[1]—British occupation does not meet with the same geographical conditions in all tropical colonies. In America they are insular territories, sometimes very small, but thickly populated and highly cultivated; in Africa they are vast areas, scarcely inhabited, and even little known at present; in America plantation colonies more than three centuries old; in Africa trading-stations, long established on the coast, and quite recently extended toward the interior—in short, there are two different types of colonial settlements.

The English, whose colonial career started in the Antilles, still give them their early name of the West Indies. In former days they made the fortunes of Liverpool and Glasgow, and they represent always the advanced type of tropical colony, in which man directs and regulates natural production amid artificial conditions of work and existence. On the one hand, we have intensive cultivation—plantations—under the direction of white planters, valuable products giving a heavy yield in a small space—sugar-cane in Jamaica, Barbados, St Kitts, Nevis, Antigua, Trinidad, Tobago, and Guiana; coffee in Jamaica and Guiana; cacao in Trinidad, Tobago, Grenada, St Lucia, and Jamaica; cotton in the Leeward Islands; and rubber in Honduras. On the other hand, in those colonies which have become

---

[1] Ashley, **2**, pp. 170–185; Caldecott, **15**, pp. 85–95; Leroy-Beaulieu, **47***a*, *passim*; Zimmermann, **70**, pp. 665–680; Fletcher, **36** and **37**.

regular factories for costly commodities we find the food crops and the local resources insufficient for the needs of the population, and therefore enormous imports of flour, rice, clothing, meat, and timber. This plantation system, this exploiting to the uttermost of a single valuable product, involves the dangers of all monoculture. For a hundred years the West Indies have lived, as it were, in a state of crisis. The eighteenth century turned Jamaica into a huge sugar factory, some estates yielding such fabulous incomes as £75,000 or even £100,000. But all this wealth gradually crumbled away before the competition of younger or less exhausted lands, such as, to begin with, other tropical colonies like Trinidad, Guiana, and Mauritius; secondly, foreign countries like Cuba and Brazil; and, finally, Europe with its cultivation of the sugar beet. So Jamaica turned to the cultivation of tropical fruits, such as bananas and coconuts. The tropical plantation, as a commercial undertaking, was subject to the vicissitudes of world commerce, and had to adapt itself to its requirements.

The population also, like the general economy of the country, is the work of colonization. The natives having been exterminated in the early days of the European conquest, the colonists turned to African slaves for the labour they required. The settlement of the islands was the result of a transplantation *en masse*. To-day, however, the black race dwells as mistress in these hot and fruitful islands, dominating the white element : Jamaica has scarcely two white inhabitants in every hundred. This black race multiplies rapidly, and reaches a density of population greater than that of many industrial countries. Thus there are 1000 inhabitants to the square mile in Barbados, 500 in Grenada, and 200 in Trinidad and Tobago. That intensive cultivation which the Dutch developed later on in Java had been practised by the English in the West Indies for two or three centuries. But though the work was original it has no longer the importance in the Empire that it had formerly. With their 12,000 square miles and their 1,840,000 inhabitants (excluding Guiana and Honduras) the West Indies are responsible for scarcely more than 1.8 per cent. of the imports and 1.4 per cent. of the exports of the whole of Great Britain's colonial empire.

So far as economic development is concerned the African tropical colonies are the reverse of the Antilles. They comprise vast territories in which cultivation has always been carried on in accordance with ancient extensive methods, or even on primitive fruit-picking lines. Apart from Egypt and the islands of Zanzibar and Mauritius, where old trading relations and contact with advanced civilizations were favourable to the plantation system, the colonization of Africa has hardly begun, retarded as it is by the obstacles that the ' Dark Continent ' opposes to white penetration. These obstacles are as follows : difficulty of communication with the interior ; a scanty population, difficult to arouse, and sometimes depressed by a long *régime* of wars, raids, and despotism ; the ravages of the tsetse-fly that kills domestic animals and the sleeping sickness that works havoc among men. Tropical Africa has not yet become for the European a sort of black West Indies : it has scarcely risen above the level of native civilization. Only here and there, in certain limited spots, have attempts at plantations met with success : cotton, coffee, and sisal hemp in East Africa (Uganda, Kenya Colony, and Tanganyika) ; cotton and tobacco in Nyassaland ; and cotton and cacao in West Africa (Nigeria, Gambia, Gold Coast, Sierra Leone, Togoland, and Cameroon). To these must be added Egypt, whose cotton is much sought after in the markets of the world ;

Mauritius, with its sugar plantations; and Zanzibar, with its clove-trees. But, taking it all round, European methods of exploitation have scarcely touched the native communities, and what they yield for commerce proceeds for the most part from the patriarchal cultivation of their fields or the rapid gathering of wild products, such as palm-kernels, palm-oil, ground-nuts, and cola-nuts in West Africa, and oil-seeds, copra, and rubber in East Africa. In 1918 British tropical Africa exported oil-yielding products to the value of nearly £10,000,000, almost all coming from the Guinea coast. At a time when oil is taking an ever larger and larger place in industry the oil-palm is becoming the chief wealth of West Africa, and the trade of that region is therefore being directed toward Liverpool, the great centre of oil and soap works. For the moment the initiative of the African native can be turned only toward the production of this easily acquired form of wealth, whereas time is requisite for the establishment of plantations. Similarly, in the islands and archipelagos of the Pacific a primitive economy still obtains : except in the Fiji Islands and some others, where the sugar-cane is cultivated, the articles of external commerce are for the most part the products of the coconut palm and the banana-tree.

Negro and Indian Emigration.[1]—Whatever stage of economic evolution they may have reached, the tropical colonies are alike in this, that they are almost all unfavourable to the permanent residence of the European. Except in the case of such islands as Barbados and Jamaica the colonist can neither settle nor work there. A strict hygienic *régime* is imposed upon him by the conditions of existence. Thus in India the English escape during the summer to the fresh and temperate

[1] Zimmermann, 70 ; Caldecott, 15, pp. 191–193 ; Mondaini, 54, vol. i, pp. 82–84 ; Avalle, 5, pp. 134–136 ; Lucas, 49, p. 184.

mountain heights. The activity of the European consists particularly in directing, controlling, supervising, and advising. For manual labour he uses the natives, if they are willing. When there is no labour available on the spot, he appeals to hardy races which are acclimatized to the Tropics. In many hot countries, therefore, British colonization can be traced by the migrations that accompany it; it has played a great part in the distribution of races. Above all, it has recruited its workers from among negroes and Indians. Crossing the seas in British ships, these peoples have reached regions sometimes far distant from their native lands, and hence have arisen profound ethnographic transformations, presenting grave problems to the colonist.

The successful exploitation of the West Indies was due to the employment of black labour. The Portuguese were the first to conceive the idea of transporting to their American plantations the negroes of their African trading-stations. The Spaniards, too, having no possessions in Africa, bought slaves from the Portuguese for their colonies of Cuba and Porto Rico. This lucrative traffic attracted British shipowners, and in the year 1562 they started their career as slave traders. In the course of an expedition to Sierra Leone the famous John Hawkins, having burned down a large village, seized the inhabitants and sold them in the West Indies. Becoming possessed of plantation colonies, the English soon began to recruit black labour for themselves. Bristol and Liverpool grew rich on this trade, carrying to the islands in some years as many as 50,000 negroes, while in 1771 Liverpool possessed 105 slaving ships, on which 28,500 slaves crossed the Atlantic. For more than two hundred years, thanks to these slaves, the plantation trade brought a stream of wealth to Europe. But in producing so much the land became exhausted.

The defects of slave labour were realized: it could produce fruit from a fruitful soil, but not from one which needed to be made fertile. It was only then that those generous-minded men who wanted to suppress slavery as an inhuman scourge could make their voices heard. The anti-slavery movement started in England in 1772, but it was necessary to wait fifty years before slavery was abolished. The British Parliament voted the abolition of the slave trade in 1807, and the abolition of slavery in 1833. In its passing, however, the system left a living mark upon the spot where it had flourished in the shape of the thousands of negroes who people the West Indies to-day. They form two-thirds of the population of the islands, and every day they are out-stripping more and more the white element. The race conflict which sets white and black against each other in the United States has reached the West Indies: the Antilles alone contain upward of a million and a half blacks against barely a hundred thousand whites. There is a sentiment of solidarity among the blacks, and white supremacy is no longer uncontested.

After the emancipation of the negroes many of the tropical colonies had to seek for another source of labour, and found it in the free emigration of coolies from India. In 1837 Mauritius received 20,000 of these for her sugar plantations. The West Indies followed her example in 1844, South Africa in 1860, and the islands of the Pacific in 1880. These labourers are engaged for a fixed period, on conditions controlled by the State. When their contract time is completed many of them settle down in the country instead of returning to India. At the present time they constitute two-thirds of the population of Mauritius (about 158,000), half that of British Guiana (about 150,000), and a third of that of Trinidad (about 130,000). Then there are upward of 150,000 in South Africa, and 60,000 in the

Fiji Islands. Thus the extension of the British Empire has widened the area inhabited by the Hindu race. Just as the United Kingdom has peopled the temperate regions of the Empire with her emigrants, so it may be said that India is ' the old country ' for some tropical colonies. A centre of tropical exploitation herself, she furnishes human material for the exploitation of other hot countries. But these Indians, coming in contact with other races, especially in Africa, are preparing difficult problems there for imperial statesmen to solve.

II. COLONIZATION IN TEMPERATE COUNTRIES

In peopling with her children the temperate lands beyond the seas Great Britain has fashioned them in her own image, making them truly her colonies, daughters of her blood and of her spirit.

Disappearance of Native Races.[1]—Hardly anything in the nature of human action has hindered the expansion of the Anglo-Saxon race and of British civilization in the colonies. Over immense areas they have been faced only by small and scattered populations, with no strong ties binding them to the soil—unstable communities of nomads and hunters, incapable of resisting the occupation of settlers. Wherever the Anglo-Saxon has established himself the native races have disappeared. Nowhere has he formed a mixed race with them, as the Spaniards and Portuguese have done in Central and South America : no fusion has taken place. In North America the French colonists had got into touch with the Redskins and put confidence in them. Merivale, speaking of the French, said that no other European people had ever displayed so much talent

---

[1] Caldecott, 15 ; Lucas, 49 ; Zimmermann, 70.

in conciliating savages and adapting itself to their customs and habits, and that the French traders and hunters intermarried with the Indians. The Anglo-Americans, on the contrary, have never succeeded in effecting an assimilation, nor have they, it would seem, even tried to do so. They have driven back the natives and caused them to disappear. In North America the Indians are threatened with extinction. Between them and the whites there have been terrible fights for the possession of the soil, and as late as 1756 a reward was payable in New England for the head of every Indian killed. The stories of Fenimore Cooper and Mayne Reid describe the adventures of those who hunted the Redskins—episodes in that unequal contest between the two races. Dispossessed little by little of their hunting-grounds, trapped and driven back, then attacked anew and penned up and isolated in their Reserves, the Indians at length succumbed. In the face of over 90 millions of whites they numbered no more, in 1918, than 327,000, scattered over the area of some 56,000 square miles that has been reserved for them. Even there, however, the voracity of the white colonists is threatening their last refuge.

In Canada the Redskins scarcely exceed 105,000 in number as against eight million whites. In Australia there are only 75,000 natives left ; they have the desert to themselves, while the white men have kept the wheat lands and the pastures. Tasmania has had no natives since 1876—they were exterminated by the early nineteenth century colonists. In New Zealand the Maoris were compelled, after putting up a valiant defence, to hand over their lands to the white men : they dwell to-day, to the number of 50,000, in the North Island. In South Africa every day sees the Bushmen and Hottentots driven farther into the solitudes of the interior. By the disappearance of primitive tribes the place is everywhere left free for the kind of agricultural life that is brought from Europe by the British colonists.

Appropriation of the Soil by the Colonist.[1]—Anglo-Saxon colonization in temperate countries has been essentially the work of small cultivators, driven from their homes by economic crises and coming to the colonies in the hope of acquiring land. Spain and Portugal sent soldiers, adventurers, and traders to their colonies, whereas Great Britain supplied hers with peasants, either agricultural labourers or artisans. These humble folk carry with them their passion for land and for ownership. British colonization has therefore been distinguished from others from the beginning by a land system which secures freedom and independence to the colonist. In Spanish and French colonies, on the contrary, the feudal law still holds good in the matter of grants of land. For the British colonist the possession of land is the necessary condition of existence, and consequently a democratic organization of the system of appropriation of land is forced upon every colonial establishment. The idea that directs colonization and settlement is that the soil has no value without man and that the home of every colonist ought to be accompanied by a plot of land. Colonization should associate together these two forms of wealth, which can do nothing without each other : if it gives no land to those who wish to produce it is merely emigration, while if it gives lands to those who do not work it is just speculation. In order to improve the land it is needful to plant it with men ; and for men to settle down it is necessary to give them land. There are many needs and circumstances that have sometimes hindered the rigid application of these principles, and we have seen huge concessions monopolized by

[1] Leroy-Beaulieu, 47a; Mondaini, 54, vol. i; Avalle, 5; Siegfried, 62; Duval, 30.

companies and individuals. But, despite all, the tendency of the appropriation of the soil in Anglo-Saxon lands has been for a hundred years toward direct ownership.

After experience of the huge grants of land—free and unlimited in extent—which resulted, at the end of the eighteenth and the beginning of the nineteenth centuries, in the squandering of public lands and the setting up of enormous uninhabited estates, the practical notion was arrived at that to settle men on the land it was necessary to bind them to it by a material bond. So in the distribution of lands recourse was had to the system of sales instead of free grants. Thus even before cultivation was begun a personal bond was established between the man and the land—the bond of ownership that is so powerful in the case of these humble folk of rural origin, dispossessed landowners or uprooted agricultural workers. It is a curious fact, however, that the conception of sale was not the same in all parts of the Anglo-Saxon world : we might even say that there was a Southern conception and an American one.

By the Southern system, which was applied to the Australasian colonies under the influence of Gibbon Wakefield, the lands were put up for sale publicly at a high enough price to discourage the needy. The produce of the sales was paid into a special fund for assisting emigration and conveying to the colony the emigrants of the mother country. To apply this system Wakefield founded the South Australia Company in 1830, and then, extending the system to New Zealand, he created the New Zealand Company, whose first colonists landed in 1839. In 1842 the Governments of the five Australian colonies, New Zealand, and Tasmania were authorized by Act of Parliament to make a cadastral survey of the uncultivated lands and to sell them publicly, by auction, at the price of £1 per acre. This system evidently aimed at giving the country its value by peopling it with colonists attached to the land. But it was worked in such a way that this appropriation of the land could not be immediate, for newcomers were required first to enter the service of already established landowners, and to work for them for at least a year or two. To prevent these workers from becoming landowners too quickly the selling price of the lands was fixed sufficiently high to deter them from an immediate purchase and to enable them to obtain the purchase money only after several years of saving. This system, ingeniously contrived so as to develop settlement colonization, seriously limited the freedom of the colonist.

A good deal more elastic, more free, more methodical, and more effective was the American system. It arose in the United States, the most advanced Anglo-Saxon colony in North America, and was adopted by Canada later on. To begin with, all alienation of land was preceded by a survey. Bands of surveyors and engineers measured, surveyed, and divided into lots the public lands that were to be sold. Then the Federal Government put up for sale every year the amount of available lands in each state, at the moderate price of a dollar and a quarter per acre. After 1820 every sale was made for cash. Each colonist was able, on his arrival, to purchase a plot of land, whose title-deeds he received without delay, thus becoming the owner at little cost and very speedily.

But other facilities also exist for the acquisition of land. Thus by a law of 1854 lands offered for sale, which would otherwise remain unpurchased, may be sold for a dollar an acre after ten years, 75 cents after fifteen years, 50 cents after twenty years, 25 cents after twenty-five years, and 12½ cents after thirty years. The distinctive feature of American colonization, therefore, is the ease with which the colonist can become a landowner. It is no doubt for this reason that British emigrants so long preferred United States territory to that of the British colonies. In the year 1850 the United States census revealed the presence in the Union of 150,000 Canadians, attracted thither by the low price of land. Moreover, as soon as Canada undertook its own colonization it adopted a similar system of land sales to that of the United States : from 10s., 15s., and 20s. an acre the price fell, after 1854, to 4s. and even much lower ; payment by annual instalments was permitted ; and a stream of emigrants soon arrived to make Canada a land of small proprietors.

For all these new countries, rich in land and poor in population, man is the chief form of wealth. They need colonists if they are to live and grow and have their soil put into cultivation, for of what value is the land without creative labour ? And nowadays it is no longer the colonist who is in search of a plot of ground, but the land which is offered to the colonist. In the United States, by the famous Homestead Act of 1862, plots of land were granted free, under certain conditions as to residence and cultivation. In distributing these plots the desire was to make them proportional to the needs of a family of cultivators, and they were guaranteed against confiscation. This care in providing land for colonists is to be found nowadays in all British colonies which require men. Great private landowners and companies still continue to sell, but, generally speaking, in the case of public lands the system of grants prevails. The State regards it as a duty to make payment in land for the fortune that each new colonist brings with him in his own person, and since the end of the Great War it is this land policy which has carried the day.

TYPES OF BRITISH COLONIZATION

Land Systems of Australia, New Zealand, and Canada.[1]—In Australia the earliest colonists were provided by deportation. Few free emigrants chose to go there, on account of the cost of transport : between 1815 and 1825 there were only 3000, and from 1825 to 1829 only 5000. But after the adoption of the Wakefield system more than 220,000 assisted emigrants landed during the years 1830 to 1850, and when the gold rush brought along its stream of adventurers this systematic scheme of colonization had already established a solid foundation of settlers upon the country. Unfortunately, however, they were only inhabitants, and not true colonists. In view of the high price of land few emigrants could settle down as agricultural proprietors ; they went instead as workers on sheep-farms and in the town factories. Then, under the influence of natural and economic conditions, the country turned rather in the direction of stock-raising than of cultivation. There was a fortune to be made out of wool, and vast areas were required for these immense flocks of sheep. The land became concentrated in the hands of a few great squatters : in 1845 four of them alone held nearly eight million acres in New South Wales, and in 1851, of a territory of 36 million acres in Victoria, 640 squatters held more than 29 millions. The greater part of the available lands, even the best arable land, belonged to this cattle-breeding aristocracy. In this great system of pastoral exploitation there was little room for the ploughman colonist : these *latifundia* —these sheep-runs—drove away the men.

A profound change in the peopling of the country came about, however, when the gold-mines drew thousands of smaller folk thither. And, just as had been seen in California, the gold-seekers, giving up their hazardous fortune-

---

[1] Ashley, **2** ; Mondaini, **54**, vol. i ; Leroy-Beaulieu, **47a** ; Dilke, **28** ; Siegfried, **62** ; *The Times*, May 24, 1921 ; Webster, **66**.

hunting, turned to the regular profit to be derived from the land. But to obtain land and set up agricultural estates it was necessary to dispossess the squatters. The demand for this became very keen about the year 1870, and from 1890 onward the rural democracy gradually became uppermost in the appropriation of the land : certain great pastoral estates were split up by legislative means, and their reconstitution was forbidden. Through a system of very long leases which were equivalent to actual possession of the land agricultural settlements were founded, and cultivation made slow but steady progress. Australia is still a land of large estates, but she is tending to become a land of small proprietors. After the Great War she realized still more strongly that her organization required the solid basis of a rural population. So she made urgent appeals to demobilized soldiers throughout the Empire, arranged for the training of those who were ignorant of agriculture, placing them on farms where they were initiated into the principles of the craft, promised them lands of their own, and undertook herself the cost of settling them. By November 1920 the Commonwealth had in this way received 22,000 colonists since the end of the War, of whom 4960 were settled in New South Wales, 8795 in Victoria, 3285 in Western Australia, 1870 in Queensland, 1570 in South Australia, and 1755 in Tasmania.

New Zealand shows us the type of British settlement by a class of small and medium cultivators. This group of islands is not connected with Australia except in the minds of Europeans. Geographically the two countries are as different from each other as Europe and America. As Sir Charles Dilke observed, it is as far from Wellington to Sydney as from Manchester to Iceland or from Africa to Brazil. Physically Australia is a land of brilliant sunshine, mild winters, warm summers, and arid plains, whereas New Zealand recalls Great Britain in her damp climate, her restless atmosphere, her cool summers, and her greenness. British colonists found in New Zealand a less exotic environment and a more familiar aspect of nature than in Australia. She very quickly came to exercise a particular attraction over them, and owing to the Wakefield system she became a land of good fortune. Though scarcely known even in 1840, she soon received a regular stream of colonists—humble peasants who arrived with their modest capital and a taste for agricultural pursuits. This was a family form of settlement which from the very beginning bore a fairly close resemblance to the older kind of society of Great Britain. There did not arise a landed aristocracy in New Zealand as in Australia. It was only at the beginning that grants of large estates were made to the earliest colonists. There arose very quickly a desire to prevent the formation of extensive properties, and to provide by law for the splitting up of the old ones, and this movement has made continued progress. In 1912 there were still ninety estates of over 50,000 acres each, making a total of eight million acres, while in 1919 only sixty-two remained, with a total of 5.3 million acres; and many of these were ill fitted for division, as they extended into the mountains. The characteristic feature of colonization and society in New Zealand is the small or medium-sized estate cultivated by its owner. To this class is given the name of yeomen-farmers, and it is they whose increase it is desirable to encourage by making the land accessible to all immigrants. In the matter of terms of ownership two opposing tendencies were visible between 1880 and 1910. One was favourable to the system of freehold—that is to say, the granting of the land in full ownership, on condition that the preliminary labour of cultivation and settling was accomplished within a given time—while the other was in favour of the leasehold system, or long and renewable leases, reserving the right of ownership of the State and securing to it the profits arising from the increased value of the land. The first of these tendencies is now in the ascendant, and with it a development in the direction of complete ownership and a social state in which the land is fairly equally divided between families. In 1919 out of a total of 80,468 agricultural estates 48 per cent. ranged from 1 to 100 acres in extent, 43 per cent. from 101 to 1000 acres, and 9 per cent. were over 1001 acres. The ratios of these three categories to the sum total of the lands under cultivation were 4 per cent., 28 per cent., and 68 per cent. respectively. It is easy to see what an important place is held by the large estates in the matter of extent, especially those engaged in stock-rearing, but also what social importance attaches to those of small and medium size.

In Canada more definitely than anywhere else the colonizing tendency is toward the establishment of cultivator-owners. Throughout the whole of the early part of the nineteenth century British peasants were arriving, the possessors of modest hoards of money, in search of a secure plot of ground. Nearly all of them came from Scotland, whose rigorous mountain climate had already prepared them for that of Canada. They were uprooted husbandmen with but one idea— to settle on the land and incorporate their labour and their savings in their own particular plot. Under the influence of the democratic legislation that had spread from the United States the approach to the land was easily accomplished. In 1872 the principle of free grants was put into practice by the Homestead Act. Every colonist could obtain a free grant of cultivable land amounting to 160 acres at the most, and at the end of three years he became the owner of the plot if he had carried out by himself the requisite labour of preparing and cultivating it. There are other laws by which he is assured of credit for commencing operations, and guaranteed freedom from distraint for a portion of his property. The lands thus granted are public lands, and there still exist in the prairie regions nearly 25 million acres of them. Newcomers have other reserves of land at their disposal also ; for example, there are the vast estates granted to colonization societies and railway companies as a form of subsidy. Among these great private landowners the Canadian Pacific Railway, the Hudson's Bay Company, and the Canadian Northern Railway hold nearly 30 million acres in the prairies, and they sell these lands at reasonable prices, averaging about 20 dollars an acre. Generally speaking, the public lands are found somewhat far to the north, in a harsh climate, and on poor soil. The private lands, on the contrary, occupy the best parts of the prairies, and it will be readily understood that colonists with some savings to invest prefer to buy good lands rather than to receive bad ones for nothing.

In any case, these public and private lands, all easy to obtain, whether they are given away or sold at moderate prices, attract emigrants to the prairies. They stream into these corn lands, where it is possible for anyone to set up an estate, and by them the country is rapidly being peopled. Between 1901 and 1916 the population of Manitoba rose from 255,000 to 553,000, that of Saskatchewan from 91,000 to 647,000, and that of Alberta from 73,000 to 496,000. The number of farms in Saskatchewan increased from 13,612 in 1901 to 96,371 in 1911. This freedom and profusion of rural settlement is every day impressing its democratic character more deeply upon Canadian colonization. A class of small rural landowners is thus growing up which is giving Canadian society a complexion quite different from that of British society. The Great War, which upset the economic condition of the mother country, has simply hastened this conquest of the earth. An association called the Western Canada Colonization Association has been formed, under the highest patronage, with the object of encouraging the settlement of demobilized soldiers on those western lands where three-quarters of the great corporate properties remain unoccupied. It makes advances not only for the purchase of land, but also for the expense of putting it into cultivation. At the end of the year 1920 20,122 ex-Service men had received from this association more than 80 million dollars of advances; at the end of January 1921 76 per cent. of the colonists had duly made their payments for the year; at the beginning of 1922 62,688 claims had been received, and 27,416 colonists had been permanently settled. In this way new homes are being multiplied, founded upon that form of capital which is the most precious in those empty lands—the might of the human arm and a steadfast faith in work.

CHAPTER III

BRITISH CIVILIZATION

THE British colonies are scattered over the earth, always far away from the mother country, separated from each other by enormous distances, and divided in some cases by opposing interests. And yet—what is one of the most astonishing things in the history of colonial expansion—they remain united among themselves by the possession of a common stock of customs, tendencies, and ideas : from one end of the earth to the other they are alike in the forms of their material and moral life, for a single civilization draws them together and binds them to each other.

I. MATERIAL LIFE

Food.—A man's material habits—his manner of feeding, clothing, and housing himself—are dependent upon his means of earning his living. From his circumstances of ease and fortune the Englishman has developed a taste for comfort and well-being : his standard of living has risen with the growth of the profits he has drawn from his labour. There has been formed in England a classic type, which has become legendary, of a big, fat, well-fed man, ruddy and substantial. This popular figure of John Bull is not, properly speaking, an ethnographic type : it stands rather for an artificial product, the outcome of a particular type of civilization. It is not long since the labourer in many country parts of Britain was

meals, and the first one, the morning meal, is the biggest of them all. This system has become so habitual that it is retained by colonists at the other ends of the earth, even in lands where the climate would make a different plan more suitable. During the Australian summer, which lasts for more than half the year, instead of working in the cool morning hours and devoting the hot middle of the day to rest, most Australians remain faithful to the customs of Old England, having breakfast at eight or nine o'clock, and lunch at one.

If the English eat a great deal, however, it is impossible to say that they eat well. Among certain other races good cookery is valued : it is an art that demands care and taste. But in Great Britain there is hardly more than one kind of soup, of roast, and of vegetables, from one end of the country to the other, and the cook never departs from these, any more than a manufacturer varies the kind of article that he turns out. Industrial life, by extending material well-being to almost all classes of society, has made it unoriginal, uniform, and commonplace. It has fashioned a mode of life that is simple and rapid, made for convenience rather than for pleasure, and which, like all other British customs, has been transported to the colonies.

This impression of uniformity tends to be increased in the eyes of the foreigner by the use of certain commodities which have been introduced into the country by commerce and have become objects of prime necessity. Thus in the course of her long colonial career England has acquired a taste for sugar and tea : she is unhappy only when these foreign products are dear. She consumes an enormous quantity of sugar with her fruit and her puddings and pies, while tea, the precious leaf that brought wealth to the East India Company, has become her national beverage. Three hundred years ago the use of tea was unknown ;

to-day it is hardly ever drunk by the masses in France and Germany ; but in Great Britain it is to be found everywhere, and its use is as widespread as that of bread and salt. Each inhabitant of the United Kingdom consumes annually 80 pounds of sugar and 6.47 pounds of tea, while in Australia the annual consumption of tea amounts to 7.3 pounds per head of the population, and in New Zealand to 7.9 pounds.

Clothing and Housing.—These habits have been spread all over the world by British colonists wherever they have settled, and the foreigner comes in contact with them in every British home. In the same way he notices a like concern for what is comfortable in the matter of clothing and general appearance. There is no longer any sordid poverty, except in certain quarters of the large towns. Externally the humblest resemble the richest. The English have made famous throughout the world the appearance presented by their practical and suitable garments—their heavy cloths, their big brown leather boots, their flat caps, and their collars. In obscure parts of the country, and as far away as the Scottish islands, where one would expect to see the peasants wearing worn and dirty clothes, a Frenchman is surprised to find so much neatness and cleanliness among the people who work on the land. Care for one's personal appearance is one phase of the taste for comfort, and it is to be found spread widely among different classes in Great Britain. At railway stations the traveller is astonished to see the correct attire of the workman with a flower in his buttonhole ; it is rarely that the working man has the manners of a beggar. This correctness of clothing may even be pushed to the point of discomfort when it is observed, through mere conservatism, in opposition to the requirements of the climate. Thus the heat of the Australian summer has not yet triumphed over the black coat and tall hat, those dignified garments that the social code requires of members of ' Society.'

Perhaps it is in his home, however, that the Englishman best shows his taste for comfort. Even in far-off Australia his habitation is stamped with the imprint of British originality. The Englishman likes the inside of his house to be nice ; he improves it, and he adorns it. He knows that what he spends on furniture and carpets will be repaid to him in the feeling of rest and satisfaction. Furniture, fireplaces, pavements and floors, windows, staircases, doors and doorsteps—everything is washed and scrubbed and kept clean. " Saturday," says Ferri, " is the day of the universal deluge." This home, a real family sanctuary, has to be made independent and self-contained. It is a two-story house, generally surrounded by an enclosed garden, so that it is hidden behind a hedge, a wall, or a fence. In great cities no one likes to live in the heart of the town, so houses are built in the suburbs, far away from the noisy business quarter. These residential districts of small self-contained houses are a characteristic feature of urban life in British lands. They attract the notice of all who come from America, and land, say, in New Zealand, making Auckland seem to them like a provincial town in Old England. The British home gives an impression of tranquillity and intimacy. It is a pleasant and gracious dwelling, with sweetness shed around it by such climbing plants as roses, honeysuckle, ivy, and Virginia creeper. The Englishman shows a tender respect, a town-dweller's weakness, for everything that grows and blossoms, and he likes to adorn his house with such things. He has carried these tastes with him to the four quarters of the globe. In themselves, however, some of the great colonial cities are less pleasing spectacles.[1] Melbourne, with its wide

[1] Siegfried, 62 ; Leroy-Beaulieu, 47.

streets intersecting at right angles, its lofty buildings and huge monuments, and its intricate network of electric railways, can only be likened to an American city; and such, too, is the general appearance of Toronto.

Sport.—Along with this concern for the adornment of his life and the care of his body goes the Englishman's taste for unremunerated physical activity—the conviction that muscular exercise will not only give him health and pleasure, but will assist him in the performance of his daily work. This need for bodily exercise forms part of a kind of national system of hygiene, to which all classes of society submit themselves, and which is followed by each class according to its tastes and means. It is described by the eminently British name 'sport,' which is applied alike to tiger-hunting and to fishing, to the most violent of exercises and the quietest of games. With this passion for physical exercise is associated a love for the overcoming of difficulties and the pursuit of danger for danger's sake. It is well known how important a part the English have played in the ascent of the lofty mountains of Europe and Asia, and how much energy they have displayed in Polar expeditions.

Among games that have attained to worldwide importance in Anglo-Saxon communities must be placed cricket, the popular national game beyond all others. It was played as early as the beginning of the eighteenth century, and quickly became the subject of an extensive literature, while in 1774 was held the first "Cricket Parliament," which settled the rules of the game.[1] Nowadays nearly every village has its cricket-ground and its matches, and teams of British professionals are trained for contests abroad with colonial teams. But other games have also won the popular favour:

[1] H. Neelmeyer, *Grossbritannien*, Leipzig, 1886, pp. 19–22 and 47–49.

such are football, hockey, golf, and lawn tennis; the passion for games has never become exhausted. Then besides games there are athletic exercises—running, jumping, swimming, rowing, and boxing. Boxing has no longer the vogue that it once enjoyed, but as late as the middle of the nineteenth century it was for the English what gladiatorial combats had been for the Romans, what bull-fighting is for the Spaniards, or what horse-racing is to-day for the English themselves.

If we see the place that sport occupies in the individual life of the English we can understand the part that it claims in their social life. The greatest popular festivals are race-meetings, regattas, and cricket and football matches. The Derby at Epsom, the Oxford and Cambridge boat-race, Henley Regatta, and the cricket-match between Eton and Harrow attain to the importance of national events, and are talked about all over Great Britain and throughout the whole Empire. Not only so, but all over the Empire we find the same amusements, the same kinds of sport. Even in hot countries the colonial throws himself eagerly into his games during the fine weather. Polo is played throughout the whole of India, and has its ardent devotees everywhere, ranging from the competitors in the great championships of Calcutta and Meerut down to the players in the modest games of the district officials. Horse-racing arouses the same enthusiasm in India as in the mother country and the Dominions; its most popular centres are at Calcutta, Bombay, Poona, Lucknow, Meerut, Bangalore, and Rawalpindi. At Lucknow, a great garrison town, the principal spring event is a great pony race, and at Calcutta, sometimes called the Newmarket of India, the chief race, the Viceroy's Cup, dates from 1856. In India, too, there are other less classical and more original forms of sport, such as boar-hunting, which is known as pig-sticking and involves an active excursion into the jungle. A line of elephants and beaters drives the boar out of the long grass in which it is lurking; once it is turned out the riders make a dash for it on horseback, and then begins a regular steeplechase over all the irregularities of the ground and the obstacles presented by the vegetation until the beast is killed by spear-thrusts. This boar-hunt, called the Kadir Cup, takes place in the neighbourhood of Meerut. And what is to be said of tiger-hunting, the sport of princes, in the jungles of the Sunderbunds and the Terai?[1]

In the Dominions the colonists from the different parts of the United Kingdom have taken with them their favourite sports and pastimes. The game of curling, or bowls played on the ice, has migrated from Scotland to cold countries like Canada and Nova Scotia: it is played on the St Lawrence every winter. In Australasia and South Africa horse-racing is a veritable passion. The Melbourne Cup stirs society for months in advance. "The day it is run," says Leroy-Beaulieu,[2] "at the beginning of November, it is impossible to engage in any other subject of conversation, not only in the large towns, but on the remotest sheep-rearing stations of Queensland as well as in the mining camps in the depths of the western deserts, 800 or 1000 miles from Melbourne, and the betting reaches enormous figures." Cricket too is played everywhere, regardless of the heat of the summer. "Despite the temperature," says Leroy-Beaulieu again, "I have seen the young people of Adelaide rowing on the Torrens River, and others in the mining camps of Western Australia playing cricket in 85° or 95° of heat, with the same energy as in England."[3] Throughout the Empire on Saturdays

[1] *The Times*, November 17, 1921.
[2] Leroy-Beaulieu, 47a, p. 455.
[3] Leroy-Beaulieu, *Revue des deux mondes*, 1897, p. 137.

the open-air life rules supreme ; from continent to continent challenges are launched ; matches are arranged between Australia and England ; champions and teams cross the seas ; and pan-British reputations are set up, like the pan-Hellenic ones of old, the symbol of the unity and universality of Anglo-Saxon civilization.

II. SOCIAL LIFE

There are other bonds, as powerful as material habits, which draw all Anglo-Saxons together. By their use of the same language, by the similarity of their religious aspirations, and by their employment of the same political institutions they form one great community, whose members, despite their individual interests, feel themselves united throughout the world in mutual dependence.

The English Language.—Outside the British Isles there are more than a hundred million people who speak English. Of these the most important group inhabits the United States, and these have slipped from the authority of Great Britain. English is not the mother tongue of all the inhabitants, but every one speaks it. Spread over vast spaces from the Atlantic to the Pacific, it develops and alters, becoming impregnated with slang and variegated by local inflections, so that an Englishman from England often smiles when he hears the talk of his American cousins. But this extension of their language beyond their own political community means for the English an extension of their material and moral heritage, and a source of benefit and influence. The ideas and the merchandise of Great Britain penetrate America more easily than those of other nations, because the English tongue is the vehicle of the one and an instrument of exchange for the other.

BRITISH CIVILIZATION

To the 46 millions of Englishmen in the British Isles, the 110 millions in the United States, the 8.5 millions in Canada, and the 8.5 millions in the Southern Dominions, all forming more or less compact masses, must be added the sprinkling of English communities that trade has given birth to along the great sea-routes, at Calcutta, Bombay, Rangoon, Singapore, Hong Kong, and Shanghai. Being carried everywhere by the sailors and merchants of a nation that does business with the whole world, English tends to become a universal language. In the Far East it forms the groundwork of a jargon called pidgin-English,[1] a sort of *lingua franca* that is widespread in all ports open to international traffic. It is the only means by which Europeans can converse with their servants ; it is spoken at Hong Kong and the treaty ports by Chinese of the lower classes ; and it even happens that Chinese from different provinces, who do not understand each other's dialect, converse in pidgin-English. In Japan and China many documents of general interest are published in English. In the polyglot land of India English is the only tongue in which all Indians can communicate with each other : by giving her subjects this common language the conquering race has bestowed upon them a formidable instrument of unity. English serves as an intermediary between the educated native classes and the Western world. Almost everywhere, even outside the colonies, it enters into current usage, either through the special terms employed in industrial and commercial life, or through the weights and measures and currency imposed upon the whole world by the economic hegemony of Great Britain. Thus the English tongue overflows the bounds of the Empire, offering, as it were, a picture of British expansion, which it has aided by its own special characteristics. With three-quarters of its words

[1] Smith, 63, pp. 37-38.

Germanic and Scandinavian, it is easily accessible to the Germanic peoples, while its numerous borrowings from the Latin tongues in the realms of the arts, science, politics, and commerce make it appear at times to the Latin peoples under a familiar guise. Owing to the simplicity of its grammar and syntax it can be learned by foreigners without difficulty, even with only elementary instruction. It constitutes one of the finest supports of British influence.

It is still more easy to understand what strength of internal cohesion the English tongue provides for the British community, and how powerful a bond it establishes between the mother country and the colonies, and between the colonies themselves. Geographical nomenclature alone[1] extends already over all British lands like a familiar air : it is, as it were, a mirror reflecting the memories of a long common history. The swarm of Victorias scattered throughout the Empire shows the importance of the great queen's reign in the growth of the Empire. Her name has been bestowed upon lakes, territories, waterfalls, countries, and cities. Place-names remind us everywhere of the sovereigns, the great personages, and the *savants* of the mother country : James I (Jamestown) ; Charles II (Charleston, Carolina) ; George II (Georgia) ; Prince Edward, father of Queen Victoria ; Queen Adelaide, wife of William IV ; Prince Edward, son of Queen Victoria ; the Earl of Halifax, President of the Board of Trade in the eighteenth century ; Lord Sydney, Colonial Minister under Pitt ; Lord Melbourne, Prime Minister in 1837 ; as well as Darwin, Cook, Wellington, Nelson, and many other great names in the history of the nation.

From one end of the Empire to the other the English tongue provides a common foundation for human

[1] Lucas, 48.

thought. Despite local peculiarities it sets the same imprint upon men's minds : they are brought up on the same books and the same ideas. Some colonials, dreaming of a more individual part for their young Dominions to play, deplore their too great dependence upon the thought of the mother country. They remark, for instance, that Australia does not possess a single magazine of her own, or a single important review, that she gets nearly all her reading matter from Great Britain, and that she imports books and periodicals to the value of more than £500,000 a year. " Now it cannot be healthy," says Rowland,[1] " for a nation to rely in this way solely on imported art. Art should be the sincere expression of a people's feeling. But the Australian . . . lives, through his imported art, in a perpetual air of make-believe." These regrets of an Australian enable us the better to comprehend how great an influence can be exerted by the possession of a common mother tongue on the mentality of all who speak English.

British colonists have always, from the very beginning, taken great trouble over the education of the young. In 1647 the Massachusetts Assembly passed the following law : " To the intent that learning may not be buried in the graves of our forefathers, every township, after the Lord hath increased them to the number of fifty householders, shall appoint one to teach children to write and read ; and when a town shall increase to the number of one hundred families, they shall set up a grammar school." [2] They saw to it that elementary instruction was given on the spot. As for the cultivated classes, for many generations they had their children taught in England, and it was from her that they drew their intellectual inspiration. The stamp of Oxford education is noticeable throughout the Empire,

[1] Rowland, *op. cit.*, p. 156.   [2] Quoted by Caldecott, 15, p. 237.

and it has even been observed that the pupils of the higher schools of Jamaica used to pass the Oxford examinations in botany on a study of the flora of Britain, and not that of the Tropics. Of course the Dominions have set up universities, but these young foundations are far from possessing the means and resources of Oxford and Cambridge. Many of the young people of the colonies, therefore, either carry out or finish their studies in the mother country. In the universities and university colleges of the United Kingdom in 1921 there were 4470 students from the colonies, of whom 1576 came from Asia, 1187 from Africa, 781 from America, and 281 from the Pacific.[1] On the other hand, many of the chairs in colonial universities are occupied by professors drawn from Great Britain.

There is also a tendency toward establishing official collaboration between British and colonial universities. By their new regulations the universities of Oxford and Cambridge may become affiliated with universities or colleges in the colonies; six months spent in the colonial institution counts for the same period of study in England. There is mutual agreement also as to the equivalence of diplomas: thus the Royal College of Physicians and the Royal College of Surgeons of England have accepted the diplomas of the Australian colleges for the exercise of the medical profession in England. A similar reciprocity does not exist, however, between, say, the English Bar and that of Australia any more than between the Bars of the different colonies.[2]

In other directions there are numerous associations working to maintain this intellectual union by recruiting their members from the whole of the Empire.[3] Thus

---

[1] *United Empire*, 1922, p. 327.   [2] Caldecott, 15, p. 242.
[3] Hall, 41, pp. 294–301, 372–376.

in the realm of science we have the Universities Bureau of the British Empire, founded in 1912, the Imperial Bureau of Entomology (1901), the Imperial Bureau of Mycology (1918), the British Medical Association, the Society of Comparative Legislation, and the British Association for the Advancement of Science, which has held some of its conferences at Toronto, Cape Town, and Sydney. In the economic sphere there are the Federation of British Industries, the British Empire Producers' Organization, the Empire Resources Development Committee, the Workers' Educational Association, and many others. Very significant also are the great imperial leagues designed to awaken and support the sentiment of British solidarity. Such are the Victoria League, the League of the Empire, the British Empire League, the Royal Colonial Institute, the Navy League, the Overseas League, and the Patriotic League. Then there are other institutions which gather together periodically certain groups of Englishmen and colonials on the ground of their common aspirations or ideas. Thus in 1919 an exhibition was held at Burlington House, organized by the Royal Academy, and containing the works of Australian, Canadian, South African, and New Zealand artists. In the face of all these existing manifestations of British unity we are reminded of Froude's cry of exultation years ago in *Oceana* : " The people at home and the people in the colonies are one people. The feeling of identity is perhaps stronger in the colonies than at home. . . . We, the people, always regarded them [the colonists] as our kindred, bone of our bone and flesh of our flesh." [1] The existence of this vast community of the same tongue and often of the same way of thinking enables us to understand why the English are sometimes content to converse, to think, and to live among themselves, so little inclined

[1] Froude, 38, pp. 13-14.

to learn foreign languages, and sometimes, too, so incurious as to what happens beyond their own borders. Did not Bernard Shaw say that Great Britain is an island where the natives regard their manners and customs as laws of nature ?

Religion.—Another feature of the British environment which contributes still farther to create moral unity is the abundance of the religious influences that penetrate the social life of the country. A religion that is national and, so to speak, insular, freed from all foreign authority, and concerned solely with spiritual education, has formed the moral and social habits of the people for hundreds of years. A foreigner arriving in Great Britain notices on all hands the everyday nature of this religion. He finds it not only in the splendid churches where prayers are said in common in the mother tongue, but he meets it also in the streets, the highways, and the public squares, where it assumes a modest, and at times even a vulgar, aspect in order to reach the hearts of the humblest. Religious life flourishes in this land of liberty : in no other country have there arisen more Christian sects or more inspired churches. This ferment of the religious spirit has been communicated to the colonies. In Canada, besides the four great sects—Methodists, Presbyterians, Anglicans, and Baptists—there are no less than thirty others, including Lutherans, Congregationalists, the Salvation Army, the Disciples of Christ, and so forth.

In no part of the world is more moral importance attached to sundry religious observances than in British countries. The keeping of the Sabbath, in its traditional strictness, has grown from a thoroughly national institution into an imperial one. Though it is observed less rigidly than it used to be in certain countries and among certain classes there are other places where its observance is as rigorously adhered to as ever. Not only are all forms of recreation suppressed, but all economic life is suspended, every shop is closed, and trains and posts are at a standstill. In London and some of the largest cities this severity is beginning to be relaxed : most of the museums remain open, and it is possible to go for a walk in the country, as means of transport are available for the purpose. All the same, however, there is nothing to equal the tedium of a London Sunday : the town is, as it were, dead. But what shall we say about Sunday in a small town in Scotland ? There the silence of night is prolonged until a late hour in the morning ; in the deserted streets the policemen pace slowly along past the closed shops ; the doors of the railway station are fast locked ; the hotel landlord serves his scanty meals with a mournful air ; the stranger feels like an exile in a town whose citizens have fled ; once or twice during the day the streets are disturbed by an unusual movement, when, with prayer-book in hand, the faithful betake themselves in silence to their sanctuary ; then everything slips back into tranquillity. You feel as if some unlucky star had led you, on a day of public mourning, into some grief-stricken place ; and yet that is the appearance of the town on one day in every week. That is the British Sunday throughout the world—the Australian Sunday, the Canadian Sunday, and the Scottish Sunday. This tradition is the more respected as its religious value is the more realized. Colonial society, recruited largely from among the Puritans, remains more rigidly faithful to it than that of the home country, and it is perhaps in such places as Melbourne, Auckland, Toronto, and Winnipeg that this original feature of British mentality is best seen remaining in all its purity. " Winnipeg," says Siegfried,[1] " though in many ways so American, is Scottish on Sunday. The Presbyterians

[1] Siegfried, 61, pp. 316–317.

exercise a kind of moral dictatorship there, as in Edinburgh, Sydney, and Melbourne, and to this every one must submit, whether he will or no."

The religious cast of mind is more strongly marked in the colonies than in Great Britain, because the colonists come to a very large extent from those parts of the British Isles where religious life flourishes most abundantly. Statistics show that the proportion of Scots and Irishmen is far greater in the colonies than in the United Kingdom ; the number of Protestant Dissenters and Catholics in the churches of the colonies is therefore relatively much greater. In Canada the Anglicans form only 14 per cent. of the population, while the Catholics are 40 per cent., the Presbyterians 16 per cent., the Methodists 15 per cent., and other Protestant sects 9 per cent. In New Zealand 43 per cent. are Anglicans, as against 25 per cent. Presbyterians, 14 per cent. Catholics, 10 per cent. Methodists, and 6 per cent. other Protestant sects. In Australia there are 39 per cent. Anglicans, 21 per cent. Catholics, 13 per cent. Presbyterians, 12 per cent. Methodists, and 10 per cent. other Protestants. The Protestant element in the colonies comprises, therefore, a large proportion of Dissenters, recruited from among those minorities, " of a bolder, more restless, and more independent spirit," [1] which have so mightily influenced the democratic mentality of the new Anglo-Saxon communities ; they are to be found in the front rank among reformers, whether it be on a question of political liberty, of social equality, or of feminism. Still more strongly does the religious spirit burn in countries like Canada, where Protestants and Catholics face each other in opposing camps. There the Protestants, divided into four great sects, are drawn from different

[1] Leroy-Beaulieu, *Revue des deux mondes*, 1897, pp. 139–140, and 47, pp. 457–458.

provinces : the Methodists from Ontario, among the manufacturers, business men, and farmers ; the Presbyterians from Nova Scotia and Manitoba, among the farmers ; the Anglicans from Quebec and British Columbia, among the well-to-do ; the Baptists among the working classes.[1] These sects are divided among themselves by internal differences, but they are all at one in their opposition to Catholicism. In the heart of every Protestant there still remains a rooted antipathy to ' Popery,' and this social division, which corresponds to a difference of race, is found also in the political sphere.

Of all highly civilized countries the British lands are perhaps those in which the influence of the religious spirit penetrates most deeply into the structure and life of society. This religious spirit becomes itself a motive force for the national spirit : by its means Christianity has become the pioneer of British expansion. Especially since the end of the eighteenth century, after the religious revival that blossomed forth under the influence of John Wesley, have Protestant missionaries spread throughout the world. With that mixture of common sense and generosity that appears to be a fundamental characteristic of the British heart, they came to believe that the best protection for the propagation of their faith lay in the might of the British Government : the beginning of many a territorial annexation is to be found in a Christian mission. It was by missionaries that British influence was first established at Lagos, and then, as the slave trade did not end, it became necessary to annex the island officially in order to protect the natives. The journeys of Livingstone, the great apostle of the Christian faith, opened up vast areas of tropical Africa to British expansion. In several parts of the Indian Ocean and

[1] Siegfried, 61, pp. 72–75.

the Pacific Ocean British missionaries have often con-
founded the interests of their religion with the interests
of their country. Recognizing no foreign authority,
the Protestant faith is not to be distinguished from the
national faith, and thus religion becomes an agent of
political influence. The different sects do not act in-
dependently in each country : they are bound together
in regular relations by the federation of their churches.
Thus every ten years a pan-Anglican conference is
held at Canterbury, bringing together all the Anglican
bishops.[1] There are similar councils also for Presbyterian and Methodist pastors, and these federal
assemblies are one aspect of the moral unity of the
British communities.

III. POLITICAL LIFE

There is yet another institution which is to be found
in every part of the globe where British colonists are
gathered together. This is a type of government
modelled on that of England in respect of its external
features, but with a bias toward the federal form owing
to the very conditions of its geographical development.

Self-government.—British colonists took with them
their political habits as well as their moral ones.
Wherever they set up their new homes they regarded
themselves as possessing the rights and liberties they
had enjoyed in the mother country. " For it hath been
held," says Blackstone,[2] " that if an uninhabited country
be discovered and planted by English subjects, all the
English laws then in being, which are the birthright of
every subject, are immediately there in force."

In every new-born colony, therefore, the principle of

---

[1] Caldecott, 15, p. 250.
[2] Blackstone, *Commentaries on the Laws of England*, Introduction,
Section IV.

representative government was established. In 1619 the colony of Virginia,[1] scarcely twelve years old, received a representative assembly composed of twenty-two deputies elected by the owners of land, who passed laws and voted taxes and met in session at least once a year. Beside this assembly was an executive council and a Governor. This was the prototype of the colonial governments, and the ancestor of the constitutions by which the colonies of Britain are ruled to-day. To each of the American colonies which afterward broke loose and became the United States was granted, as soon as its population permitted, a political organization made in the image of that of the mother country. It consisted of a Governor, nominated by the sovereign and representing the home country, whose powers were limited to the performance of certain constitutional duties; an upper chamber, which was sometimes difficult to fill in these new countries with no past and no aristocracy; and a lower chamber, from which authority proceeded, because it was drawn directly from the colonists themselves. Shortly after the emancipation of the United States the Canadians also demanded colonial assemblies, and from the year 1791 their two provinces of Upper Canada, whose population was mainly British, and Lower Canada, which was mainly French, each possessed a legislature and a Lieutenant-Governor. The representative system, however, was only one part of political liberty. In Great Britain it had developed during the latter part of the eighteenth century into self-government, or the complete control of affairs by the elected representatives of the people, combined with the principle of ministerial responsibility. One after another the colonies were led in the same direction, and the Parliamentary system of the mother country was extended by degrees to her

[1] Caldecott, 15, p. 129.

daughters. It was applied first to Canada, in 1839, and the interesting feature of this early experiment is that it settled which of the two forms of free government in use in Anglo-Saxon countries—the American form and the British form—should be adopted for the great British colony in America.[1] Under the American system the power of the president and the power of the national representatives both proceed from popular election, and the president, being elected for four years, can govern during that time without being in agreement with the national representatives. Under the British system the ministry is merely an emanation from the national representative assembly, and resigns if it ceases to be in agreement with that assembly. The British system carried the day, and it was the English constitution that was transplanted in Canada and afterward became the charter of autonomy of full-grown colonies. It was recognized in Nova Scotia and New Brunswick in 1848, in the Australasian colonies between 1846 and 1859, in Cape Colony in 1872, in Natal in 1893, and in Western Australia in 1890. The grant of self-government is made only when no imperial interest is menaced by the existence of the new political entity. Western Australia received it quite young, at a time when she had scarcely more than 50,000 inhabitants, though her territory was nearly eight times the size of the United Kingdom. In South Africa, on the other hand, the white colonists did not attain to self-government until fairly late. In Cape Colony it was not resolved on until the construction of the Suez Canal had diminished her strategical import-ance ; [2] Natal had to wait till it was certain that her colonists were capable of administering a country where the great majority of the population were natives.

In these colonial Parliaments formed on the model of

[1] Caldecott, 15, pp. 130–135.   [2] Mondaini, 54, vol. i, p. 388.

that of Britain one often gets the impression of being still in Old England, so great is the similarity of their rules, forms, and methods of work. " The House of Commons in London is the model that is referred to most readily in Ottawa. Its forms have been minutely copied, and the assembly hall of the Canadian chamber is roughly a reproduction of the celebrated House at Westminster. The seats are arranged not in an amphitheatre as at Paris, but facing each other, with the Speaker, prim and venerable, seated on a kind of throne between the two parties, having the Government party on his right and the Opposition on his left. The sessions are opened and closed, as in the Parliament of the mother country, with that antiquated ceremonial which seems a little out of place in its setting of colonial simplicity. . . . Each member speaks from his own place, taking off his hat and addressing not the assembly but the Speaker. The general impression is clearly British." [1] In Australia likewise we find the same copying of British forms and ceremonies. The Governor in Australia says " my Government " in speaking of the ministers, as the King does in London. So, too, there is the same judicial ceremonial. " At the beginning of business in the courts an usher addresses the people with the old French formula, ' Oyez, oyez, oyez,' as is done even at Washington, in the Supreme Court of the United States. . . . All the Australian judges, like their English brothers, are clad in robes and powdered wigs. They are irremovable, and surrounded by universal consideration." [2] This respect for tradition and for the preservation of ancient things is a sentimental force in the British temperament which draws together the men of the old and the new Englands.

Colonial Federations.—That political evolution, the

[1] Siegfried, 61, pp. 222–230.   [2] Leroy-Beaulieu, 47, pp. 455–456.

offspring of the principles of freedom, which has led the British colonies to adopt the representative system and Parliamentary government has also led them naturally, through an internal force of development, to the adoption of the federal system. Canada, Australia, and South Africa have all of them, like the United States, adopted that form of political syncretism which seems to be a distinguishing feature of Anglo-Saxon communities beyond the seas. As a matter of fact, this development is the outcome of a victory over the particularism to which all the parts of these colonies were originally prone, owing to their geographical situation. At the beginning they consisted, as it were, of so many isolated and autonomous cells, separated in many cases by long distances, opposed to each other in their economic interests, and animated by egoistic tendencies. Thus in the United States there were the thirteen colonies on the Atlantic coast ; in Canada there were Upper Canada, Lower Canada, Nova Scotia, New Brunswick, Newfoundland, British Columbia, and the young provinces most recently formed ; in Australasia were New South Wales, Victoria, Queensland, Tasmania, and New Zealand ; in South Africa Cape Colony and Natal, and later on the Orange Free State and the Transvaal. Such is the first stage—dispersion, rivalry, and sometimes hostility. In Canada disagreement long prevailed between Upper and Lower Canada. In Australia each colony built its own railways on a different gauge from the rest, as if they were foreign states,[1] so that to-day this diversity forms a serious hindrance to general circulation, and the Commonwealth Government looks upon the adoption of a uniform gauge as a national necessity. In South Africa there is conflict between the colonies on the coast, which are Protectionist and anxious to support their infant

[1] *United Empire,* 1919, p. 423.

industries, and the inland colonies, which are adherents of Free Trade and desirous of maintaining free markets for their exports. Tariff wars have more than once broken out when there has been a question of favouring some port—Cape Town, Durban, or Lourenço Marques. When there is no opposition of interests there are often curious differences of tradition and custom. Nothing surprises the foreigner so much as the variety of legal codes and systems of jurisprudence that persist all through the Empire alongside of the English law. At Quebec the legal system is founded on the old French law known as the Custom of Paris; at Mauritius the Napoleonic Code is in force; Dutch law is applied to Guiana, Cape Colony, Natal, the Orange Free State, the Transvaal, and Ceylon; Spanish law is in force in Trinidad, and Sicilian law in Malta, while against the common law of England Roman law still holds sway in a part of the Empire.[1]

These original and individual peculiarities, however, have never been operative long enough to overcome the effect of geographical proximity, in virtue of which all the units at the same stage of civilization and fixed upon the same portion of the earth show a tendency toward political union. As soon as certain primitive colonies have become welded together in a material sense by the progress of settlement they have sought to combine in a federal union, and have evolved into a type of state that is in singular contrast to the old centralized states of Europe, and which seems to have become the regular model for political life in lands colonized by the British. The earliest of these federations gave birth in 1776 to the Republic of the United States of America. Nearly a century later, in 1867, the second one was founded in Canada, while

[1] *British Empire*, 11, pp. 228–240; Caldecott, 15, p. 136; Avalle, 5, p. 2.

Australia's turn came in 1901, and that of South Africa in 1909.

These young federal states do not all reveal precisely the same structure. Their constitutions are not absolutely alike, because each of them, owing to its origin and development, possesses individual characteristics which would have made a general assimilation impossible. This constitutional difference may be observed, for example, between Canada and Australia.[1] In Canada the federal bond is tighter, and leaves less power to the provinces than in Australia : the powers of the provinces are delegated to them by the federal power ; the federal Parliament possesses the chief power, and it alone represents the country before the Crown ; and at the time when the federation was made the public debt was allotted almost entirely to the Dominion. In Australia, on the other hand, the federal bond is looser, and woven, as it were, for application to provinces jealous of their rights. The federal power is delegated to the Commonwealth Government by the colonial states ; each of these states retains direct relations with the mother country, and its Governor is nominated directly by the Crown, just like the Governor-General of Canada, who nominates the provincial governors. The public debts of each of the Australian states are not merged in the federal debt : each state assumes responsibility for its own. The very name given to the form of government reveals these differences : Canada adopted the term ' Dominion,' which had become somewhat vague, while Australia took the far more precise name of ' Commonwealth.' Similarly South Africa occupies a peculiar situation. In order to guarantee to the whites their supremacy in a country peopled by many natives it was necessary to ensure the strength of the

---

[1] Lucas, 49, pp. 170–172 ; Ashley, 2, pp. 45–46, 218–219 ; Mondaini, 54, vol. i, pp. 435 ff. ; Caldecott, 15, pp. 145–150.

central Government. The principle of association here
is not a pure federation, but a union, the Union of South
Africa, in which the federal Parliament holds the chief
power.

These colonial federations were established in the
purest spirit of loyalty to Great Britain : it was simply
a matter of assuring to a group of colonies the right
of self-government which each one of them possessed
already. But it is indisputable that each federation,
under the influence of its geographical centre, shows a
tendency to live as an independent nation. The word
'Dominion' itself, whose meaning has been weakened by
usage, was chosen originally because the term 'colony'
had, as it were, a flavour of subordination about it.
When Canada was seeking for a name for her confederation the term 'Dominion' was preferred because it
called up the idea of an independent power, and was
connected in meaning with the word 'kingdom,' which
had been thought of at first.[1] At the origin of all
these colonial united states there is always to be found
a keen national feeling which instinctively calls forth
the energy of the colonists against any common danger.
The reason why the Canadians were desirous of organizing themselves as a dominion is that they were afraid
of being absorbed by the powerful republic on their
borders. In this fear British and French Canadians
were united. Upper Canada, which was British, remained profoundly loyalist, while Lower Canada, which
was French, was unwilling to be merged in a huge
Anglo-Saxon community where she was in danger of
losing her personality. By becoming a federation
Canada may be said to have asserted her nationality
and her opposition to the United States. The first
care of the new confederation was to create a powerful
material bond between its members by constructing a

[1] Lucas, *Scientia*, 1917, p. 136.

M

transcontinental railway. This railway became the visible framework, as it were, of the nation. Similarly, in the formation of the Australian confederation we must recognize the decisive influence exerted by German threats in the Pacific. The Australians quickly became aware of their isolation, and felt the necessity of forming a solid national front against all perils from without. In South Africa it was a different kind of danger that cemented the union : it was needful for the whites, both British and Dutch, to form a compact union of their forces against the swarming multitudes of negroes.

This political development—the abandonment of colonial particularism and the formation of federal states—is connected, in Anglo-Saxon communities, with the development of a national consciousness which stands next, in the colonist's mind, to the feeling of loyalty to the mother country. These two sentiments seem to have co-existed hitherto without injuring each other. But this fact must not prevent us from propounding the problem of political geography whose terms are supplied to us by the situation at the present day. Are these young nations preparing to form dissentient entities destined for complete independence ? Or are they to become members of a great federal entity, a single world-embracing state that shall include all the communities of the British world ?

BOOK III
IMPERIAL PROBLEMS

CHAPTER I

CHARACTERISTICS OF IMPERIAL UNITY

BETWEEN the constituent parts of the British Empire there are certain unifying elements. First of all, there is the material bond of the sea. Despite the continental acquisitions of the Empire, it always keeps in touch with maritime circulation : the sea is its internal highway, as it were. In the second place, there is that community of traditions, of customs, of sentiments, and of interests which makes the citizens of the Empire feel as if they belonged to a single country. But at the same time there are elements of disagreement that are no less certain. The variety and ubiquity of the Empire present a serious problem in respect of its unity. It possesses lands in every zone, and peoples of every race, every religion, and every kind of civilization. Moreover, being geographically scattered, it contains some centrifugal tendencies by the very nature of things. Not only do its Dominions themselves possess a political status which is practically equivalent to independence, but in the environment which their geographical position gives them they have individual interests which are not those of the whole Empire. It is necessary to inquire wherein exactly imperial unity lies, and what is the content of this notion of unity. Does it actually exist ? If not, can it be created ? If it exists or is created, how can it be made to last ? These are vital questions which have been for more than a generation in the foreground of British thought and action.

I. ORIGIN AND EVOLUTION OF THE IMPERIAL IDEA

The idea of imperial unity is quite modern. Down to about the year 1860 many Englishmen believed that sooner or later the colonies would be bound to part from the mother country, thus sharing the opinion of Turgot that " a colony, when it is full grown, detaches itself from the mother country as a ripe fruit falls from the tree." The example of the colonies of North and South America was quoted, and it was thought that the days of the Empire were numbered. It was remarked that the self-governing colonies protected themselves by customs tariffs, even against the United Kingdom. The seeds of conflict over colonial questions were everywhere to be seen—in America with the United States, in Asia with Russia, and in Africa with other colonial powers. People imagined that a ruinously expensive fleet must be maintained for the defence of such an empire. In 1857 John Bright asserted that it would be a fortunate day for England when she no longer owned an acre of land on Asiatic soil. In 1863 Goldwin Smith declared that the Empire was a burden on the mother country. But these "Little Englanders" were soon to be faced by the advocates of a Greater Britain.

The profound transformations which the development of means of transport has brought about in the mutual relations of human societies have given rise to a new conception of the relationship between the mother country and the colonies. Transcontinental and transoceanic lines of communication have made the world smaller ; they draw the sister nations together and bind closer the bonds of kindred. But there are yet

180

other causes operating to reinforce the idea of union. So long as Great Britain was able to find a free field for her commerce among all nations she felt less need of a colonial empire. But as her production increased and the competition of other nations grew keener she began to be afraid that she might not have enough markets, and she had to make sure of sources of supply of raw materials and foodstuffs, as well as of outlets for her manufactured products. She came to understand that she could find in her colonies a privileged estate, capable of providing her with food, producing raw materials for her, absorbing her capital and her men, and purchasing her manufactured articles. The time had come, not to relax, but to draw tighter the bonds uniting the mother country to the colonies. The colonies, on their side, felt the need of this union in order to protect their national existence. Thus Canada was afraid of seizure by the United States; the South African colonists saw their weakness in face of the Boer element and the native hordes; while in the Pacific Ocean the appearance of the great European powers and the progress of Japan impaired the feeling of security and the love of isolation in Australia. In this way the mother country and the colonies became necessary to each other, and during the last third of the nineteenth century the notion of imperial unity took shape in men's minds, and attempts were made to give it life.

The British Empire, then, appears no longer as the last survivor of a family of states destined to disappear. It is regarded instead as a new type, whose constitution is still to seek, but whose material is there, all ready, active, and alive.[1] It is worshipped almost as a religion, and its cause is proclaimed by its advocates with

[1] On this movement see Leroy-Beaulieu, 47, pp. 440–442 ; Bérard, 7, p. 64 ; British Empire, 12, p. 33 ; Mondaini, 54, vol. ii, pp. 399 ff.; Boutmy, Annales des sciences politiques, 1899, pp. 537–563.

apostolic fervour. In 1868 Sir Charles Dilke published his picture of the Empire in his book *Greater Britain*, whose very title reveals its programme. A new edition appeared in 1890, after the author had made a voyage round the world. The imperial idea made headway. It was defended by Seeley in his work *The Expansion of England*, which appeared in 1884. Froude, in his *Oceana, or England and her Colonies*, exclaimed that in traversing the earth he had seen with his own eyes that besides Old England there were other Englands where the race was flourishing with all its ancient talents. Rudyard Kipling popularized the conception of the Empire by celebrating it in his poems. Business men and practical folk adopted it with all the more ardour as they felt their interests threatened by foreign competition. Public opinion vibrated to the burning words of Joseph Chamberlain, the first statesman to work for the practical realization of the Empire. The conception of imperial solidarity became concrete and widespread. Attempts were made to keep it everywhere to the fore by the action of leagues, associations, institutions, and periodical conferences by which the imperial idea was gradually created and animated. In 1868 was founded the Royal Colonial Institute, originally called the Colonial Society, with the object, as defined in its charter of incorporation in 1882, of " promoting the increase and diffusion of knowledge respecting Our Colonies Dependencies and Possessions and Our Indian Empire and preserving a permanent union between the Mother Country and the various parts of the British Empire." It soon provided a meeting-place at its London headquarters for people from the colonies, and a centre for the exchange of views where the imperial spirit was shaped. In 1884 the Imperial Federation League was founded for studying the application of the federal principle to the relations of Great

Britain with her colonies. In 1888 arose the Imperial Institute, which was set up at South Kensington on the initiative of the Prince of Wales, its full title being "The Imperial Institute of the United Kingdom, the Colonies and India, and the Isles of the British Seas." Supported by subsidies from all parts of the Empire, its function was to study the interests common to all members of the Empire, to organize a permanent museum of raw materials and manufactured products of the whole Empire, to publish economic information of interest to the Empire, and to summon conferences. It is resorted to by merchants and manufacturers in increasing numbers when they want technical advice on any economic subject of imperial interest. Since 1907 it has been a department of the Colonial Office, its executive committee being composed of both British and colonial ministers.

Since 1900 the Botanical Gardens at Kew have become an imperial institution for the study of problems in botanical economy and for spreading knowledge to all parts of the Empire, and similar institutions, staffed by a personnel trained at Kew, are working in the colonies of Asia, America, and Australasia. Since 1895 the British Empire League has endeavoured to secure the permanent unity of the Empire by calling periodical conferences of colonial representatives to discuss commercial questions, preparing commercial agreements between members of the Empire, developing imperial trade by more direct and less costly means of communication, and standardizing commercial legislation throughout the Empire.[1]

Thus there are being built up in the Empire a common consciousness and a common life. The Empire

[1] On these institutions see Boutmy, *op. cit.*; Caldecott, 15, p. 149; White, *Scottish Geographical Magazine*, 1892, pp. 431–436; Ashley, 2, Preface; *British Empire*, 11, p. 599; Bruce, 13, pp. 38–42.

183

is like a building whose various parts have to be joined together. And just as in the Dominions the individual colonies have become federated, is it not possible to federate all these imperial lands that are sundered by the sea? Despite their diversity and their distance, do there exist sufficient common interests among the constituent parts of the Empire to form a federation— a state, that is to say, of a new type, in which individual interests would be subordinated to the general interest? In what form might this federation be realized? On what basis could an agreement be concluded which would respect the rights of individuals while consolidating imperial unity? This agreement might be made either in the political or in the economic sphere. In the political sphere a single imperial authority would be required to manage the general interests that were treated in common, to settle the internal business of the Empire, to direct its foreign relations, to make commercial treaties, to guide its diplomacy, and to decide upon questions of peace and war. Is there room in the Empire for an authority of this kind? In the economic sphere it would merely be a matter of setting up a customs union between Great Britain and the colonies. A system of reciprocity would be created which would set aside foreign countries and make the Empire an economic whole whose trade would be essentially internal. Can the Empire live thus isolated, and be sufficient to itself?

II. THE QUESTION OF POLITICAL UNITY

By one of those contrasts that are often seen between facts and ideas, it seems as if while the idea of imperial unity was gaining strength in men's minds it was losing ground in practice. The political diversity of the Empire increased as new nations were born to it, and each nation, resolving freely to follow its own path, became a centre of egoistic energy which set a limit to the extension of imperial authority.

Attempts at Political Unification.[1]—The granting of self-government to the larger colonies had seemed to many minds like the first step toward independence. Contrary to this opinion, however, a breath of union began to blow during the period 1860–80. It was considered possible, and was almost a matter of common agreement, that imperial affairs should be left to the management of Great Britain. The true-born colonies showed themselves disposed to admit the principle of guidance proceeding from the British Government, and therefore gave their confidence and affection to the mother country. It was necessary, however, to make practical applications of this principle, and such was the object of the conferences, first colonial, and then imperial, that were held for the first time in 1887. They may be said to mark the beginning of an experiment in the organization of international government within the Empire. Conferences were held in 1887, 1894, 1897, 1902, 1907, and 1911, all at London, except the one at Ottawa in 1894. They revealed the existence of two tendencies : first, the determination of the colonies not to give up their independence ; and, second, their sincere desire to come to an understanding among themselves and with Great Britain on certain questions of imperial interest.

So far as their independence was concerned they were opposed to any project tending to a centralization of government. On several occasions they rejected the proposal for a permanent Imperial Council of State, seeing therein a danger to the freedom of their own

---

[1] Hall, 41 ; *British Empire*, 12, *passim* ; Pollard, 55, pp. 773 ff.; *Empire and Century*, 34, pp. 73 ff. ; Scott, 59, pp. 327 ff. ; Mondaini, 54, vol. ii, p. 394 ; Keith, 45 ; numerous articles in *The Round Table*.

Governments. They opposed also the idea of a Parliament of Imperial Defence in which their representatives would be seated beside those of the United Kingdom, as well as the idea of a monetary contribution from the colonies toward the cost of the Army and Navy, preferring to reserve to themselves the right to create their own military and naval forces. Meanwhile they neglected nothing which might put them on a footing of equality with the United Kingdom. In 1907 it was resolved that the conference should thenceforth take the title ' imperial ' instead of ' colonial,' that the term ' colonies ' should be replaced by ' dominions,' that the imperial conference should be presided over by the Prime Minister of the United Kingdom instead of the Secretary of State for the Colonies, and that it should consist of the Prime Ministers of the Dominions, and thus become an assembly of heads of states, all equal in rights.

On several important points an understanding was arrived at : first, on the matter of imperial Protection, which raised the question of economic unity ; and secondly, and more important still, on the question of military defence, which is one aspect of the problem of political unity. It was in the military sphere that imperial collaboration was most effectively practised. For a long time the mother country alone was responsible for the defence of all her possessions. England made no demands upon them for the maintenance of her fleet, and every English colonist who belonged to a wealthy nation enjoyed the privilege of paying nothing for the defence of his country. The idea of colonial participation was imposed upon the colonies by force of circumstances, because they formed an essential part of the Empire, and therefore had an interest in supporting it if they did not wish to be left weak and isolated before the world. In the face of great imperialist powers like the United States, Japan, and Germany, rich in men and strong in material resources, Great Britain could no longer defend her worldwide interests single-handed; it was incumbent upon her colonies to help her forge her weapons, and in particular to aid in maintaining her Navy, the Empire's shield. It was realized that Great Britain's relations with her colonies depend upon the mastery of the seas—upon naval supremacy. This was expressed by Lord Selborne in 1902 at the intercolonial conference,[1] when he said that the peril he feared for the Empire was that Canada, South Africa, and Australia, being really continents, might tend to become too continental and not sufficiently maritime in their ideas and aspirations. He pointed out that the Empire owed its existence to the ocean, and could continue to exist only if all its parts continued to regard the ocean as their true source of life and strength. Through a kind of feeling of self-preservation the colonies frankly adopted these principles of solidarity, realizing that the centre of their military defence lay beyond the sea, outside their territorial boundaries. This necessity for common defence was without doubt the most powerful bond in the Empire. Colonial forces were very soon found co-operating with British forces in various parts of the world. Thus in 1885 contingents from New South Wales and Canada took part in the Sudan expedition; in 1899 the Australasian colonies sent troops to South Africa against the Boers; and in 1900 an Australian force operated in China against the Boxers. These instances of intervention showed the readiness of the colonies to pool their military forces. From year to year the organization was perfected under the influence of the Imperial Conference. Yet at the same time it respected the particularist views

[1] Siegfried, 62, p. 342.

of the colonies, allowing Australia to form her own navy, and Australia and Canada to fit out their own naval stations at Sydney, Halifax, and Esquimalt. But preparations were carefully made for fighting in concert, which was an essential point in case of war; uniformity of organization, equipment, and training was achieved, as well as unity of command. In 1907 the British General Staff became the Imperial General Staff, comprising officers drawn from all parts of the Empire and training them on uniform lines. After the conference of 1909, and in consequence of Lord Kitchener's visit to Australia, that country adopted compulsory military service, and opened a military school for officers at Duntroon. New Zealand also instituted compulsory service in 1910, and South Africa in 1912. Officers were exchanged between the mother country and the colonies, and an Imperial Defence Committee met periodically.

This military agreement explains how, at the time of the Great War of 1914, the surprising sight was seen of several colonial armies taking the field under a single command. Even more definitely had the mobilization and concentration of the fleets been arranged in agreement with the British Admiralty. It is true that the colonies had rejected the principle of a monetary contribution to Great Britain, because that would have implied that there was only one navy. They had preferred the plan of national navies, and after the mission of Rear-Admiral Sir Reginald Henderson in 1911 Australia had built a fleet. It was understood, however, that in case of war the Australian squadron would pass under the orders of the Admiralty. This junction took effect automatically in 1914, and in November of that year the Australian cruiser *Sydney* successfully engaged the German cruiser *Emden* near the Cocos Islands.

CHARACTERISTICS OF IMPERIAL UNITY

Throughout the whole of the War the co-operation of the colonies was secured to Great Britain. No appeal for help was addressed to the Dominions; their assistance was warmly welcomed, but no form of pressure was exerted upon them. They offered an astonishing spectacle to the world: the whole of the British communities making common cause with the mother country and bringing her their wealth and their sons. The impression produced was that of a spontaneous solidarity, arising from the possession of a single soul. In the month of November 1918 the number of men carried overseas or in course of training in camp amounted to 458,218 for Canada, 331,814 for Australia, 112,223 for New Zealand, and 76,184 for South Africa. These figures represent a proportion of from 11 per cent. to 19 per cent. of the male white population. Canada had 55,175 killed, Australia 55,585, and New Zealand 16,132. If we add to these numbers of killed the numbers of missing and wounded we obtain a proportion to the total number of troops of 45 per cent. for Canada, 63 per cent. for Australia, and 50 per cent. for New Zealand. Canada and Australia suffered more losses than the United States.[1] And what about the cost of the War? The five Dominions expended in war expenses and capitalized value of pensions the sum of £862,434,600. Between 1914 and 1919 the Australian debt (federal debt and state debts) rose from 327 million to 695 million pounds. The federal debt alone per head of the inhabitants increased from £2 to £62 for Australia, from £68 to £334 for Canada, and from £84 to £170 for New Zealand.[2] Nothing has drawn the inhabitants of the Empire closer together than the Great War. When it was over the colonies saw that the British Navy was their strongest

[1] *The Round Table*, March and June 1919.
[2] *The Times*, May 24, 1921.

bulwark against the foreigner. Without it, what would be their defence ? This position was clearly explained by Mr Hughes, the Australian Prime Minister, in May 1921. " The Dominions," he said, " must share the burden [of maintaining the Navy]. . . . Any scheme of Imperial Naval Defence must necessarily provide for the defence of the Pacific Ocean, where the future of Australia will be decided. . . . Naval defence is for us a Pacific question. . . . We have a coast-line nearly three times as long as that of America. They have over 100 millions of people to defend a country slightly smaller in size, and only vulnerable from seas on two sides. It is evident we want a much larger Navy than the Commonwealth itself is able to maintain."[1] Questions of defence bulked large on the programmes of the Imperial Conferences : thus in 1921 there was a discussion as to the type of warships that should be built. The Navy is at present the most concrete aspect of the imperial idea.

The Sentiment of Independence in the Dominions.— The sacrifices entailed by the War and so loyally accepted have none the less given the Dominions a keener sense of their own interests. Hitherto complete freedom was permitted them, in practice, in dealing with their internal affairs, and they preserved their constitutional independence even in respect of customs duties and Army and Navy. But, on the other hand, the control of foreign policy was taken from them. It often happened that the Foreign Office went counter to the wishes of the colonies.[2] Thus it forbade Queensland to annex New Guinea, thwarted the ambitions of Australia in the Southern Pacific, imposed its policy upon her in the New Hebrides and upon Newfoundland over the question of fishing rights on the Grand Banks, and left the

[1] *The Times*, May 24, 1921.
[2] Colomb, 20, pp. 235–237 ; Keith, 45, pp. 15 ff.

Dominions, against their will, in ignorance of the resolutions proposed and passed at The Hague at the Peace Conferences of 1899 and 1907, as well as of the clauses of the Declaration of London in 1911 on the subject of naval warfare. And not only so, but the Dominions might even be drawn into war without being consulted or having any voice in the matter. Lord Rosebery declared plainly in 1888 : " When you declare war you do not declare war alone, but Canada declares war, Australia declares war, every dependency in the Empire declares war, without having an official voice in the control of our policy." [1]

Consequently, having given thousands of their sons and contracted enormous debts for the defence of the Empire, the Dominions are asking to be allowed for the future to collaborate in the control of imperial diplomacy. They desire a place in the councils of the Empire, and a voice in the conduct of affairs that are common to them all. In their view the mother country can no longer take control single-handed of foreign affairs. Even during the War colonial opinion was sometimes refractory and had to be appeased. On many occasions it required care to avoid infringement of what the Dominions might regard as their prerogatives, in respect of procedure as to prizes, or of trading with the enemy, or of the compulsory service of colonial citizens living in England.[2] Care was needed also to avoid hampering their action in the course of military operations conducted by them. Thus in New Guinea the terms of capitulation of the German forces were arranged by the Australian commander of the expeditionary corps, and the same thing was done by the New Zealand commander in Samoa and by General Botha in South Africa.

Moreover, the principle of Dominion control of the

[1] *British Empire*, II, p. 591. [2] Keith, 45, pp. 21–22.

foreign policy of the Empire is now admitted.[1] In March 1917 the Imperial War Cabinet, composed of the ministers of the home country and the colonies, brought forward the grave affairs of the time. The Dominion ministers were seated there by the same right as the British ministers, and through them each Dominion had a deliberative voice in questions of war, peace, and foreign policy. Even the principle of the equality of all national statutes has been declared; the Dominions are recognized as autonomous nations belonging to an imperial federation (including India); their right to be consulted on every imperial question has been proclaimed; and such was the practice throughout the whole of the War. At the end of the War the Dominions and India were represented at the Peace Conference. They were recognized as members of the League of Nations on the same footing as the United Kingdom, and they received colonial mandates. At the Imperial Conference of 1921, which sat for seven weeks, the British Government applied itself to the task of drafting an imperial policy in agreement with the Dominions; in the intervals between the sessions it considered it its duty to apply this policy. From the outside there was no apparent change in the structure, but in reality a revolution had taken place in the British system. This revolution made itself felt in the international relations of the world, since for the first time the young Anglo-Saxon democracies penetrated within the political system of Europe. Thus at the 1921 conference they gave their opinion on the question of Upper Silesia. We may say that British policy in Europe is now no longer that of Great Britain alone, but that of New Zealand as well.

Under the same influence of the non-European countries

---

[1] On this question see *The Round Table*, June 1921, pp. 535–540; Keith, 45, *passim*; Mondaini, 54, vol. i, Preface; Hall, 41, pp. 159 ff.

that make up the Empire European problems are tending to recede into the background. In consequence of the trade of Australia, New Zealand, and Canada with the United States, Japan, and the Far East, the Pacific Ocean is becoming more and more the main theatre of imperial politics. Because the Dominions were anxious to form a close alliance with the United States in regard to Pacific problems Great Britain was compelled to give up her treaty of alliance with Japan. In the opinion of colonials Europe no longer holds the same position in the world as she did before the War, and Great Britain ought not to concern herself so closely with European affairs. Other countries have gained what Europe has lost in international importance, and policy ought to take account of this change. Speaking at the Imperial Conference of June 1921 General Smuts declared that during the coming half-century the real world problems would be those relating to the Pacific. It was incumbent upon the Imperial Conference, he added, to give guidance to the interested Powers, Great Britain, the United States, China, and Japan, and to bring them to a friendly conference. The centre of gravity of imperial politics is shifting toward the Far East and the Pacific ; it is there that the national interests of the Dominions lie. Thus the Great War, which aroused the common loyalty of all the Dominions, has no less developed in each of them a national consciousness. Each of these nations has individual interests which are not always precisely those of the Empire as a whole. It follows that, for the defence of these interests, each one may wish to have her own representatives in foreign capitals. Canada will henceforth have her own ambassador at Washington. This places a new difficulty in the way of imperial unity, for unity of action will have to be secured between the diplomacy of London and that of the Dominion.

N

THE BRITISH EMPIRE

There is another event that must weigh heavily upon the destiny of imperial unity. This is the birth of a national consciousness in colonies inhabited by natives, like India and Egypt, and their progress toward the status of Dominions. Formerly, when people spoke of British federation, it was only a question of self-governing colonies of European settlement, and not of dependencies and possessions. But to-day the dependencies are aspiring to Dominion status. India had her delegates in the Imperial War Cabinet and at the Peace Conference. She has representative institutions, elected assemblies, and ministerial responsibility. She seems impatient with her dependent position, and is anxious to be associated, like the Dominions, with the management of imperial affairs. How, then, is the political unity of the Empire to be organized? Is there room in the confederation of colonies of British blood for a tropical nation, entirely different in race, in mentality, in civilization, and in material life? Some of the Dominions are strongly opposed to any idea of imperial centralization. Would not a Hindu Dominion be still more refractory?

The Slenderness of the Constitutional Bonds.—To what, then, is the political unity of the Empire reduced? Very light and slender are the constitutional bonds that bind its various members to Great Britain. Of these the first and the most respected is the monarchy. The King is the personification of unity. He remains the sovereign of all British lands. He is the concrete, living image of the Empire. In each Dominion this common sovereign is represented by a Governor-General, who plays the part locally of a constitutional sovereign, having officially renounced all personal opinions, and promulgating the laws passed by the colonial Parliament, even if he disapproves of them. This Governor may be a man of great personal worth, and he may carry out his representative function with great dignity, but his authority is scarcely more than nominal in face of the Parliament in which sovereign authority resides. And the question has arisen whether even this position should not be lowered. There are some who ask whether the choice of the Governor should be left in the hands of the Crown, or whether each Dominion should not have a veto on the person chosen, or even the right to nominate him, and, in the latter case, whether the person chosen ought to be a citizen of the United Kingdom or a citizen of the Dominion. There are others who even inquire whether the office of Governor-General ought not to be abolished, and whether in that case the Dominions should not have their diplomatic representatives in London and the other colonial capitals.

There is one institution in existence which maintains another constitutional bond. This is the Judicial Committee of the Privy Council, which is a supreme court of appeal for the whole Empire. Each Dominion has its own courts of law, but from all colonial tribunals there lies an appeal to the Privy Council. In principle the source of all judicial authority is in London, as the source of political power. But there is a tendency in some colonies to contest the authority of the Judicial Committee. The political constitution of imperial unity is composed in reality of a slender tissue of traditions.[1]

The builders of governmental machinery [2] are therefore seeking for a constitution for the British confederation, a constitution that will reconcile the principle of unity with the principle of diversity. To organize the participation

---

[1] On these constitutional bonds see *The Round Table*, June 1921 ; Siegfried, 61, p. 327 ; Keith, 45, p. 7 ; Mondaini, 54, vol. ii, pp. 389 ff.
[2] See Hall, 41 ; Caldecott, 15, pp. 155 ff. ; Webster, 66, p. 294 ; Keith, 45.

of the Dominions in imperial politics by means of a constitution is, in fact, to create a new type of state. How is it to be done? Is there to be a kind of federal super-state to which each state in the Empire will relinquish a portion of its independence? And in that case will there be an imperial Parliament to which each state will send its deputies? The present Parliament in London would then have to occupy itself only with purely national affairs. Or will the Empire remain a group of autonomous states, ordering its common affairs by a kind of internal diplomacy? In that case, if the Empire is not to be a meaningless term, some means would have to be found of organizing the continuous consultation of all its members, either by general conferences of Prime Ministers, or by special conferences of particular ministers, or by conferences of delegates. The second method would obviously be merely a continuation of the existing system, adapted and improved, whereby imperial unity is maintained simply by a kind of tacit agreement. The first plan would be an innovation—a political entity to be created from the very beginning. Has this new kind of state any chance of coming to birth and remaining in existence?

It does not look as if the centralization of imperial business in a Parliament sitting in London would stand any chance of being accepted by the Dominions, for it would conflict with their invincible desire for the preservation of their independence. A colonial people, born and growing up in a distant land unlike its mother country, may be said to have a tendency toward political independence. As it grows and spreads it becomes conscious of its personality, as has been shown already in the case of the United States and other European colonies. From this consciousness there emerges a force which is no other than the national sentiment, and which is always accompanied by egoism. Most of the Dominions, therefore, reject the idea of political federation, some more emphatically than others. Australia and New Zealand, colonies of pure Anglo-Saxon blood, would not be absolutely opposed to it, but Canada and South Africa, the offspring of two different European elements, would not take to it readily. India too would resist, and would not the enormous extent of this heterogeneous mass upset the equilibrium of the whole edifice? This state of mind is plainly revealed in the utterances of some colonials, for whom the very name of empire is ill suited to the commonwealth of the British nations. We have no name that would adequately describe this system, and we should assuredly go wrong if we tried to give it the ancient name of state. General Smuts, of South Africa, speaking of the Dominions, declared in 1917 that they were a system of nations—not a state, but a community of states and nations. They were far greater than any empire that had ever existed, and formed a world in themselves, composed of many states and nations and communities of every kind, collected under the same flag. They were a system of states, he said, and not an unalterable one, but a changing and progressive system, advancing ever toward new destinies. It is a significant fact that a statesman, an artificer of imperial politics, should feel himself unable to define the Empire with precision. Another colonial, Mr Hughes, Prime Minister of Australia, spoke in 1921 of those " enthusiastic but inexperienced persons " whose object " is to redraft the Empire constitution, and to substitute for the empirical, illogical structure, fashioned by time and circumstances, under which we have lived and flourished, a constitution built according to some logical plan which they have devised. . . . They hint at a central council endowed with powers over various parts of the Empire. . . . They forget that it has existed for centuries without any of these things. . . . The pillars of this temple of Empire are firmly embedded in the rock of liberty. No wonder other nations find it difficult to understand the relation between the different parts of the British Empire and the Mother Country. . . . The surest way of destroying this mighty Empire, one of the chief bulwarks of civilization, is to tamper with its constitution. Complete autonomy of the parts is the foundation upon which its unity rests. . . . This assurance of perfect freedom of each of several parts ensures a spiritual unity which binds us together. The basic principle underlying the relations between Great Britain and the Oversea Dominions is freedom of action." [1] In other words, the bond of sentiment is the only powerful bond that unites the British communities to each other, and there appears to be no political machinery in existence that is capable of strengthening it.

III. ECONOMIC UNITY OF THE EMPIRE

Cecil Rhodes saw clearly that sentiment cannot provide a permanent foundation for a political edifice. In 1891, speaking of South Africa, he said : " Can we invent some tie with our Mother Country that will prevent separation ? It must be a practical one, for future generations will not be born in England." [2]

There is no doubt that bonds of sentiment between nations become relaxed in course of time : some material adhesive is necessary for a political aggregation. From these considerations arises the idea of an economic union as the foundation of imperial unity.

[1] Quoted in *The Times*, May 24, 1921.
[2] Quoted by Ashley, 3, p. 205.

The Foundations of an Economic Union.—The idea of an economic union is justified by the importance of the commercial relations between the mother country and the colonies. Commerce appears capable of providing a solid support for imperial unity. English colonists, scattered over their vast domains, are consumers of English products, while, on the other hand, their young and thinly populated countries provide such crude products as the foodstuffs and raw materials required by the mother country to feed her people

VALUE OF BRITISH GOODS IMPORTED PER HEAD
OF THE POPULATION [1]

Country	1913			1921		
	£	s.	d.	£	s.	d.
Australia . . .	7	3	0	8	7	4
Canada . . .	3	3	2	2	4	4
New Zealand . . .	10	2	10	12	4	5
South Africa . . .	3	11	5	4	5	11
United States . . .		6	1		8	2
Netherlands . . .	2	9	8	3	18	11
Sweden . . .	1	9	1	3	11	1
Switzerland . . .	1	1	9	1	8	6

and set them to work. Of all that Great Britain purchases from the world a fifth comes from the Empire, and of all that she sells a third goes to the Empire, while generally speaking colonial trade accounts for more than a quarter of her total foreign commerce. The share of the tropical colonies, and of India in particular, is large, but the colonies of European settlement also occupy an important place in this trade. Canada does two-fifths of her foreign trade with Great Britain, Australia one-half, New Zealand two-thirds,

[1] After *United Empire*, 1922, pp. 279–280. See also Ashley, 3, p. 144.

and South Africa four-fifths. The value of goods exported by the United Kingdom to South Africa in 1918 was greater than that of her exports to the United States, and more than half of that of her exports to India. The 5½ millions of Australians buy more from the United Kingdom than the 110 million inhabitants of the United States. This means that the colonies import British goods to a very much greater value than do foreign countries, reckoning per head of the population. The simple table given on the preceding page will supply the commentary on this economic fact. As *United Empire* remarked in 1922, a New Zealander is worth thirty Americans, an Australian twenty-one, a South African ten, and even a Canadian five.

This colonial trade unites Great Britain with countries in their full vigour and vitality. It must be borne in mind that between 1875 and 1915 the foreign trade of Canada increased fivefold, and that of New Zealand nearly fourfold ; that four out of the five countries that send wool to England are British—namely, New Zealand, Australia, South Africa, and India ; and that Canada, Australia, and India rank with the United States, the Argentine, and Eastern Europe among the corn granaries of the mother country. Colonial trade has for a long time been increasing faster than trade with foreign countries, and its progress has been noted in all statistics since 1870. Between 1900 and 1913 British exports to India increased by 130 per cent., to Canada by 100 per cent., to New Zealand by 97 per cent., to South Africa by 70 per cent., and to Australia by 60 per cent. Her exports to colonial markets have made up to Great Britain for the decrease in her exports to the markets of Europe.

But besides the direct and simple exchange of goods we must also measure all that the colonies stand for in the commercial system of the United Kingdom. They furnish a portion of that *entrepôt* trade that is always such a valuable element in British business. Much of the merchandise that they send to the mother country is re-exported by her to other lands—for instance, the gold and diamonds and wool of South Africa. Similarly, among the goods imported by the colonies from Great Britain many are not the produce of the United Kingdom, but come from foreign countries and are re-exported : such are oil, sugar, tea, coffee, and rice. In proportion to her total trade with each country Great Britain re-exports more colonial than foreign merchandise. Again, nearly all the trade of the colonies is carried on in British ships. Before the War the British flag covered three-quarters of the tonnage trading to Canada and Australia, four-fifths of that to South Africa and India, and nearly the whole of that to New Zealand, the colonies thus providing freight for British merchant shipping. And finally Great Britain possesses an invaluable source of trade in the capital she has lent to the colonies. This capital has almost all passed in the shape of goods, and the interest returns in the form of produce and raw materials, grain crops, and mineral ores. Colonial investments contribute thus to the development of British commerce ; owing to their financial dependence the colonies remain almost compulsorily among the customers of the mother country. These financial relations very often explain how it is that the trade of the colonies is directed toward the mother country, in spite of the geographical proximity that would otherwise attract it to markets closer at hand. Thus New Zealand has little trade with Australia, and—what is very curious—Canada's economic front is not all turned toward the United States, despite their wealth and their extent.

This solidarity of interests between Great Britain

and her colonies was bound to strike many people as a possible basis for an economic federation. Did not the interest of the country, rightly understood, require us to base British commerce resolutely upon that of the colonies? Froude was already writing in *Oceana*, " It has become doubtful even to the political economist whether England can trust entirely to free trade and competition to keep the place which she has hitherto held." This development was hastened by the pressure of two dangers : the economic nationalism of the colonies and the competition of foreign countries. Along with their political autonomy the colonies had obtained the control of their customs tariffs : they could not only impose taxes on British products, but they could also conclude commercial treaties with foreign countries. As Sir Charles Dilke said, we were paying dearly for the defence of Canada, and she kept out our goods by prohibitive duties levied at her ports.[1]

In the period 1880-90 *ad valorem* duties of 40 per cent. were common in Australian and Canadian tariffs.[2] While men were discussing whether the Empire was not threatened with dissolution, that dissolution was being slowly accomplished as each Dominion turned itself into an economic fortress.[3] About the same period Great Britain came up against formidable international competition in her own traditional markets. Inquiries and statistics bore terrible witness to the multiplication of indisputable facts which seemed to presage an approaching downfall. Foreign manufactured products were invading the British market itself, while the manufactured products of Great Britain were finding increasing difficulty in entering foreign markets. The foreigner was extending his trade in colonial markets.

[1] Dilke, 28.
[2] Bérard, 7, p. 242.
[3] Ashley, *Revue économique internationale*, 1907, p. 466.

CHARACTERISTICS OF IMPERIAL UNITY

The regular shipping lines of France, Germany, and other European countries were diverting Australian wool to Dunkirk, Hamburg, and Antwerp. German firms were furnishing plant for the South African mines. American, Japanese, and European merchants were disputing the trade of China with those of Great Britain. Even in the markets of the Empire British commerce was losing ground. It was no longer so far in front of its rivals as it had been. Between 1875 and 1900 the proportion of imports from the United Kingdom to total imports fell from 77 per cent. to 65 per cent. in the case of India, from 49 per cent. to 24 per cent. for Canada, from 73 per cent. to 61 per cent. for Australia, and from 83 per cent. to 65 per cent. for South Africa. Out of all these menacing facts sprang the idea of an imperial economic union. In 1885 the delegates of the Chambers of Commerce of Birmingham and Sheffield discussed the question of an agreement with the object of giving to the colonies the monopoly of the British market for their raw materials, and to Great Britain the monopoly of the colonial markets for her manufactured goods. In 1895, for the first time, a British minister, Joseph Chamberlain, publicly declared himself an advocate of an economic union of the Empire.

Attempts at Economic Unification.—There exists at the present time within the Empire a rough draft of economic federation, made up of measures for facilitating trade and, above all, of preferential tariffs. Since 1898 the Empire has formed a single postal area, with a uniform charge for the conveyance of letters. The construction of the Canadian Pacific Railway was an achievement of imperial unity. It set up a trade movement between East and West at the very time when the attraction of the United States was tending to give that movement a North and South direction.

THE BRITISH EMPIRE

The trans-Pacific cable between Canada and Australia is an imperial work, the cost of which was shared between the United Kingdom, Canada, Australia, and New Zealand. Attempts are made to direct British emigrants to the Dominions rather than to foreign countries. Whereas in 1900 33 per cent. of them proceeded to imperial lands, in 1911 these destinations received 80 per cent., and the proportion remained almost the same in 1919. Organizations have been set up for the study of imperial commerce. Thus in 1907 the Board of Trade instituted four Trade Commissioners,[1] residing respectively in the four Dominions, whose duty it is to watch the development of commercial conditions between the United Kingdom and the colonies and to record them in regular reports. This organization has already succeeded in diverting certain currents of trade from foreign lands to British lands. Conferences of Chambers of Commerce are held periodically : the first one met in London in 1886, and others have been held at Montreal and Sydney. They strengthen the feeling of community of interests in the Empire. For the first time in 1901 the Board of Trade published its *Statistical Abstract of the British Empire*, which condenses the statistical returns of the whole Empire. Everywhere, to some extent, plans are being prepared which when realized will mark a new stage in the progress to unity. These projects include the uniformity of naturalization laws, the uniformity of legislation concerning patents and trade marks, and the uniformity of methods of official information services and statistics. There are plans for the deepening of the principal ports of the Empire, so as to make them all accessible to the same vessels of deep draught, and it is proposed to reserve the coasting trade of the Empire for British ships.[2]

[1] Grice, 40, p. 61 ; Ashley, 2, Preface.
[2] See Drage, 29.

It is in a customs union, however, that imperialists hope to find the strongest guarantee of the integrity of the Empire, so far as the economic aspect is concerned. Such a union does not appear easy of accomplishment between two parties, both of them undoubtedly permeated by a feeling of their mutual solidarity, but opposed to each other in their economic tendencies— Great Britain a Free Trade nation and the colonies Protectionist. How is the Empire to be made an enclosed domain, with no internal barriers, but with barriers against the outer world ? The colonies were originally little disposed to sacrifice their infant industries even to those of the mother country, while, on the other hand, Great Britain was reluctant to cut herself off from the world market on which her factories were dependent. It appeared more practicable to adopt a system of preferential duties, by which certain British products would pay lower customs duties, or be exempted altogether, on entering the colonies. Inspired both by interest and by sympathy, the Dominions welcomed this policy. But they were alone in welcoming it, and Great Britain gave them no reciprocity. Their action, however, was dictated by their affection for the mother country ; for Mr Deakin, the Prime Minister of Australia, preference could not be reduced to a matter of financial gain—its aim was to ratify a union.[1]

The example set by Canada in 1897 was followed by South Africa in 1903, by New Zealand in 1907, and by Australia a little later. Having developed her wheat production in the west, Canada had to turn to Great Britain, the great importer of cereals. It was to the

---

[1] On preferential tariffs see Pulsford, 56 ; Asquith, 4 ; Caldecott, 15, pp. 180 ff. ; Ashley, *Revue économique internationale*, 1907, pp. 468 ff. ; Mondaini, 54, vol. ii, p. 403 ; *British Empire*, 11, p. 605 ; Bowman, 9, p. 19 ; Leroy-Beaulieu, 47, p. 448 ; Grice, 40, pp. 55 ff.

interest of both countries to come to an understanding. Freightage conditions were favourable, as the same ships which had brought the Canadian wheat to England could return laden with British products. So in 1897 Canada set up a preferential tariff reducing by 12½ per cent. the customs duties on Canadian imports from Great Britain, and the reduction was increased to 25 per cent. in 1898, and to 33⅓ per cent. in 1900. This preferential treatment was gradually extended by Canada to other parts of the Empire : to India, the Straits Settlements, Ceylon, New South Wales, Bermuda, the West Indies, and British Guiana, and then to New Zealand and South Africa, as well as to certain products of West Africa, Mauritius, the Falkland Islands, and Honduras. The system ran a grave risk in 1910, when the question was mooted of a treaty of commercial reciprocity between Canada and the United States. But imperial preference, though attacked by the manufacturers and the railway companies, carried the day, and the advocates of imperial solidarity were victorious.

Almost from its birth in 1903 the South African Union admitted the system of preference for most of the goods of the United Kingdom. The rate of preference amounted on an average to only 3 per cent., and seemed lower than was granted to Australia (5 per cent.) and New Zealand (13 per cent.). But it was applied to a greater number of articles, and, moreover, the possibility of increasing it was not ruled out. Preference was extended by South Africa to Canada in 1904, to Australia in 1906, and to New Zealand in 1907. This latter country granted preference to the United Kingdom in 1907, and then to other colonies, while for certain commodities South Africa enjoys advantages that the United Kingdom herself does not possess. Australia in her turn has set up preferential tariffs for many articles of British manufacture, as well as for some South African products.

For a long time colonial preference brought no reciprocity from the mother country : the colonies gave without receiving anything, and even, as a rule, without asking for anything. But Free Trade lost ground during the Great War and no longer appears as the panacea that is to set trade upon its feet again. In February 1916 the Association of Chambers of Commerce proposed a preferential and reciprocal tariff for all parts of the Empire, and in February 1917 the committee on commercial and industrial policy, presided over by Lord Balfour of Burleigh, published the following resolution : [1] " We therefore recommend that H.M. Government should now declare their adherence to the principle that preference should be accorded to the products and manufactures of the British overseas Dominions." For the first time in April 1919 the British Chancellor of the Exchequer proposed to grant a preferential tariff to certain colonial products, including the wines of Australia. On September 1, 1919, the British Finance Act prescribed preferential tariffs applicable to all the Dominions, to India, and to the protectorates : the reduction in the duties was to be one-sixth on tea, coffee, raisins, fruits, sugar, molasses, motor spirit, and tobacco ; one-third on motor-cars, musical instruments, and watches ; 40 per cent. on wines not exceeding 30° of proof spirit, and $33\frac{1}{3}$ per cent. on wines exceeding 30°.[2] The same policy was continued in the Budgets of the following years. Great Britain took a fresh step toward Protection—that is to say, toward economic imperialism.

There are certain facts which seem to justify this policy. Preferential tariffs ensure an appreciable amount

[1] Quoted by Webster, 66, pp. 325–326.
[2] Keith, 45, p. 44.

of relief for imports from Great Britain. It has been calculated that this amounted in 1913 to £1,573,000 for Canada, £1,244,000 for Australia, £760,000 for New Zealand, and £555,000 for South Africa.[1] It has been noticed that these tariffs have everywhere given an impetus to commercial relations between the different parts of the Empire. It is certain that they have arrested the decline of Canadian imports from Great Britain, and this is a noteworthy result, considering the almost irresistible force that was drawing Canada toward the United States. Similarly, since the beginning of the twentieth century there has been a general growth of trade within the Empire. It would seem as if the system of preference had borne fruit and might reasonably be regarded as a factor of imperial unity. Ought not, therefore, the foundation of an imperial state to be a Protectionist confederation, with a preferential system working universally within it ? Will the political union have an economic union as its prelude and condition ? To answer these questions we must first analyse the characteristics of imperial commerce.

Characteristics of Imperial Commerce.—To effect the economic union of the Empire two conditions are requisite. In the first place, there would have to be no tendencies in the Dominions toward forming trade relations with non-British countries, and, in the second place, the Empire as a whole would have to be self-sufficing—capable, that is to say, of producing all that it consumes and absorbing all that it produces.

Now is it possible for the Empire to live in isolation from the rest of the world and be economically self-sufficing ? Supposing that the United Kingdom can provide manufactured goods for the whole Empire, can she obtain from her colonies all the raw materials and

[1] Raffalovitch, *Journal des économistes*, 1917, pp. 202–215 and 384–393.

foodstuffs that she needs ? Let us find out from a study of the table appearing on p. 210 which articles of consumption in the United Kingdom are of British origin.

On reading this list of products we may to a certain extent agree with Sir Charles Lucas that the Empire is a gigantic wholesale trading-house under British management. In the case of many essential materials it supplies all the consumption of the United Kingdom, and even more, and in the case of others there is no doubt that the production of the Empire is bound to increase. Thus there is every reason to think that the United Kingdom might obtain more iron ore from Newfoundland, more rubber from her tropical colonies, more meat and butter from Australasia, and more wheat from Canada and Australia, while there is nothing to prevent Great Britain herself from cultivating the sugar beet. But she remains in close dependence on the foreigner for oil, chemical manures, cotton, silk, flax, wood pulp, coffee, and sugar, not to speak of other wants of minor importance, and she cannot hope in the near future to obtain her resources entirely from within the Empire. Nor can she do without the foreigner as a seller of what she is in need of, any more than as a purchaser of the goods she manufactures. Of the imports of the United Kingdom in 1919 65 per cent. came from foreign countries and only 35 per cent. from the Empire, and of her exports 74 per cent. went to foreign countries as against 26 per cent. to the Empire. It was her foreign trade in particular—with Eastern Europe, Western Europe, and the Far East—that caused the economic crisis from which Great Britain suffered so severely at the end of the Great War. Her commercial life, indeed, is closely bound up with the world market, and she could not be entirely dependent upon the Empire.

THE BRITISH EMPIRE

CONSUMPTION OF THE UNITED KINGDOM [1]

Percentage of Goods of British Origin

Products	Per-centage	Principal Places of Origin
ORES AND MINERALS		
Coal . . .	100	Great Britain
Iron ore . .	67	Great Britain
Tin . . .	60	Straits Settlements, Australia, Great Britain
Lead . . .	25	Australia, Burma
Copper. . .	25	Australia, South Africa, Canada, Great Britain
Oil . . .	3	India, Scotland, Trinidad
TEXTILES AND OTHER RAW MATERIALS		
Jute . . .	100	India
Wool . . .	80	Australasia, South Africa, Great Britain, India
Rubber . .	75	Malaysia
Raw hides . .	50	India
Cotton. . .	25	Egypt, India
Wood pulp . .	10	Canada
Silk . . .	3	India
FOODSTUFFS		
Tea . . .	90	India
Cheese. . .	80	Canada, United Kingdom, Australasia
Oats . . .	80	United Kingdom, Canada
Meat . . .	70	United Kingdom, Australasia
Barley. . .	60	United Kingdom, Canada, India
Rice . . .	60	India
Butter. . .	55	United Kingdom, Australasia
Cocoa . . .	50	West Indies, Ceylon, West Africa
Wheat. . .	50	Canada, India, United Kingdom, Australia
Coffee . . .	11	India, West Indies, Guiana
Fruits . . .	10	Canada, Jamaica, United Kingdom
Sugar . . .	6	West Indies, Mauritius
Tobacco . .	6	Borneo, Nyassaland, India
Maize . . .	5	Canada, South Africa

[1] This table has been drawn up with the aid of information furnished by Cunningham (23), Grice (40), and Bowman (9, p. 15). The figures must be understood as applying to *gross* consumption—that is to say,

Let us now turn to the British colonies, and see what direction their business relations take.

TRADE OF THE BRITISH COLONIES

Colonies	Exports to the Empire expressed as Percentages of Total Exports			Imports from the Empire expressed as Percentages of Total Imports		
	1902	1913	1918 or 1919	1902	1913	1918 or 1919
Canada .	60	51	46	25	24	11
Australia .	73	56	72	72	72	61
New Zealand	97	92	80	83	82	70
South Africa	93	93	62	70	67	67
India . .	47	—	43	68	—	53

This table shows, in the case of certain colonies, the importance of their trade with the Empire. Of this New Zealand offers us an interesting example. She turns neither to Australia, the great country that lies nearest to her in the Southern seas, nor to the United States, a land peopled by the same race and of the same social structure, nor to the swarming multitudes of the Far East, but to the United Kingdom, at the other end of the earth. Despite the nearness of the United States, Canada sends nearly half her exports to the mother country. Two-thirds of the trade of South Africa and of Australia is carried on with the Empire. These trading relations with the Empire are for the most part with the United Kingdom, but they are also, and to an increasing extent, with other colonies : a quarter of the colonial trade may be reckoned as intercolonial. Canada exports to the

in the case of commodities not produced in the United Kingdom to all that enters the country from abroad, including, therefore, a certain amount of merchandise that is re-exported. It follows that the *net* consumption in the United Kingdom of these commodities (such as wool, jute, rubber, tea, etc.) is more than abundantly covered by the production of the Empire.

West Indies, Newfoundland, Australia, and South Africa, and imports from India, the West Indies, and Newfoundland. Australia sends foodstuffs to India, Hong Kong, the Straits, and South Africa. India does an active trade with Hong Kong, the Straits, Egypt, Mauritius, Australia, and East Africa.

This internal trade of the Empire, however, does not represent the whole of its commerce. It is true that the trade of the colonies with the Empire has increased absolutely, like their total trade, since the beginning of the twentieth century; but relatively it has decreased, and the trade of the Empire with foreign countries has continually increased its proportion almost everywhere. Of the trade of Canada and India the foreigner takes a large share. We cannot imagine the commercial system of Canada without the United States or without Europe; that of India without Japan, the Dutch East Indies, and the United States; or even that of Australia without the United States and Japan. These colonies could never obtain the fullness of economic life while remaining isolated within the Empire. The unity of the Empire may indeed profit by an imperial agreement in regard to commercial questions, but it could not derive its entire support from this source: without the foreigner there is no such thing as British trade. The drafting of plans for a customs union based upon the preferential system has not established a pan-British union. Moreover, there are some Britons who wonder whether this union resting upon material bonds would strengthen the cohesion of the members of the Empire, already drawn together as they are by their language, religion, customs, and education. In their view the moral bonds are the stronger, and it would be dangerous to put them to the test of a too strict economic alliance. Such is the opinion even of practical men. As Mr Lloyd George said in his speech before the Lord Mayor on

CHARACTERISTICS OF IMPERIAL UNITY

December 7, 1920: "Such a combination is either the strongest in the world or the weakest in the world, according to what you make of it. It is the strongest when you have attachments and goodwill. . . . Therefore everything depends upon the event, the force that strengthens the invisible bonds of attachment to the Empire."

CHAPTER II

THE DOMINIONS

THE Dominions, as nations, have individual interests which are neither those of the Empire nor those of the United Kingdom. It was remarked by Sir Charles Dilke that British emigrants very quickly come to love the corner of the world in which they have set up their new home; whereas the Frenchman is frequently homesick, the Englishman when transplanted looks back with less regret upon what he has left behind—the present is closer to his heart than the past. Wherever a man is comfortable, there is his native land. So every English colony quickly became a centre of particularism, and, as it were, of local patriotism, a sensitive and irritable sentiment which sometimes inspires the colony with opposition even to the mother country. In the realm of practice the Dominions adopted Protection as soon as they became masters of their own customs systems, and they developed gradually in the direction of economic independence. On the other hand, however, there is a kind of law of gravitation which impels them to live within the orbit of their nearest neighbours—thus Canada turns toward the United States, as also does Australasia, each tending to create its own individual sphere of action in its own corner of the world. Each Dominion, being situated in the temperate zone, wishes to acquire territory in the tropics. To surround themselves with satellites producing cotton, sugar, and tropical commodities appears to the lands of wheat and sheep as a natural step, and one that is necessary to their complete economic development. The United States made this union of the two zones on its own territory ; the nations of Europe have accomplished it by creating their colonial empire. The Dominions, which are nations in their youth, are preparing the same thing for their own benefit in their own hemisphere : thus Canada is aspiring to the West Indies, South Africa to the lands on the Zambezi, and Australasia to the archipelagos of the Pacific Ocean. In each Dominion there is now both a nationalist and an imperialist sentiment.

I. CANADA

Canadian Nationalism.—Impatient of all control, Canadian nationalism asserts itself alike on political and on economic ground. The Canadians will tolerate no interference by the mother country in their affairs. In 1904 Lord Dundonald, the English commander of the Canadian army, having failed in his duty of subordination to the federal minister, had to hand in his resignation. The Dominion wished to keep control over her own fortresses ; about the same time she set her heart upon replacing the British garrisons at Esquimalt and Halifax by Canadian ones. " Instead of imperializing the national services," remarks Siegfried, " they nationalized the imperial services." [1] The national feeling showed itself no less punctilious in external affairs. In 1846, at the time of the partitioning of Oregon with the United States,[2] all Canadians combined to support British diplomacy. Later on, in 1867, the federation of the provinces of Canada was accomplished, as a measure of national defence, in answer to the aggressive intrigues of American nationalism.

[1] Siegfried, 61, p. 391.
[2] Mondaini, 54, vol. i, pp. 217–218.

The fact is that during the War of Secession, when relations between the United States and Great Britain were embittered, Canada had fears for her safety, and by thus combining the Canadians gathered together all their national strength. At the time of the settlement of the frontiers of Alaska in 1903 Canada complained bitterly that Great Britain had not supported her sufficiently,[1] and this betrayal strengthened her desire to conduct her own foreign policy and have her own representatives abroad. The principle of Canadian representation at Washington has been admitted by Great Britain, and a strong volume of opinion is pressing for the complete realization of this reform, by which the foreign policy of Canada will be subject not to the London Foreign Office, but to the Canadian Parliament.[2]

On the economic plane Canada is anxious to develop her industries and to organize her foreign commerce freely. In 1904, when the tariff giving preference to Great Britain was in course of preparation, the Canadian manufacturers made an unequivocal protest. " We approve," they said, " of the offer of a substantial preference to the mother country and her colonies ; but we are strongly opposed to any policy that would have the effect of hindering or restraining the exploitation of our own resources." [3] Canada is becoming industrialized, and her factories are entering into competition with British ones ; the movement has only just begun, but development is proceeding at an increasing pace. The iron-mines of Bell Island, in Newfoundland, rich deposits of hæmatite, belong to a great shipbuilding company of Halifax (Nova Scotia). The factories of Shawinigan Falls (Quebec) work for the export trade and receive orders from Australia. In 1913 Canada

[1] Siegfried, 61, pp. 358–363.   [2] *The Times*, May 24, 1922.
[3] Siegfried, 61, p. 376.

imported from England 73 per cent. of her consumption of woollen goods, whereas in 1918–19 she supplied 60 per cent. of her needs herself. In 1921 a great linen factory was set up in Ontario to work the flax of the country.[1] Each step taken by Canadian industry involves a danger to British industry. In the matter of commerce Canada tends sometimes to follow paths that are peculiar to herself, regardless of imperial interests. During the War, in 1917, laborious negotiations were required before Great Britain could buy the Canadian wheat crop. A first offer of 1.30 dollars a bushel did not satisfy the farmers of the West and of Ontario, who did not consider it their duty to sacrifice interest to patriotism. Agreement was reached at a price of 2.40 dollars for what remained of the 1916 harvest, and at prices considerably over 2 dollars for the crops of 1917 and 1918. A similar agreement was concluded, after some discussion, for cheese and bacon, and thus the exports of agricultural produce from Canada rose from 251.5 million dollars in 1914 to 740 millions in 1918.[2] Again, markets have been acquired by Canada to the detriment of Great Britain. Newfoundland has become an economic annex of Canada, and in 1921 52 per cent. of her imports came from that country, as against 33 per cent. from the United States and only 11 per cent. from the United Kingdom. This little colony herself is intolerant of any injury to her own interests : in 1920 she complained bitterly that the Imperial Government had not obtained favourable conditions for the sale of her fish in foreign markets. She threatened that if preference were not granted to her codfish she would negotiate directly with the United States and give a preference to that

---

[1] Various particulars drawn from different places in *United Empire* and *The Times*.

[2] Keith, 45, pp. 52–53.

country on her manufactured goods.[1] Corresponding to all these moves in the direction of commercial independence there are also measures calculated to free the maritime communications of the country from foreign control. Thus by means of regular steamship services direct relations have been established with Australia, India, the Straits, the Far East, and West Africa. In 1920 the Dempster Company started a line from Montreal to Lagos, and since 1921 a new service has been in operation between Vancouver and South Africa, under the guarantee of the Canadian Government Merchant Marine.

Canadian Imperialism.—Among her foreign trading relations there are some which Canada regards as more and more essential to her system in virtue of a kind of regional co-ordination. She has a tendency to associate with herself the British colonies of tropical America, and the idea has even sprung up recently of a political union between Canada and the West Indies.[2] Canada, a temperate land, turns naturally to the Antilles, which are tropical lands yielding sugar, cotton, cocoa, and bananas. The sugar plantations of the West Indies have been suffering from a severe crisis since the end of the nineteenth century ; in the British market they have been faced by the competition of European sugar ; and their natural tendency is to turn to the American mainland, which is close by and whose market is open. In fact, they do more business now with the United States and Canada than with the United Kingdom. Could not Canada, therefore, under cover of their common political allegiance, extend her influence in these tropical colonies ? A joint conference was held at Ottawa in 1911 to establish a system of preferential duties between the two colonies, and in 1912 Canada

[1] Keith, 45, p. 59.
[2] Ashley, 2, pp. 175 ff.; *United Empire*, 1919 and 1921, *passim*.

granted a specific reduction of duties on sugar from the West Indies and a preference of 20 per cent. on certain of their tropical products. The West Indies in return granted a specific reduction on Canadian flour and a 20 per cent. preference on certain articles from Canada. During the War the two countries were dependent upon each other for sugar and flour respectively. Between 1909 and 1919 Canadian exports to Jamaica almost doubled. Efforts of the same kind are being made with a view to drawing Canada and British Guiana together : the tropical colony, in search of capital to develop her resources, applied to the banks of the Dominion. In this way a Canadian Empire within the British Empire is being organized in America.

Americanization of Canada.[1]—There is one fundamental influence that bears heavily upon the destinies of Canada. This is the powerful, almost irresistible attraction exercised over her by the United States. As far as sentiment goes, Canada has no wish to become ' debritannized,' but by force of circumstances she is compelled to become Americanized. Geographically the two countries present close affinities, and along their common frontier no change is apparent on passing from the one to the other. Each part of Canada communicates more easily with the adjacent part of the United States than with the neighbouring provinces of the Dominion ; the Canadian prairie is a continuation of the American prairie ; in the maritime provinces of Canada there are the same conditions of life as in the greater part of New England ; and the factories of Ontario burn the coal of Pennsylvania. Across the whole wide continent the frontier marks no separation, for American life penetrates Canadian life as if by a kind of osmosis. It

[1] On this subject see *The Round Table*, June 1921 ; Siegfried, **61**, *passim* ; *The Times*, May 24, 1921 ; Ashley, **2**, pp. 219 ff. ; Drage, **29**, p. 60 ; Mondaini, **54**, vol. i, pp. 215 ff.

was noticed by Sir Charles Dilke that the great commercial enterprises of Canada were in the hands not of Britons, but of Americans, and that the gold-mines of Nova Scotia and the coal-mines and forests of British Columbia were owned in New England and New York. He made the prediction, which has been fulfilled, that as soon as Montana was peopled we should hear of the colonization of the Red River district by citizens of the United States. American capital is invading Canada, especially in her industrial undertakings. It was calculated in 1911 that while five-sixths of the British investments in Canada since 1905 had gone mainly into Government securities and town bonds the Americans had devoted nine-tenths of theirs to private enterprises. The dollar was driving British capital from the factories. And the War has simply confirmed and extended this supremacy. *The Times* of May 24, 1921, estimates that four-fifths of the capital invested in the pulp and paper industry of Canada belongs to Americans. The total amount of Canadian investments in the United States is reckoned at 524 million dollars, and the total of American investments in Canada at 1250 millions (1920), while the number of industrial establishments owned by Americans is put at 600, and the sums paid annually by Canada to the United States as interest, dividends, cost of transport, and insurance are estimated at 75 million dollars. Finally, there are 140 branches of American firms in Toronto and 53 in Hamilton.

A stream of colonists flows from the United States to Canada. Since the lands of the Canadian West have borne vast fields of wheat, and especially since the beginning of the twentieth century, many farmers from the Dakotas, Minnesota, and elsewhere have gone to settle on the Canadian prairie. The number of American emigrants to Canada increased from 9000 in 1898 to

18,000 in 1901, 50,000 in 1903, 53,000 in 1919, and almost the same figure in 1920. Between 1910 and 1920 562,000 Americans have set up their homes in Canada, either by purchasing lands or by settling in the towns. To this human migration must be added an extensive movement of goods. The shortness of the distance, making transport charges less heavy; the nearness of the two countries, which makes knowledge of the markets easier; and the fact that the Canadian factories are working with capital, materials, and sometimes also with a personnel drawn from the United States—all these advantages make the latter country one of Canada's chief purveyors. Despite the vicissitudes of the customs system Canadian imports from America show a progressive increase: they were 36 per cent. of the total imports in 1868, 46 per cent. in 1884, 50 per cent. in 1895, 60 per cent. in 1902–7 (yearly average), and 62 per cent. from 1908 to 1913. In the year 1918–19 82 per cent. of the imports of Canada came from the United States, and only 8 per cent. from the United Kingdom.

Then there is also some penetration of American customs and civilization from the United States into Canada. The towns are alike on both sides of the frontier; the houses, hotels, railway stations, and theatres of Winnipeg and Toronto are built after American models; Canadian bookshops display American novels and magazines; Canadian cinemas are supplied with American films; and Canadian papers depend upon American agencies for their news. In the border regions of the two countries the railways form practically a single system; the railway trade unions being international, any rise of wages that is granted in the United States applies automatically to Canada also. Many professional associations and learned societies are recruited indifferently from both countries. What we are witnessing is the Americanization of Canada : the entire civilization of America is pressing at the doors of Canada and entering with irresistible force.

Some surprise may be felt that so many powerful bonds have not already sealed the union of the two countries, and it may well be asked if, some day, nine new stars may not be added to the American flag. The question arose several times in the course of last century. When England repealed her Corn Laws in 1846 and adopted Free Trade her new policy inflicted a terrible blow on Canada, who not only exported her wheat and flour to the United Kingdom, but also purchased American wheat, turned it into flour, and sent this flour to England as a Canadian product. The murmurs of discontent in the towns rose to such a point that annexation by the United States was talked of. A little later on, when the commercial treaty between the United States and Canada expired in 1866, the former country would not agree to its renewal. Canada suffered severely from this, and many people thought then that it would be to her interest to be absorbed by the United States. There were others, it is true, who preferred a closer union with Great Britain ; it was they who carried the day, and it was the same party that determined the federation of the Canadian provinces. The United States, on their side, had never exerted any pressure on Canada, but they looked upon her as a neighbour who was destined sooner or later to share the same house with them. They therefore greeted the formation of the Canadian Confederation as an act almost of hostility, and the American Congress went so far as to declare that the continuance of British domination in Canada could only make relations more difficult between the United States and Great Britain. Later still, in 1910, a new opportunity occurred of airing this serious problem. A treaty of commerce between the United States and Canada was being prepared by the Liberal Party in Canada. This treaty, if it had been passed, would have turned the commercial relations of Canada decisively toward the United States : it would have given free course to the natural stream of trade from one country to the other. The project collapsed before the opposition of the Conservatives, but this episode in the political life of Canada revealed once more the force and permanence of the attraction of America. Is this attraction irresistible ? Is Canada called upon to follow the economic slope, to obey this material law ? Will she be absorbed ?

There do not appear at present to be any symptoms of secession. On the contrary, Canada is showing plainly by her loyalty to Britain and especially by her native patriotism her wish to preserve her independence. It is true that there is always a strong tradition in Canada of faithfulness to the mother country, but the real moral binding force of the Canadian state resides in a national feeling, already of long standing, which is incompatible with American nationalism. This sentiment derives its strength from the British race consciousness, which is far purer in Canada than in the United States, from the influence of the schools in teaching patriotism, and, curiously enough, from the hostility of the French Canadians to any idea of fusion with the United States. The French Canadians are fearful of losing their individuality in the great Anglo-Saxon melting-pot, and so, by a kind of paradox, they form one of the strongest props of imperial unity in Canada.

As a matter of fact, the political independence of Canada does not appear for the moment to be threatened. From the point of view of the American Government there is no danger in sight for the Canadian Government. But in the words of Siegfried,[1] " it is rather American

[1] Siegfried, 61, p. 411.

civilization that is threatening to supplant British civilization in Canada." And he adds : " Not that Canada will give herself voluntarily and consciously to her powerful neighbour. The peril lies not there, but in the daily unconscious transformation which is steadily Americanizing the colony, her people, her capital, and her customs. . . . Canada is running the risk of one day finding herself so completely transformed that the name of ' English colony,' though always theoretically correct, will cease to be applicable to her in practice." [1] A commercial union between the two countries, founded on their necessary trading relations and supported by the concerted desire of their Governments, would strongly resemble a political union. It is conceivable that the two countries might coalesce economically without effecting a political fusion. Moreover, federation is a more flexible system on American soil than our European method of centralization, and it is not unnatural that the question of the flag should be solved there without war.

II. SOUTH AFRICA [2]

In South Africa too we find national interests which are sometimes opposed to British and imperial interests, and complicated, in addition, by the race problem.

South African Nationalism.—The political union of South Africa was accomplished under the British flag. But the two white elements in the population of European origin, the English and the Dutch, remain facing each other without combining. Certain sections of the Boers

---

[1] Siegfried, 61, pp. 309–310.

[2] On South African questions see, *passim, United Empire*, March 1921 ; *The Round Table*, December 1917, March 1920, December 1921 ; *The Times*, May 24, 1921. Also Keith, 45, pp. 128 and 328 ; Bowman, 9, pp. 37–42 ; Mondaini, 54, vol. i ; Caldecott, 15, p. 196.

have not abandoned their hatred of the English, and there is a nationalist Boer party whose programme includes separation from the British Empire and the setting up of an independent republic. When the Empire entered upon the war with Germany in 1914 armed rebellions broke out in the Transvaal and the Orange Free State against British authority, and a campaign was necessary to reduce the insurgents. This extremist tendency, to be sure, does not show itself in the majority of the Boers, and the Union of South Africa maintains an attitude of loyalty among the Dominions. It even looks as if the opposition between the two white elements would be mitigated by time. Their geographical distribution can only contribute to this end, for whereas in Canada the French and English do not mix, but dwell in different provinces and practise different religions, in South Africa the Dutch and the British are scattered all over the country and mingled with each other. This mode of distribution will probably gradually lead both elements in the direction of mutual assimilation, and the need for unity in the face of the native peril will accomplish the rest. In the economic realm internal dissensions are already subsiding, and a particularist spirit has been born in South Africa which stands up for South African interests when these appear to be threatened by imperial interests. The farmers complained bitterly during the War that the British Government had requisitioned their wool in 1917 at lower prices than those of 1916, and lower in particular than those that would have been offered by the United States and Japan if the market had been free. The industrial system developed in South Africa under the influence of the War, as in so many other colonies. Factories are working and producing regularly; the country possesses tanneries, dairies, cement works, match

P

factories, soap works, and engineering shops. To these industries and to those yet to be created the nation will give its protection when the proper time comes, as has been done in Canada and Australia.

South African Imperialism.—The national sentiment that watches over the economic interests of the country is no less vigilant upon her frontiers, and territorial extension keeps pace with the consolidation of national unity. In conquering German South-west Africa General Botha was thinking less of the Empire than of the Union of South Africa. At the time of the negotiations for peace South Africa opposed the restoration of this country to Germany, and she retained it by mandate of the League of Nations in 1921. But her attention is directed chiefly to the north—to the region of the Zambezi and the tropical zone. In those parts extend the lofty tablelands of Rhodesia, so favourable to European settlement, and the river plains destined for tropical plantations. A profound change is under way in the situation of Rhodesia. Administered hitherto by the British South Africa Company, she is now preparing a new system. Is she to be a Crown Colony, a self-governing colony, or a province of the Union of South Africa ? This third alternative, so congenial to the taste of the country, is winning. Rhodesia is already closely attached to the Union ; life has always come to her from the south ; it is thence that she has received her colonists ; her railways are continuous with those of the Union, and her commerce takes the same direction. In April 1922 delegates from Southern Rhodesia met the South African Prime Minister to discuss the conditions of annexation. Northern Rhodesia was to stay out of the Union for the time being ; strictly speaking, she is merely a native reserve, containing no white colonists except along the railroad. Yet from one end of Rhodesia to the other, as far as the Zambezi, the same system was to be applied to the railway. Thus the Anglo-Boer confederation will soon extend alike over the temperate and the tropical lands of Southern Africa.

The Race Problem.—The South African colonists are finding themselves up against a very serious problem caused by the presence of a huge mass of natives, prolific, aggressive, and formidable. The question for them is how to retain a footing on the land their forefathers conquered, and how to stem the black tide that rises from the tropical plains and threatens to submerge the tablelands where the whites are able to dwell.

Ever since their arrival in South Africa the white colonists have encountered civilized and organized tribes of blacks. Between the two races there was savage warfare, and the history of the Boers is full of these terrible memories. The hatred felt by the Boers for British domination arose to a large extent from the fact that the English treated the natives kindly. It was because they felt the abolition of slavery as intolerable that thousands of the Boers emigrated from Cape Colony in 1835 ; and thus began the series of *treks* which were the origin of the colonies of Natal, the Orange Free State, and the Transvaal. Later on their anxiety to defend themselves against the blacks made the two Boer republics resolve upon federation. The English themselves had to face the natives, and English columns fell back more than once before the Basutos and the Zulus : each advance of the British power into Kaffir territory was made at the cost of hard fighting.

British peace has not solved the problem, which still remains acute. As in all lands of European occupation, the native population increases rapidly : between the Cape and the Zambezi it forms four-fifths of the total population, while in Natal there are more than nine hundred blacks to every hundred whites. This swarm of natives, in contact with Europeans, is becoming gradually conscious of itself; the War affected it profoundly; some of the blacks saw Europe at war, and observed her weak points; others were armed by the Germans, and fought against the whites in South Africa, while others again, taught on European lines, are able to reflect upon their own servile position. The natives are understanding better and better the complaints that they make against their masters. They have at heart the Natives' Land Act of 1913, which restricts the right of those of them who are farmers to buy and rent land, and also the settlement of 1916, which reserves 87 per cent. of the land for 1,250,000 Europeans and leaves the rest for the 4,500,000 natives. In the gold-bearing regions the black labourers have seen the white miners obtain increases of wages by means of strikes, while their own attempts at strikes are violently repressed. The whites feel themselves hated. Force and brutal repression have had their day, and are no longer adequate to maintain order. In 1908 Natal was busy organizing native representation on the legislative council, and there was a desire to create local assemblies of natives. In 1913, during a strike of miners on the Rand, Bloemfontein found itself cut off from communication with the sea— that is to say, with the imperial power—and the town was at the mercy of a black rising which was already in preparation. The black peril is one to be feared.

This fear, inspired by the five millions of blacks in South Africa, explains the attitude of the whites toward the Asiatics: they are not anxious for a Hindu peril to be added to the native peril. The first Hindu coolies arrived some fifty years ago on the tea and sugar plantations of Natal, and their number to-day exceeds 150,000. Their competition is dangerous for the whites : living sparely, and being content with low wages or modest profits, they are driving them out and taking their places. On the Witwatersrand in 1913 there were three companies whose shareholders were Hindus, and in May 1919 there were 370. European firms, burdened with expenses, become bankrupt. At Krugersdorp there are only four European grocers as against twenty-seven Hindu. So the whites protect themselves by restrictive laws. In 1913 the South African Parliament passed a law making Indian immigration difficult and almost impossible. In the course of the discussion the Minister of the Interior asserted that it was a matter of self-preservation for the whites of South Africa, and that it was important to declare openly that they regarded European civilization as the only civilization desirable for the progress of the country. In 1919 another law, the Asiatic Trading and Land Act, forbade the granting of new trading licences to the Hindus, and prohibited them from becoming owners of land in the Transvaal, either as shareholders in companies or as mortgagees.

The Asiatics, supported by their political leaders in India, have protested indignantly against this violation of their rights as subjects of the Empire ; they do not want their legal status to be lower than that of Europeans, and they turn to the mother country to demand equality of treatment. The whites reply, " Everything that turns out a European with his standard of life, and replaces him by a coloured man with his lower standard of life, constitutes a step back-ward." The imperial authorities find themselves in a delicate position in regard to these race problems, for if they support the whites they displease the Indians, who are awaking to national self-consciousness, while if they support the Indians they come up against the interests and feelings of the European colonists.

III. AUSTRALASIA [1]

Australasian Nationalism.—The Australasian colonies long dwelt in isolation in their vast continent. When their federation was once accomplished the sentiment of solidarity which had united them developed in the direction of nationalism. In the political sphere there is scarcely any room for nationalist claims. The Commonwealth can hardly wish for more independence than it already possesses, and nowhere in the Dominions, it must be added, is more loyalty shown to the mother country than in these colonies of Australasia, of purely British blood. In the economic realm we are witnessing progress in an independent and egoistic direction, which will certainly not shake the predominant position of Great Britain, but which may constitute a danger in the future. The merchants of Australia are fond of travelling widely, and they have a choice between several routes between their own country and England. They can travel by way of the Suez Canal, through Canada, or through the United States, while before the War they used to go round by the Far East and the Trans-Siberian Railway. On their way they saw countries manufacturing more cheaply than England, and others, like the United States, that were clever in producing goods suited to the requirements of new countries. These discoveries made them customers of the United States and Japan, and when the War

---

[1] On Australasian questions see Hall, **41**, *passim* ; Ashley, **2**, p. 54 ; *The Round Table*, December 1918, March, June, September, December, 1920, December 1921, March 1922 ; Scott, **59** ; *United Empire*, 1919, pp. 155 and 331, and 1922, p. 296 ; Fletcher, **36** and **37** ; Bowman, **9**, pp. 27, 526 ff. ; *The Times*, May 24, 1921.

supervened these relations became more frequent, and their trade with Britain grew smaller. On the other hand, Australian industry is gathering strength. The federal Government supports it by tariffs and bounties, and though it is certainly not yet working for the world market it means to capture the home one. Australia possesses a metallurgical industry: in 1918 her blast furnaces produced over 150,000 tons of metal, while her rolling mills and wire mills turned out 160,000 tons of rails, steel bars, steel plates, and wire. These factories themselves supply the metal for the works that build railway trucks and agricultural implements. Spinning and weaving mills are also being set up in this land of wool, which has hitherto done no weaving. European industries are coming to settle in Australia so as to be near their raw materials and to profit by the cheapness of labour. Thus the firm of Lysaghts is establishing a galvanized-iron factory at Newcastle, Cadbury and Pascall are setting up confectionery works at Hobart, and Nestlé a dairy in the west of Victoria. This latter colony and New South Wales possess workmen's cities of the modern type, even outside the great towns. The country is moving toward a more complete and independent economic life.

Australasian Imperialism.—Busily occupied in the direction of economic nationalism, these young nations are no longer bound by their insular mentality, but are extending their outlook over the seas by which they are surrounded. Australia has already been dreaming for a long time of a kind of Monroe Doctrine for keeping Old Europe out of the Southern Pacific. When France resolved in 1863 to make New Caledonia a penal station the Australian colonies protested against the presence of such undesirable neighbours, and in 1898 France gave them satisfaction, and sent no more criminals to the gates of the irascible continent. So, too, the Australians submit with a bad grace to the presence of the French in the New Hebrides, where in 1882 a French company, having purchased lands in the archipelago, established regular trading relations between it and New Caledonia. British missionaries uttered a cry of alarm in the Presbyterian churches of Australia, and the Foreign Office speedily made it known to France that the annexation of the New Hebrides would be an affront to Australia. By agreements concluded in 1887 and 1906 a Franco-British *condominium* was established which satisfies no one, and the question to whom the archipelago ought to belong will no doubt arise in the near future. Australia, who regards it as a maritime station on the Panama route, makes no secret of her desire to annex it.

For a long time also Australia and New Zealand had their eyes on the tropical approaches to their territories, and in New Guinea, the Bismarck Islands, and Samoa they saw portions of their future colonial empire. When Great Britain annexed the Fiji Islands in 1874 she did so under pressure from the Australians, who were growing anxious about German ambitions. Since that date almost all the trade of the islands has been with Australia and New Zealand, to whom they send their bananas and their sugar, while at the time of the recent strikes among the Hindu coolies New Zealand troops were landed to restore order. The Fiji Islands are officially a Crown Colony, but in reality they belong to Australasia. Again, in 1883, when Germany established herself in New Guinea, the Australasian colonies felt themselves threatened ; Queensland took alarm and seized the island " in Her Majesty's name, pending her definite decision "—a compromising move which was disavowed by Great Britain, but was very significant of the state of colonial feeling. More recently still, during the War, the seizure of the Marshall Islands by Japan aroused anxiety in Australia, who saw this Power drawing near to her and penetrating far into the hot lands of the Pacific. The Australians no longer felt themselves alone in these parts of Melanesia, whence they had just driven out the Germans. The War, indeed, has established the ambitions of Australia. To the south-eastern part of New Guinea, which has belonged to her since 1887—the Territory of Papua—she has just added, in virtue of a mandate of the League of Nations, the former German possessions in New Guinea, together with the Bismarck Archipelago and the Solomon Islands, and has thus become one of the chief producers of copra in the South Seas.

New Zealand appears to dwell secluded in the distant South, but in reality she also turns her face toward tropical lands. She laid claim to the island of Nauru (south of the Equator, in longitude 167°) because she considered its rich phosphate deposits essential to New Zealand agriculture ; but since Australia claimed it too the mandate was granted to Great Britain, and by an agreement between the three the produce of the phosphate works was divided between the United Kingdom (42 per cent.), Australia (42 per cent.), and New Zealand (16 per cent.). New Zealand in return received satisfaction for the western islands in the shape of the Samoa Archipelago (Savaii and Upolu). These islands had been occupied by British troops since August 1914, and were allotted to New Zealand by a mandate of the League of Nations in 1919. She had long taken an interest in them, and in 1899 she offered them an expeditionary force for the restoration of order, but Lord Salisbury, making light of this ambition, gave up the claims of Britain in favour of Germany. Samoa and the Cook Islands, which were annexed in 1901, form the little tropical empire of New Zealand. Their exploitation is being developed ; the production of sugar, tropical fruits, cocoa, and particularly copra is being encouraged ; and attempts are being made to connect it with the Dominion by regular services of steamships. New Zealand, like Australia, is becoming a colonial power, and it is possible to speak of the imperialism of the Dominions.

The Race Problem. — There is one question in Australasia on which national sentiment is not agreed, and which causes many difficulties for imperial diplomacy. This is the race question. The need of keeping Australia for the white race is an article of faith with all Australians. The vastness of their country, their small numbers and low birth-rate, and the exploiting of the tropical part of their country all seemed to counsel them to appeal for yellow labourers—Malays, Japanese, and Chinese. At first they were welcomed, but these sober and laborious workers, whose competition was feared by the whites, were soon excluded. At its birth the Commonwealth passed the Immigration Restriction Act of 1912. This law did not in principle exclude the coloured races, for there was no wish to embarrass relations between the United Kingdom and Japan, but in practice it had exactly that effect, since it imposed upon immigrants a written examination in the English tongue. The same policy is pursued in New Zealand : when several hundreds of Chinese and Hindus were landed at Wellington and Auckland in 1920 the associations of demobilized soldiers made a great demonstration to demand the expulsion of the yellow men. The popular desire for a white New Zealand was proclaimed. This aversion to the yellow races unites in a single sentiment of solidarity all the white men dwelling on the Pacific coast, whether in Australasia or America. They indignantly resist any encroachment on the domain of their race, and their wrath re-echoes from shore to shore of the great ocean. Before this race consciousness, active and almost fierce, the Anglo-Japanese treaty of alliance, already broken down by the Dominions, was bound to disappear.

CHAPTER III

INDIA

LIKE the Dominions, India lives her own life, which does not always square with the life of the Empire. But the two types of colony differ profoundly. Conscious of their rights, the Dominions have never disregarded their duties. The community of memories and of civilization which attaches them to the mother country is a factor that makes for union, and there are thinking men in the Empire who consider that British unity has no more solid foundation. India, though also conscious of her rights, has not the same reasons for admitting her duties. She has nothing in common with the English but the memory of two centuries of domination. In her religions, her races, her tongues, her customs, and her ways of living she is different from Europe. She belongs to the Empire, but the union rests on force and not on free association. If India herself becomes a force, of what nature will be her relations with the Empire? Now even from contact with her masters India has come to know herself through opposing them.

I. THE UNITY OF INDIA

The diversity of India has often been exaggerated, though British diplomacy has managed to make clever use of it by setting races, religions, and castes against each other, so as to rule by creating division. As a matter of fact, there exist in India the foundations of

236

moral unity. She possesses in Hinduism a dominant religion, counting 200 millions of adherents, and entering intimately into the entire life of the natives, both material and moral. The Brahmins, by whom it is taught, associate it with a thousand trivial daily observances which draw the faithful together. When they go back to its sacred origins and ancient traditions they are speaking of their native land, and thus out of the conception of religion they cause the idea of nationalism to arise.

The English themselves have co-operated in this unification of India. Their railways have made travelling and pilgrimages popular. The trains bring crowds of people to Benares during the religious festivals. Statistics for 1913 show nearly 440 million travellers on the Indian railways,[1] and of this total the number of Europeans, even including the movements of troops and the yearly migration to the hill stations, remains very small. The Hindu community is thus stirred by broad streams of life and thought, and its mental horizon is widening. It is true that the British peace has been of use to India in warding off the dangers of internal anarchy and foreign invasion, but it has also awakened the self-consciousness of the nation. This self-consciousness is shown in a certain conception of the rights of India which creates a feeling of disaffection by setting the governed country in opposition to the ruling one. Many far-sighted Englishmen have noticed this for a long time. Thus Sir John Strachey[2] speaks of the English in India as the representatives of a belligerent civilization, who stand for peace imposed by force, while Curtis[3] remarks that it is not in the nature of things for a people that has governed so many races to be loved by its subjects, and that the essential fact is that England's

[1] Webster, 66, p. 141.
[2] Strachey, 65, pp. 368–369.   [3] Curtis, 24, p. lii.

dominant position has made her no friends. India has hitherto been living under a colonial *régime*, but she seems now, as the result of this new spirit, to be evolving in the direction of a national *régime*.

II. THE COLONIAL RÉGIME

British Exploitation.—For the nearly two centuries during which India has been under British control she has been for her masters the richest and most valuable of their colonies of exploitation. In proportion to the value of the country she has cost little to conquer, and we have seen that, in Seeley's ingenious words, she has, rather, conquered herself. This method of utilizing the Indians for the conquest of their own country has been extended by Great Britain to the whole of her Empire. India forms a reserve of troops who are excellent for warfare in hot countries. She has fought for the Empire more or less in every part of the world, having supplied soldiers for service in Burma, Afghanistan, Persia, China, Abyssinia, Egypt, the Sudan, and Natal. During the Great War she recruited over a million men, of whom more than a hundred thousand perished;[1] it may even be said that it was India who conquered Mesopotamia and vanquished Turkey.

The flood of wealth that has flowed into Great Britain since she has been exploiting the tropical world has proceeded to a large extent from India, and it was there in particular that the fortune of the merchants of London was made. Vast and populous as India is, and rich in costly produce, she represents a treasure-house of inestimable value. To her the East India Company owed that unheard-of prosperity of which Macaulay said that history knows nothing to equal it. During the twenty-three years following the Restoration

[1] *L'Asie française*, January 1919, p. 150.

the value of the annual imports from the delta of the Ganges increased from £8000 to £300,000. In the year 1676 each shareholder in the Company received a bonus equal to the value of his shares, and on the capital thus doubled he received for five years a dividend of 20 per cent. But the activities of the Company did not consist only of splendid commercial operations, for there were also, especially during the second half of the eighteenth century, extortions and robberies whose victims sometimes found eloquent defenders in England. This was the shameless exploitation which made the scandalous fortunes of the British ' nabobs.' By tribute imposed on the Indian princes, by taxes levied on the people, by the personal profits of the Company's agents, and by the export of gold, precious stones, and fine textiles, there were built up enormous ' Indian fortunes,' which came to England at the very time when the country was heading for the Industrial Revolution and had most need of capital. With this wealth the coal-mines, the blast furnaces, the iron works, and the cotton and woollen mills of Great Britain were enabled to set up their new machinery and assume industrial supremacy in the markets of the world.[1]

As the nineteenth century progressed British capital came to India for investment in increasing quantities, and helped to build up the European form of civilization that was superimposed upon the traditional modes of life of the country. The total amount has been estimated at more than 390 million pounds.[2] Public works, modern factories, tropical plantations—almost all this apparatus of the economic revolution has proceeded from British enterprise and pays dividends to British

[1] On the subject of the exploitation of India there are some interesting but tendentious works : Lajpat Rai, 46 ; Hyndman, 43 ; Digby, 27 ; Sarkar, 58.

[2] *The Statist*, January 1916.

capitalists. If India does not exploit all her wealth herself and for her own benefit, neither does she govern herself. She employs a small army of high British officials, whose salaries she pays and whose savings are sent to Great Britain every year for investment, and she pays into British coffers the interest on her public debt, the pensions of retired civil servants, and the home expenses of her administration. Not all these sums constitute a mere draining of India's wealth to Great Britain, as some Indians assert, for the colony has received services and supplies in exchange for these sacrifices—the security of the country against anarchy and invasion, imports of machinery and raw materials, and the work of engineers, scholars, and technicists. In any case, it is a good investment for British capital, as the amount that India pays in the United Kingdom to her shareholders, creditors, and officials is estimated at over £30,000,000 a year. India is thus completely and permanently a debtor country, and to this position she owes that excess of exports over imports which is a standing feature of her foreign trade. She pays her foreign debt in raw materials, and in her balance of trade there are not sufficient imports to set against these exports.[1]

Besides this standing wealth, the fruit of centuries of saving, there is also the wealth that is made every day through trade—the raw materials that India sells to Great Britain and the manufactured goods that she buys. In 1919 Great Britain imported Indian goods to the value of 108 million pounds ; the only countries which sent her more than this were the United States (543 million), Australia (111), and Canada (115). The mother country is the great market for the tea and jute of India, and she also demands great quantities

[1] The excess of exports was 6.6 millions sterling in 1851, 14 in 1900, and 14 in 1914.

of rice, oil-seeds, wheat, wool, and cotton. So, too, in 1919 Great Britain exported goods to India to the value of 71 million pounds, her only better customer being France (147). India has enriched the cotton-spinners of Lancashire : in 1919 she bought from them manufactured cotton goods to the value of 30.5 million pounds. These dealings in such enormous values and quantities are accomplished by means of a vast business organization and a fleet of merchant shipping, which are both of them for the most part British.

In her exploitation of India Great Britain, so clever in making profits, has managed also to restrict her losses. As soon as she had in India a huge market for her manufactures she did her best to destroy the native industries. Until the middle of the nineteenth century India was an exporter of hand-made articles. In her towns and larger villages there were crafts practised in former days whose products were known throughout the world. For more than a century and a half the East India Company was enriched particularly by trade in the fine textiles and embroideries of India and their sale in the markets of Europe. But the development of the cotton industry in Great Britain made Manchester cottons the rivals of those of India, and to secure a market for them heavy and practi-cally prohibitive duties were levied upon Indian textiles. Between 1814 and 1835 the number of pieces of cloth imported by Great Britain from India fell from 1,266,000 to 306,000. On the other hand, the cheapness of the British cloths opened the Indian market to them, and caused them by degrees to supplant the native cloths : Indian imports rose from 818,000 yards to 51,777,000 yards between 1814 and 1835. Native crafts came to an end, and industrial life died out more and more in many places where it had formerly flourished. A House of Commons committee of inquiry reported in

1840 that the town of Dacca, renowned for its beautiful fabrics, had only 30,000 or 40,000 inhabitants, as against 150,000 at the end of the eighteenth century.[1] India became an almost entirely agricultural country, producing raw materials and receiving manufactured goods from abroad.

After the period 1875–80, however, the modern manufacture of cotton arose in India, and Lancashire grew anxious, and manœuvred to retain the Indian market. Before that time cotton goods from outside had always paid a small import duty for the purpose of providing revenue for the Indian Treasury, but in 1877 all duties were abolished on goods of ordinary quality, which meant, in fact, on those consumed by the Indian people. Later on, in 1896, the state of the Budget necessitated the reimposition of these duties at a higher rate. A uniform tax of $3\frac{1}{2}$ per cent. was levied on all imported cottons, as well as on those manufactured in India : this was to tax the produce of the mother country lightly, while hampering the trade in that of the colony. In 1917 the duty on imported cottons was raised to $7\frac{1}{2}$ per cent., to the great dissatisfaction of Lancashire, but Indian cottons continued to pay the $3\frac{1}{2}$ per cent.[2] A decisive change, inspired alike by budgetary embarrassment and the particularist spirit that was beginning to penetrate Indian legislation, was made in this system in 1921, when the import duty on British cottons was raised from $7\frac{1}{2}$ per cent. to 11 per cent., seriously aggravating the situation of the Lancashire merchants,[3] who seemed now to have nothing to count on in the economic contest except the superiority of their workmanship. Until a very recent period, at all events, India was treated, in the interests of British manu-

---

[1] Fisher, 35, pp. 35 ff.
[2] Lajpat Rai, 46 ; Mondaini, 54, vol. ii, pp. 144 ff.
[3] *The Times*, January 31, 1922.

facturers, in such a way that she could easily purchase British fabrics, but could sell her own only with difficulty. India, as a colony of exploitation, formed an essential part of the colonial system which enriched Great Britain for nearly three centuries.

Relations between Natives and Europeans.—From the Indian point of view the colonial *régime* consists not only in the economic exploitation of the country for the benefit of the English, but also in the obligation to live in contact with a foreign race with whom all assimilation appears impossible. The bare fact is that in the Indian Empire there are only 120,000 British in face of 315 millions of natives—a proportion of one European to 2520 natives. The position is forcibly described by Hyndman in the following terms : [1] " Not only is there no white race in India, not only is there no white colony, but there is no white man who purposes to remain. . . . No ruler stays there to help, to criticise or educate his successor. No white soldier founds a family. No white man who makes a fortune builds a house or buys an estate for his descendants. The very planter, the very engine-driver, the very foreman of works, departs before he is sixty, leaving no child, no house, no trace of himself behind. No white man takes root in India, and the number even of sojourners is among those masses imperceptible." British power has therefore only a somewhat loose and superficial hold over Indian society. It has not enough Europeans at its disposal to set up direct and profound relations between itself and the natives ; contact is made indirectly through the intermediary of native agencies.

Included in India there are more than 700,000 square miles, with over seventy million inhabitants, that are withdrawn from the direct influence of Great Britain.

[1] Hyndman, 43, pp. 212–213.

These are the native states, ' India of the Princes,' in which the Indian rulers retain their functions under the control of a high British official. There are seven hundred of them, and they vary in size from the Mohammedan state of Hyderabad, with an area of 83,000 square miles and thirteen million inhabitants, or Mysore, with its 20,000 square miles and six million inhabitants, down to those that are mere groups of villages. In these lands British authority depends for the most part on the loyalty of the princes.

As for the provinces that depend directly on the Imperial Government, it would have been impossible to provide them with the army of British officials needed for the minor posts, and it was better, even in the interests of administration, to make use of the natives. Between 1820 and 1830 a provincial governor declared that the natives were in general more amenable, more patient, more hard-working, and better informed as to the state of the country and the manners and customs of the inhabitants.[1] Consequently the bulk of the officials in India are natives : there are 2,650,000 of them in the administrative services, and 1,730,000 in the police, while to these may be added the five millions employed on the railways and in the postal, telegraph, and telephone services. There remain only about ten thousand Englishmen holding the highest and best-paid posts—a meagre staff for such a huge army.

The real administrative unit of India, and the smallest one that has a European chief, is the district. Now in the whole of British India there are only 267 districts, and some of them contain over a million inhabitants. These officials, therefore, who are generally men of mark, are too far removed from the people, and cannot ensure the advantages arising from their personal presence everywhere. The people at large can only see

[1] Digby, 27, pp. 48–49.

and judge the British rule through a host of inferior agents by whom it is disguised, and who frequently cause them to hate it. The Englishman cannot get near to the people ; often he ignores them ; sometimes he despises them ; he has done nothing to bridge the distance that separates him from them. " There are villages in British India," says Dilke, " where the people have never seen a white man, and off the main roads, and outside the district towns, the sight of a European official is extremely rare. To the inhabitants of the greater portion of rural India the governor who symbolizes British rule is a cruel and corrupt Hindoo policeman." [1] These causes of misunderstanding have increased with the progress of time. In former days— the days of sailing-ships, when the voyage from England lasted months—many of the English made their homes in India and lived in contact with the natives. But the coming of the steamship made the return to England easy, and men now leave India as often as possible. Some Anglo-Indians see the danger of this : they would like to see England and India united by ties of affection arising from mutual understanding, and they wish that more men of birth and education would go and live in India so as to create an Indian mentality and Indian friendships.[2] But is fusion possible ?

At all events, although the English have tried to create a British mentality among certain Indians, it seems that their efforts have contributed rather to arouse and strengthen the national self-consciousness of the Indians. They have long considered it a crime to leave their subjects in ignorance, and have felt that they could not withhold all Western culture from them. To give the native this education was of course in the

[1] Dilke, 28, pp. 539–540.
[2] Lecture by Sir Francis Younghusband, *United Empire*, January 1921.

interests of the governing race, for in this way the lower ranks of the British service were improved. Yet there were some worthy men, like Lord Ellenborough in 1842,[1] who considered that the education of the Indians would inevitably result in the political ruin of England. But as there was no question of universal education of the masses the English did not hesitate to encourage the teaching of the natives; this teaching was confined to the upper classes, who were intended to fill posts in the administrative service of the country. British education, therefore, has no effect upon the masses, but only upon a chosen few; the people at large remain completely ignorant. These schools have provided an education for many young men of the upper classes. They have turned out a body of educated men who hold learning in honour and whose capabilities are equal to those of Europeans of the same standing, and these ' intellectuals,' owing to their knowledge of the English tongue, can appreciate the causes of British superiority and show up the weak points in their masters, intellectual culture giving rise to the spirit of criticism. It is a surprising thing that the proportion of pupils receiving secondary education is greater in India than in England, while in Bengal, whose population is equal to that of the United Kingdom, the proportion of the upper classes who attend regular courses at a university is nearly ten times as large as in England.[2] In 1921 there were more than 1500 Indian students in the United Kingdom, and more than a quarter of them were studying law. There exists in India, therefore, a class of educated men whom the English have raised to their own level and who are capable of reasoning in the European manner, and from this class has come the conception of a free India, an Indian nation developing on the lines of its own native

[1] Quoted by Fisher, 35, p. 158.
[2] *The Times*, December 17, 1921.

civilization. It is in this class, too, that feelings of pity and revolt have found voices to proclaim the sufferings of the Indian people. It is no doubt unjust to attribute to British rule the woes of the peasant— that over-population, that subdivision of the land, and that lamentable poverty which cause a chronic state of scarcity and provoke periodical famines. All these scourges are not the work of the English, but there is a common tendency among those who regard English domination as wrong to hold the English responsible for them. So the Indians are impelled by their impatience with their sufferings and their consciousness of their rights to claim for themselves the management of their own affairs, thinking that an improvement would thus be effected. What their leaders want is, in pursuance of those Western ideas which they owe to their British education, to be associated with the government of their country, so that they may themselves defend the interests of their fellow-countrymen. There is now an Indian nationalism which operates both as a political and as an economic force.

III. THE NATIONAL FUTURE

Political Nationalism.—Until very recently India had no conception of political life. The English governed her as absolute masters, successors of the Great Mogul. On several occasions since 1861, under the influence of educated Indians brought up in Western lands, certain small reforms had given the country a shadow of native representation, though without any real authority or responsibility. Natives were admitted neither to the higher positions in the public service nor to the control of British officials. This exclusion left the same feeling of bitterness among the Hindus as among the Mohammedans, and gave rise by degrees to the union of the best of the natives against British rule.

It was in 1905 that the Indian nationalist movement became powerful enough to cause Great Britain anxiety.[1] It is a remarkable thing that the spirit of revolt took possession first of those provinces which might have been regarded as the least impatient of British rule. In October 1905 the whole of the historic province of Bengal protested against the decision to divide her into two provinces despite her ancient unity. British goods were boycotted, and a demand was made for the establishment of a national Bengal university, independent of British control, in which the first place should be given to native languages and the second to English. The spirit of resistance was fomented by the nationalist papers, which exalted the memory of Cavour, Mazzini, Kossuth, and Parnell, the nationalist heroes of Europe. The Indian Government tried to close the road to new ideas by prohibiting the teaching of European history in the Indian universities. But the movement gained strength, and revolts broke out, followed by harsh repressive measures which did not discourage the patriots. Japan's victory over Russia was hailed with enthusiastic applause, and a watchful eye was kept on the conduct of Europe in lands where she ruled over native races. The wars waged by the Christian nations of the Mediterranean against the Turks were wounding to the religious feelings of the Moslems, and it is a positive fact that they won over to nationalist ideas the Moslem minority in India on which the Indian Government had always counted to oppose the Hindu majority.

[1] On this nationalist movement see Fisher, 35; Stoddard, 64; Lajpat Rai, 46; *L'Asie française*, April and September 1918, and May 1922; Mondaini, 54, vol. ii; Curtis, 25; Webster, 66; Bowman, 9, p. 53; *United Empire*, April 1921; *The Round Table*, June 1921; *The Times*, May 24 and December 17, 1921.

INDIA

The Great War brought a unique opportunity for native sentiments to be freely displayed. Congresses were held at Lucknow (December 1916) and Bombay (August to September 1918), at which Mohammedans and Hindus agreed to demand self-government under the direction, but not under the domination, of Great Britain. Self-government within the Empire, they declared, could alone satisfy the Indian people, and enable them to take their place as a free nation in the British commonwealth and thus strengthen the bonds between Great Britain and India.[1] On the other hand, there was one statesman in England who had the courage to assert that if England was not prepared to repair the old machine in accordance with modern experience she would lose the right to control the destinies of the Indian Empire.[2] We are therefore witnessing the opening stages of a new political system. A new state is preparing to take its place among the Dominions. What should it be and what will it be ?

Already—and it is a fact without precedent in the history of British domination—two representatives of India have sat on the Imperial War Cabinet in London, and these two members represented their country also at the Peace Conference at Paris, while there was a Hindu among the British delegates to the Washington Conference of November 1921. As a matter of fact, however, this would be the merest window-dressing, causing only a feeling of moral satisfaction, if nothing were changed in the structure itself. But Great Britain has resolved upon a system which ought gradually to make India the equal of the British Dominions. At the end of 1917 Mr Montagu, the Secretary of State for India, set out to study the Indian problem on the spot, in concert with the Viceroy, Lord Chelmsford,

[1] Curtis, 25, p. lii.
[2] Mr Montagu, quoted by Fisher, 35, p. 181.

and at the end of July 1918 he published a monumental report recommending the adoption of a bold programme of autonomy for India. Then in December 1919 a Bill for the reform of the Government of India passed its third reading in the House of Commons.

This reform scarcely touches the central Government, but applies mainly to the system of provincial government. The central government of India still remains in the hands of the Viceroy, under the control of the British Government, and with him are associated two chambers. One of these, the Council of State, is the supreme legislative authority, composed of members partly elected and partly nominated by the Government, the latter being in a majority, while the other, the Legislative Assembly, contains a hundred members, of whom two-thirds are elected, and to this chamber the Budget is to be submitted, as well as to the Council of State. The Viceroy, however, retains the right of veto, and if the two chambers refuse to pass a Bill which he considers necessary it may pass all the same, subject to the approval of the King in Council. Alongside of the central Government there is, therefore, a measure of national representation, though limited and without responsibility. Out of a total male population of 164 millions there are only 909,874 electors to the Legislative Assembly, or one elector to every 180 male inhabitants.

In the matter of provincial government, on the other hand, there is an effective penetration of autonomy into the administration of the nine great provinces of India. It was impossible to grant complete provincial autonomy at one stroke. The Indian electorate is yet to be created : it cannot be called into existence by a stroke of the pen ; nor can the whole of the vast interests of each province be entrusted to a body of natives who are still inexperienced. The new system, therefore, provides for a division of responsibilities between British and natives which forms what is called the system of dyarchy. A certain number of questions are withdrawn from the provincial assemblies until they have acquired a wider experience of affairs. Certain kinds of business are therefore ' reserved ' and referred to the governor of the province. But there are also ' transferred ' subjects, over which the provincial assemblies may exercise their competence and control. Such subjects are provincial taxation, rural and urban administration, public education, health, and public works of secondary rank. These departments are managed by ministers, who are to be chosen from among the elected members of the provincial legislative assembly, and must possess the confidence of that assembly. Of the members of this assembly not more than a fifth may be officials— that is to say, British. These reforms are of wide scope : by giving to 5,345,870 persons the electoral franchise for the provincial councils (one elector to every thirty male inhabitants) they are preparing the provincial life of India to try a representative system that should ultimately spread to the national life.

Unfortunately this experiment was started in a troubled atmosphere. The year 1919 had been a dark one for India. A terrible famine had decimated the population ; the Afghan War had broken out afresh on the North-west Frontier ; revolts had broken out among the Moslems ; and a veritable epidemic of outrages resulted in the passing of a rigorously repressive law—the Rowlatt Bill—whose enforcement provoked a fresh wave of violence and terror. There were bloody encounters, and at Amritsar the British troops, firing upon a gathering of nationalists, made hundreds of victims. So the Indian extremists threw over all idea of agreement with their ' oppressors ' and all attempts at reform. They acknowledged that an armed revolt would break down before the British forces, but they proclaimed the policy of non-co-operation, which meant a gigantic boycott of everything British : they advised the Hindu lawyers to leave the courts, the taxpayers not to pay their taxes, the workers to go on strike, the merchants to buy no British goods, the children to leave the schools, and the electors not to vote. The elections, as prescribed by the Reform Act, took place at the beginning of 1921, but they suffered from the boycott recommended by the extremists, only a quarter of the electors voting for the provincial councils and a fifth for the Legislative Assembly. It is evident that until the Hindus are strong enough to win their independence they will have to become accustomed to the system of moderate freedom that is offered them, and to endeavour to draw from it all the advantages that accrue for the control of their affairs and the interests of their country. For in reality this reform contains the germ of a revolution : it marks the end of a tradition of autocracy inherited by Great Britain from the Great Mogul and the beginning of a system by which Indian affairs will be conducted in conformity with the wishes of the country's own representatives. She will even be able to manage directly her relations with the other Dominions, without the intervention of London. The services are to be Indianized, business will be settled at Delhi and not at Whitehall, and decisions will be made in India, and to an increasing extent by India and for India. The position of the British officials will be profoundly altered, not so much by the letter of the new law as by the force of circumstances. Becoming less and less numerous as they are gradually replaced by natives, they will find themselves more and more isolated in a social environment that is foreign and hostile. There is one administrative headquarters, for instance, which used to have ten English officials before the reform—enough, that is to say, to form a little community ; but now it contains only two. Many of the English are already growing discouraged : the older ones are retiring before their time, while the younger ones are no longer asking for posts in India ; they are all warning their fellow-countrymen against venturing on a career in a colony where they will be made subordinate to the natives.[1] Thus the contact of the English with India will become less close as the consequences of the reform spread wider.

Complete independence or supervised autonomy, whichever be the system of the future, how can we conceive the political geography of an immense country like India ? Will she remain a political entity, one huge state, or will she split up into smaller states, corresponding more or less to the great provinces ? Will it be a centralizing force that will win the day or a series of regionalist tendencies ? All that can be said now is that in the present state of India these two influences can be seen at work, but their growth is too recent to enable us to foresee what kind of grouping will prevail.

It is indisputable that India has evolved in the direction of unity under British domination. British influence has developed individualism at the expense of those collective tendencies which were penetrating the ancient society. We can see Hindus who are sufficiently free from prejudice to abandon their hereditary profession and even their caste. The employment of the same currency and the same business language has spread over almost the whole peninsula from Simla to Cape Comorin. The Brahmin caste has gained much influence ; the administrative reforms will increase their prestige ; they will be masters of the elections ; they will direct the spirit of the people and guide their political opinion. India would thus be an immense

[1] Martin, *L'Asie française*, May 1922, pp. 206–207.

state on a theocratic basis, embracing the majority of her inhabitants under the direction of their religious chiefs.

India, however, is a land of profound diversities. She is so large that she covers regions that are physically and economically distinct, and so populous that she contains very different types of civilization. The more numerous the elements of particularism, the more possibilities are there of regional groupings. If each of the great provinces grows accustomed to managing its own affairs within its own borders and with its own autonomous institutions, shall we not see formed, round the capital cities linked up with their territories by regional railway systems, great provincial personalities aiming at independence? Some of these personalities are already becoming conscious of themselves, owing to the religious or material ties which bind their inhabitants together. Such is the Punjab, with its Moslem people and its irrigative cultivation, and such above all is Bengal. It is well known that when Lord Curzon conceived the idea of dividing Bengal into two provinces, each with its own capital, he provoked a provincial revolt. He was reproached with trying to break in two an ancient historic province.

The political geography of India is therefore in process of evolution. Will she become, like the European continent, the natural framework of several independent states? Or will she, like Russia, form a single state collecting a diversity of races, regions, and religions under one sway? Or, again, will she, like the American continent, become a republic, associating under a single flag a confederation of more or less autonomous states? Time alone will tell. But this evolution will certainly not be the same if it is accomplished under the *ægis* of Great Britain as if it is brought about by the might of India alone.

INDIA

Economic Nationalism.—Political independence leads to economic independence. By directing their political affairs themselves the emancipated peoples learn to defend their material interests. This economic nationalism is seen to arise wherever political nationalism has sprung up. When British rule was established in India it opened up to business men a vast field for commercial exploitation : capital and merchandise followed the British flag. But, taught by her rulers, India became aware of her own resources. Indians are beginning to realize that their country is a powerful machine that is working for the benefit of foreigners, and to wish to run it for themselves. It is now a common thing in the Punjab[1] for the peasant not to sell his wheat when it is harvested, so as to get a better price later on : thus in 1910 the grain remained so long in the hands of the grower that serious harm was done to the revenue of the port of Karachi and the railways of Scinde. In the Presidency of Bombay at the beginning of 1918[2] the better-educated natives advised the peasants to refuse payment of their taxes. As a matter of fact, however, owing to the shortage in the autumn harvest, the British authorities had decided to suspend the tax wherever the yield would have been less than a quarter of the normal yield, so the " Home Rule League " disputed the official estimates everywhere, and advised the villagers to declare a harvest of less than a quarter of the normal. The peasant has a clear enough conception of the difference between mine and thine, and has no wish to give up what is his except consciously. In some industrial centres the Indian workmen are acquainted with the use of strikes, and the English may well ask themselves what would become of their interests if those millions of workers knocked off work.

[1] Sarkar, 58, p. 267.
[2] *L'Asie française*, April 1918, p. 52.

" Indians themselves," says Hyndman,[1] " have only to refuse to work for Europeans, and the whole white Empire would be brought to an end within a month."

The desire to protect the Indian worker gave rise some thirty years ago in the Bombay Presidency to the *swadeshi* (' home-made ') movement.[2] Certain Indians of the upper classes were anxious to create a livelihood for the people who were dying of hunger. The problem was to give the poor in the country districts some supplementary resources in case of a bad harvest and, with that end, to revive the small domestic crafts which had been killed by large-scale industry. It was regarded as a religious duty to encourage national manufactures and to avoid articles imported from abroad. The notion made gradual headway ; in 1905 it became very popular in Bengal, where its faithful adherents were collected, and it ended in a boycott of British goods. These fighting tendencies could not last, but this movement for mutual aid and humanity was not all loss, for it popularized the notion of a national industry. During the War the Government itself fostered the *swadeshi* movement, and a *swadeshi* exhibition was organized at Bombay in 1917–18, under the auspices of the Viceroy, where were sold brushes, brooms, soap, and shoes, all made in India.

One noteworthy fact that stands out in the economic situation of India is the growth of the industrial spirit among the natives. Its roots are not yet very deep ; educated men hold aloof too much from practical careers ; the workers are completely ignorant, and, as Sarkar says, there is a divorce between brain and muscle. Yet the taste for large-scale business is awaking here and there. Native capitalists, seeing the factories in which British capital is invested, are becoming familiarized with modern business tendencies. One finds native

[1] Hyndman, 43, p. 220.   [2] Sarkar, 58, pp. 327 ff.

shareholders in tea plantations, in the flour trade, in sugar refineries, cotton mills, jute factories, and even in coal-mining. They know what power is given to them in the industrial struggle by the low wages and long hours of their workmen. The most characteristic example of this transformation is to be found in the creation of the metallurgical industry, which was entirely the work of native capital. In 1902 Mr Jamsheedji Tata, a member of the Parsee community in Bombay, and one of the founders of the cotton industry of that city, was travelling in the United States when he conceived the idea of setting up ironworks in India. He sent for engineers to study and prepare the undertaking, and though he died before the scheme could be put into practice this was accomplished by his heir, Sir Dorab Tata. After vainly seeking in England for capital he appealed to the wealthy Hindus; he met with immediate success, and thus was founded the Tata Iron and Steel Works Company,[1] an exclusively Indian undertaking. The site of the works was chosen in Orissa, near to coal-mines supplying abundance of coking coal and not far from iron-mines yielding an ore containing from 60 per cent. to 67 per cent. of iron. In 1910 the American firm responsible for the building finished its task, and it was possible for smelting to begin, and by the end of 1913 the manufacture of steel was going on. When the War broke out the works were in full swing. They supplied enough rails during the War for the construction of new railway lines in Mesopotamia, Syria, Egypt, and East Africa, and in 1919 its three blast furnaces turned out 232,000 tons of cast iron and 1600 tons of ferro-manganese. The company employs 44,500 Indians and 200 Europeans. It had to apply to the West for the higher ranks of its administrative and technical staff,

[1] On the Tata works see Fisher, 35, pp. 45–46; *The Times*, December 17, 1921; and especially Chirol, 18, pp. 248 ff.

as well as for certain specialized workers, but it draws excellent mechanicians, electricians, and foremen from among the natives: it is an Indian, an old student of Harvard, who is in charge of the coke furnaces. Most of this industrial activity is concentrated in the town of Jamsheedpur, with over 100,000 inhabitants. India has thus added now to her great cotton and jute factories a metallurgical business which seems to mark the commencement of a new branch of large-scale industry, and what gives particular value to this economic phenomenon is the fact that many of these firms working with large quantities of capital are owned by natives. These are the foundation stones of economic independence and the first signs of emancipation from European exploitation. The nationalists hold that the wealth of the country ought to be for the natives, and they are grieved to see in the hands of foreigners so many concessions of land, mines, forests, and railways, through which channels the national wealth flows out of the country. They are conscious of their material power of self-realization and expansion, a power which has grown considerably of late years. There was a time when the Indian Government almost had to beg for loans in the country, but during the two years before the War it had no difficulty in borrowing 70 million pounds. Indian capitalists are to be met with throughout the Far East, and quite recently they were buying immense landed estates in Burma. Economically India has emerged from infancy, and for certain enterprises she can find in herself sufficient strength to enable her to act alone.

India's National Interests outside India.[1]—Having

---

[1] See *United Empire*, 1921, p. 84, and 1922, p. 355; *The Round Table*, September 1920 and March 1922; *The Times*, May 24, 1921, and March 7, 1922; *L'Afrique française*, June 1922; Bowman, 9, p. 531; Wedgwood, 67, pp. 79–80.

become conscious of her national interests at home,
India is beginning to recognize and defend them abroad.
In several tropical dependencies of the Empire there
are colonies of Indians. By emigrating far from their
homeland these natives have not severed all ties with
her, and now that she is taking shape as a nation they
are turning to her when in need of aid and protection.
In British East Africa there is a colony of 42,000 Indians
—36,000 in Kenya Colony and 6000 in Uganda. Many
of them went there in 1895 to work at the building
of the railway. Since that date the influx has never
ceased, and both by its numbers and its functions the
Indian community holds an important place in the
structure of the colony. A great part of the trade of
the country is in their hands or under their influence,
and it is they who are employed as labourers, artisans,
and Government officials. The majority, however, are
small shopkeepers who monopolize the retail trade,
while some of them are the proprietors of huge business
houses at Mombasa and Nairobi. Nearly all the business
of these latter is with India, which supplies 70 per cent.
of the unbleached cotton cloth imported into Kenya
Colony, Uganda, and Tanganyika. From the economic
standpoint, being satisfied with a very low standard of
life, they make all European competition impossible,
and no British firm has any chance of success unless it
employs Indian agents or obtains from the Indian firms
their tacit authorization to carry on business. Strong
in this material situation, they complain of the political and social situation in which they are left by the
Europeans, and they are formulating their demands.
As by a settlement of 1909 the higher lands of the colony,
whose admirable climate seems to promise a great
future for European settlers, are reserved for white
colonization alone, the Indians are claiming the right
to buy these lands. They also want the right to hold

the same posts as Europeans in the administration and the Army ; to enter the country in unlimited numbers, with no restriction upon immigration ; to dwell where they please, instead of being relegated on sanitary grounds to certain districts ; and, finally, the right to the same representation in the legislative and municipal councils as the Europeans. At the Indian Congress held at Mombasa in December 1920 there was even some talk of declaring Kenya Colony Indian. The national feeling is rising ; there is community of thought and action with the agitators in India, and delegates are sent to carry the complaints of the Indians in Africa to the Legislative Assembly at Delhi. The same burning questions are exercising the 150,000 Indians in the Transvaal and Natal, as well as the 60,000 who labour in the plantations in the Fiji Islands, and the smaller groups who live elsewhere. All these brothers by birth, scattered throughout the world, are now finding strong support in national India, and wherever they come in contact with the whites demands are made for race equality. In 1922 Mr Sastri, a prominent Indian native, was sent to study the question of the status of Indian subjects in Australia, New Zealand, and Canada. This mission was the result of a decision of the Imperial Conference of 1921, agreed to by all the members except South Africa, by which the inequalities of treatment from which the Indians suffer in other parts of the Empire cannot be admitted, as being contrary to the situation of India as an equal member of the Empire : differences of race are no longer to afford any ground for inequality of treatment. Any attack upon these principles wounds the national feeling of the Indians severely. Thus the return to India of a number of Sikhs who had been refused permission to land in British Columbia provoked serious disorders in the Punjab in 1916.

INDIA

What we are witnessing in India is the slow toil of preparing national solidarity in the face of European domination. It would be unwise not to admit that the future of British rule is compromised by the very principle on which this movement is founded. From the political point of view the guidance of the country will pass gradually from the hands of the English to those of the Indians, while from the economic standpoint the Indians, by managing their own affairs, will work in the interests of their own country instead of in those of Great Britain.

CHAPTER IV

NATIVE NATIONALISM AND NATIONALITY

LET us now leave the great dominions and India, whose position in the Empire we have been analysing, and also those colonies, like Aden, Gibraltar, Labuan, Hong Kong, Singapore, the Falkland Islands, and St Helena, which are first and foremost trading-stations or strategic posts. What remains then of the Empire? Simply the tropical colonies, inhabited by coloured races, in which the number of white men is insignificant compared with that of the natives. Their methods of administration are not all modelled on the same lines. They contain authority and autonomy in cleverly devised proportions, with the latter always subordinated to the former, though in principle the governed race is not ignored, especially when the proportion of whites is relatively large. But as a general rule, whatever be the variety of the machinery and contrivances of these local forms of government, all the real power proceeds from the Governor or the High Commissioner—that is to say, from the British Government or from the Crown. In other words, it is a matter of absolute power, if not without any control, yet without any autonomy or any free initiative on the part of the inhabitants of the colony.

In several of these colonies, however, as in India, a certain development of native mentality is to be noticed : some colonial peoples who have long been subjects or slaves are already conceiving the possibility of a change in their relations with their masters. A process of fermentation is in active operation here and there in the Empire, nourished either by race hatred, by religious passion, or even by outbursts of national self-consciousness. Almost everywhere a trial is pending between European and native civilizations, and occasionally even white domination is being brought in question.

I. CENTRES OF NATIVE NATIONALISM

Burma and Ceylon.[1]—Indian example and contagion have won over the adjacent lands, like Burma and Ceylon. Burma, compulsorily joined to India, is afraid of being absorbed and losing her individuality. Being profoundly Buddhist, she feels little affinity with the great land of the Brahmins, and grieves to see her trade in the hands of British, Indian, and Chinese capitalists, her lands, her forests, and her mines delivered over into the same hands, her fields invaded by swarms of Indian coolies, and her city of Rangoon almost completely Indianized. The national resistance of the Burmese started among the Buddhists in 1920, and claims the rights of small nations so often proclaimed by the Allies during the War. As soon as Burma learned of the Indian reforms the Young Men's Buddhist Association demanded for Burma a constitution and responsible government. At the same time there were violent outbreaks which showed to how great an extent the entire country was associated with the nationalist movement. The Burmese students boycotted the newly established University of Rangoon ; strikes broke out among the workers in the rice works, and in the Irawadi fleet, as well as among the officials ; an attempt was made to boycott European goods ; and there were protests against the invasion of the country by foreign capital.

[1] Wedgwood, 67, *passim* ; *The Times*, May 24, 1921 ; *L'Asie française*, February 1922.

In Ceylon it was a Buddhist revival that caused the rise of nationalism, especially since 1915. Moreover, there has grown up in the island a wealthy and educated class, the owners of numerous plantations, speaking English, and almost Westernized by their education. Why should such natives as these remain in tutelage? What they demand is a widening of the sphere of autonomy in the island, and the substitution of regional representation, which would give a majority and political influence to the Cingalese Buddhists, for representation by race groups, which splits up opinion. This would be the germ of a Cingalese nationality. Hong Kong also is demanding the improvement of her representative institutions in imitation of the Bermudas, Cyprus, and Jamaica, desiring to have the number of non-official members of her legislative council raised from six to nine, so as to give them a majority.

West Africa.[1] — The African continent has not escaped the same evolutionary process, for ideas of autonomy are penetrating the negro community. At a national congress held at Accra at the beginning of 1920 the claims of the natives of British West Africa were put forward, being voiced by a very singular class of negroes called by the English the 'Educated Natives.' These are inhabitants of the Gold Coast, Lagos, Sierra Leone, and Bathurst, who have almost completely assimilated English civilization, and have the same language, the same religion, the same laws, and the same customs as the English. They live in the towns, and are employed as officials and commercial agents, while they are also advancing into the interior of the country, along the railways, carrying British civilization and interests with them and acting as clerks and interpreters. But they have not lost their race feeling, and they uphold the cause of their brothers.

[1] *L'Afrique française*, January 1922; Baillaud, *op. cit.*, p. xvii.

They have long claimed political freedom, and they are spreading the idea throughout all West Africa. In 1920 they succeeded in collecting delegates from all parts of the country at a congress which demanded the establishment of self-government in West Africa and protested against racial inequalities. These demonstrations have called forth a measure of defence on the part of the English, namely, the grouping of all the British possessions in West Africa under the authority of a High Commissioner, the idea being to unify British rule in order to render it more effective. But an endeavour is being made to give some satisfaction to the natives by the grant of autonomy to the municipal councils of Accra, Cape Coast Castle, and Sekondi, as well as by the development of the primary schools.

South Africa.—The native problem gives no less anxiety in South Africa, as we have already seen. The blacks are there five times as numerous as the whites, and their astonishing birth-rate is continually increasing this superiority. Just at the time when the black world is becoming more formidable through weight of numbers it is losing to an increasing extent its ancient habits of obedience and servitude. The native is coming to notice that his wages do not rise like those of the white man, that he has to pay heavy taxes, that he has no political rights, and that he is treated with scorn. A feeling of solidarity is drawing him toward his race-fellows who are suffering as he is. In 1921 there was held at Bloemfontein the South Africa Native National Congress, which requested the King to exercise his right of veto over such laws of the Union Parliament as were contrary to the principle of race equality, and asked that the Bantus should be directly represented at the Constitutional Conference of 1922. These ancient communities, which used to be looked upon as fixed and immovable, are being stirred as by a ground swell.

The European can no longer ignore the fact, and it is to his interest to become acquainted with the history and progress of these races. The University of Cape Town has just set up a school of Bantu study, and Johannesburg is preparing to follow her example.

Egypt.[1]—Of all the centres of native nationalism there is none more ardent and more advanced in national activities than Egypt. The Egyptian people forms a block of thirteen million natives, speaking the same tongue, professing the same religion, homogeneous, and conscious of its individuality ever since the beginning of the nineteenth century. When the English settled in Egypt in 1882 the country, rich, populous, and well cultivated, could not be regarded as virgin ground to be tilled and made fertile. It already contained the experience and the virtues of a long period of agricultural labour, and inspired its inhabitants with that passionate love of their land which is characteristic of peasant races. As a province or vassal of the Ottoman Empire Egypt acquired during the nineteenth century a consciousness of her national individuality. Under her native prince Mehemet Ali she became a land of advanced civilization long before the English established themselves on her borders. In Mehemet's reign her population doubled and her trade increased sixfold ; public education was organized, irrigation plans were prepared, the Mahmudieh Canal was constructed, the port of Alexandria was partly laid out, and a beginning was made with the profitable cultivation of cotton and sugar. Later on, but still earlier than 1882, Cairo, Alexandria, and Port Said became modern towns ; the Ibrahimieh Canal was completed for the irrigation of Upper Egypt, as well as the Ismailieh Canal between the Nile and Suez. In view of these works and this

[1] Chirol, 19 ; Milner Report, 33 ; Stoddard, 64 ; Bowman, 9, p. 61.

progress Egypt could scarcely be regarded as a minor country, as incapable of managing herself and of producing by herself as some of the countries of Central Africa. In occupying Egypt the main object of Great Britain was to secure to herself the control of the Suez Canal and the way to India, and from the very beginning she proclaimed the temporary character of her occupation. Every time, however, that the question of the expiry of her mandate arose she found some reason to justify its continuance. The Egyptians had no control over her administration, but there were some patriots who did not despair of obtaining it one day. They thought that the time had arrived when Turkey declared war on Great Britain : they thought that Egypt, having broken the last ties that bound her to the Ottoman Empire and having taken up her stand beside England in the struggle, would obtain from her the recognition of her independence. But instead of putting an end to the system of occupation the British Government converted it into a protectorate, and thus made its own authority over Egypt more direct and immediate.

By this measure the enlightened Egyptians, from among whom the political opposition had hitherto been drawn, were roused against British rule, though the people as a whole were not troubled by it, for they were moved only when they thought their material interests threatened. At the beginning of the War, when the price of cotton fell to such disastrous depths, the British authorities did nothing to stop the fall, and the Lancashire spinners were able to buy Egyptian cotton at a low price. Later on, in 1917, when the price had risen, the British Government itself bought the entire crop of Egyptian cotton at prices much lower than those quoted in England, which meant another advantage to Lancashire. But this fall in the value of the produce of his fields touched the peasant in a tender spot, and he became seriously displeased. Another question was also exploited among the fellahs by the nationalists : they were led to fear that the British projects for barrages on the Upper Nile were a menace to the irrigation of their lands. And, finally, several other causes, touching the life of the peasant still more closely, ended by embittering and irritating him during the War, such as the recruiting of labour for Army work and transport, the requisitioning of domestic animals and grain, and the collections in aid of the funds of the Red Cross—measures which, being clumsily applied, roused anger in the hearts of the Egyptians. The landed classes then began to suspect the ties that bound their everyday life to the political system, and for the first time in many years the country districts were seen united with the towns and the peasants with the intellectuals in the same aspirations for national freedom. A period of agitation, disturbance, and even violence therefore shows the general desire of Egypt to take over herself the management of her own affairs ; the millions of fellahs, hitherto passive, are making common cause with the enlightened classes, and bringing them the brutal assistance of their savage passions. Foreign domination is on its trial ; complaints are made of the increasing number of highly paid British officials ; the English are reproached with living apart, in a closed community, withdrawn from Egyptian society ; and the national question is coming to the fore in the most acute fashion at all points of contact between Egyptians and British. The English realized, therefore, that it was inadvisable to resist a movement so deeply rooted in the hearts of the people. Egypt was declared independent in 1922, and in March of the same year she took to herself a national king, so there is now an Egyptian state, independent and sovereign, except for certain matters of imperial interest which the British Government strenuously reserves the right to settle, such as the security of imperial communications in Egypt, the defence of the country against foreign aggression, the protection of foreign interests in Egypt, and the status of the Sudan, which is to be directly dependent upon the Imperial Government. These reservations constitute a heavy mortgage on the freedom of Egypt, but none the less her independence will be a shining example for all the native nationalities that are coming to life.

II. ISLAM [1]

It appears that a certain solidarity is tending to be established between all the peoples who feel themselves strangers to European civilization, and nowhere does this solidarity appear so close as in the Moslem world. Now the relations of Great Britain with Islam constitute one of the most fundamental problems of British imperial policy. Great Britain rules over Moslem lands in India, Afghanistan, Beluchistan, Persia, Mesopotamia, Arabia, Palestine, Egypt, and the Sudan. Her sway extends over some 110 millions of Mohammedans, of whom over 60 millions live in India and over 45 millions in Africa. The roads to India pass through Moslem countries ; in Arabia they are close to the holy cities ; in Asia Minor they traverse regions where but lately the crescent flag was flying. British policy comes up against Islam everywhere, and always finds in it a latent force of resistance. As Lord Milner said in his report on Egypt, every Moslem is impatient of being subject to the laws of the Christians, and it is contrary

[1] Stoddard, 64 ; *British Empire*, 11, pp. 520 ff. ; *The Times*, May 24, 1921 ; *The Round Table*, December 1921, p. 136 ; Bowman, 9, pp. 54 ff.

to the fundamental spirit of Islam for a Moslem to b
compelled to occupy a political situation that involve
his subordination to a Christian. There is a religiou:
patriotism in the East which is an even more deeply
rooted sentiment than patriotism toward one's country
and her traditions.[1]

In India Great Britain long dwelt at peace with
Islam. It was to the interest of the Moslem community
of India to support the British rule, for it was afraid
of the fanatical tyranny of the Hindus, both for its
faith and for its civilization. The English on their
side regarded the Moslems as internal allies, and relations
were free from suspicion on both sides. In 1875 was
founded at Aligarh the Anglo-Oriental college that was
intended to provide a modern education for young
Mohammedans. The best of the Moslems welcomed
Western culture. In 1867 Sir Syed Ahmed Khan, one
of those who afterward combined to found the college
at Aligarh, recommended the study of European books.
They ought, he said, to imitate the Arabs of ancient
times, who were not afraid of losing their faith by
studying Pythagoras. Later on, at the time of the
Boer War, there were Moslems in India praying for
the success of the English. It was the very first time,
it has been remarked, that Moslems had prayed for the
arms of infidels. More recently still the Moslems resisted
the *swadeshi* movement, received grants for their schools,
and accepted titles and honours.

But this Moslem minority, the hope of the masters
of India, is undergoing a change : it is rallying to the
national idea. In 1916 a Moslem presided over the
Hindu national congress ; in 1918 the Indian Moslem
League protested against the occupation of Jerusalem
by the British Army, and demanded that the city
should be restored to a Moslem power ; in 1921, at a

[1] Milner Report, 33, p. 68.

congress of the same league at Ahmedabad, the president talked of setting up an Indian republic under the name of the United States of India. There is a certain amount of ferment everywhere : it has broken out into revolt in the Punjab, in the north-west, and in the south-west, while in 1921 some Moslem fanatics on the Malabar coast—the Moplahs—over-excited by the news from the West and the misfortunes of the caliphate, rose in rebellion, massacred Europeans and natives alike, and converted some of the Hindus by force. In India, as in the rest of the Moslem world, it is felt that the spirit of Islam is standing up against Christian domination.

After long years of impotence and discouragement we are witnessing a kind of Islamic renascence. Islam is finding once more its propagandist strength, its faith in its future, its hold over the faithful, and its consciousness of its own individuality. Never before have the pilgrimages to Mecca assembled such crowds ; they draw over a hundred thousand believers every year ; and every year at the tomb of the Prophet there is held a kind of pan-Islamic congress that discusses the interests of the faith and its propaganda. Under the influence of confraternities or brotherhoods the propagation of the faith is being extended, and the missionaries of Islam are gradually converting the negroes of Africa. A few years ago the British authorities noticed that Islam was invading Nyassaland, and on making inquiries they learned that the movement had started from Zanzibar. Ten years later almost every village in the south of Nyassaland had its preacher and its mosque in a hut, and it seemed as if Islam would not be long in crossing the Zambezi and reaching the southern parts of Africa.[1] Across the Moslem world there is blowing a wind of unity and faith. Despite the distances, despite their varying modes of life, and

[1] Stoddard, 64, p. 37.

despite the differences in their material civilizations, all the faithful are united by a powerful bond, and their unity affects not only their spiritual life, but is impressed also upon their family and social laws. It is strengthened by modern forms of activity : thus there are over a thousand propagandist papers circulating in the Moslem world : the Cairo papers are read at Teheran, and those of Constantinople in Bombay. This Moslem solidarity is opposed to European solidarity in the minds of believers, for there is hardly a country of the Moslem faith which is not at the same time a country under European rule. Thus the religious idea paves the way, as it were, for the political idea, the defence of the faith becomes mixed up with the defence of freedom, and Islam is tending to become once again a political power.

Its political power, however, had not entirely disappeared. It still persisted at Constantinople, whose sultans had been acknowledged as caliphs by orthodox Moslems. It is true that although the institution of the caliphate was still greatly venerated, the caliphs of Stamboul no longer received as much homage as their predecessors of Mecca and Bagdad. But none the less they were looked on as the defenders of the faith : the Turkish Empire was considered a bulwark of Islam. So the Moslem world was profoundly indignant when it learned, at the beginning of the twentieth century, that the attacks of the Christian nations on the Turks would result in the destruction of the material power of the caliph. In Tripoli, in the Balkans, in Morocco—everywhere Islam retreated. With the coming of the Great War the imperialist aims of Europe in the East were still more openly disclosed. From all parts of the Moslem world arose protests against any dismemberment of the Turkish Empire. At the end of 1918 the Moslems of India requested the Allies to respect the caliphate.

1919 the Punjab broke into open revolt. It was
nritsar, the scene of a bloody act of repression, that
s chosen for the meeting-place of the Hindu national
ngress. A union was effected between Moslems and
ndus, and Islam entered the political life of India.
Egypt also, behind the desire for political independ-
ce, there appeared the hatred of the Moslem for the
ristian yoke. Among educated Egyptians the influ-
ce of the great El Azhar University is much stronger
an that of any form of European culture. The
yptians have never severed their relations with Con-
ntinople. Though long divided among themselves
ey have formed an internal union, and the whole of
ypt is now solid against British rule. By granting
r the principle of independence Great Britain has
lded as much to Islamic resistance as to the claims
the nationalists. It appears, therefore, that British
stige in the East is diminishing: it is up against
tional movements, supported by religious faith, which
preparing for the Moslem peoples a *régime* of political
erty.

S

CONCLUSION

WHETHER we regard it as a political construction, an economic edifice, or an association of nations, everything seems so vast and so coherent in the British Empire that the idea of its might and solidity is the first that impresses itself upon the mind. To think of weaknesses and cleavages we must recall the memory of those other empires whose grandeur and decay have been described to us by historians. Prophets have not been lacking, even in England, to foretell the downfall of the British Empire. Between 1850 and 1870 many thoughtful Englishmen—those who were called 'Little Englanders'—regarded its disintegration as inevitable, but since that period this discouraging talk has been refuted by the expansion, the prosperity, and the worldwide sway of the Empire. A French publicist [1] wrote in 1895 that a conflict between England and a foreign country would be enough to bring about the downfall of her empire, yet never did the Empire seem more united and close-knit than during the Great War, and to see the colonies giving their men and their money gave the impression that they were defending their motherland in time of danger.

It is useless to try to read the future. But after having in this book analysed the conditions of existence of the Empire it is permissible to deduce from the facts those influences which may tend to restrict its power or disturb its life. In the conception of the Empire there appear to be three leading notions that are

[1] Festy, *Annales des sciences politiques*, 1895, p. 345.

inevitable, because they are derived both from it
geographical distribution and from its human composi
tion. These are the notion of distance, the notion o
heterogeneity, and the notion of ubiquity. It is owin
to distance that the human communities of which :
is composed, being widely separated from each othe
are lacking in territorial continuity, and tend to dwe
in isolation. The Empire thus contains an interna
disintegrating force. On account of its heterogeneit
the Empire embraces peoples so diverse in civilizatio
that any fusion between them seems impossible. The
differences would appear to be incapable of resolutio
between peoples of the temperate zone and those
the tropics. If it is true that these differences do n
imply the fundamental inferiority of the dominate
peoples, yet it is inevitable that these peoples, raisir
themselves gradually to the level of the European
should claim their right to unfettered developmen
Lastly, owing to its ubiquity the Empire is in dire
touch, as it were, with all the states, all the religion
and all the races of the world. It rubs shoulders wi
other human communities having neither the san
interests nor the same civilization. Everywhere it is
opposition to something or other, and the more it exten
the larger becomes the surface that is open to fricti
and collision.

The Empire has two weapons against distance a
geographical isolation : the freedom of the seas, whi
maintains material intercourse, and the freedom of t
peoples, which maintains moral union. Will this ki
of union be adequate to support the edifice ? Will
come to a confederation of all the members of the Emp
—that is to say, to a union arranged by treaty or
contract, and based upon equality all round ? Sh
we see a time when a colonial will be Prime Minist
of the British Empire ? And in a confederation in whi

oloured men would be five or six times as numerous
s the whites, how would the members of the imperial
'arliament be elected ? On the other hand, will con-
titutional union be impossible ? Will it be necessary
o give up the idea of an imperial state ? Will each
Dominion grow daily more and more united with the
art of the world in which it is geographically situated ?
Vill it develop toward complete independence ? It
aay be asserted that this independence will not be
ealized so long as the Dominions have to fear for their
xternal security : apart from other reasons, their
oyalty to the Empire is imposed upon them by the
eeds of their defence, for the Empire is the British
eet. One of the causes of the emancipation of the
United States would seem to have been that they no
onger had to fear French aggression and that their
ifant freedom was not at that time at the mercy of
ie foreigner. To-day the case of Australia is just as
gnificant : thinly peopled, and having a long coast-
ne, she could not protect herself alone, and when she
ecided to help the mother country during the War
ie knew that such a course was to her own interest,
o that she might herself be helped by Great Britain
iould the occasion arise. It is to her interest to belong
o the great military system based upon Colombo and
ingapore, so as always to maintain her maritime com-
unications.

Against heterogeneity there is no remedy to be looked
or in a fusion of races, or even in assimilation. The
hole of past history, confirmed every day by experience,
iows us the impossibility of this. Of all the colonial
owers Great Britain is the one that rules over the
rgest number of people in the tropics : India alone
orms a gigantic block of over 300 millions of natives.
i the future something other than clever diplomacy
id a strong military force will undoubtedly be neces-

sary to keep India. Only a policy of freedom and
equality, in gradually increasing proportions, will suc
ceed in prolonging that paradoxical association betwee
Great Britain and India, between the tiny island an
the vast continent. But will such a policy alway
suffice ?

Against ubiquity Great Britain can take action onl
by keeping up her strength. When she conquered he
empire she thought of little else than developing he
trade. But to protect that trade she had to exten
her conquests, and she found herself mixed up with th
outer world wherever there was an opening for trad
among Moslems, among the yellow races, and amon
the blacks. Behold her, then, right along the roa
to India, faced by such ticklish frontiers as those of th
Afghans, the Persians, the Kurds, the Arabs, and th
Turks. Behold her, too, in the Far East, faced b
the imperialism of Japan and the nationalism of Chin
and not long ago by the imperialism of Russia as wel
Behold her, lastly, in the American hemisphere, i
contact with the United States, not only in Nort
America, but also in the West Indies and in Sout
America. With her capital and her merchandise sh
is to be met with everywhere. But in the long ru
she is losing ground before other nations who suppo
their own financiers and traders. On all sides there a
indications of coming conflicts over frontiers and oth
matters which will impose serious obligations upon th
Empire. To solve this imperial problem will be a heav
task. It will be solved if the Empire remains stro
on the seas, but it is no longer keeping its old marg
of superiority, and has had to yield points to the Unit
States. It appears, therefore, that the security of t
British Empire depends upon a good understandi
between the two great Anglo-Saxon nations, to who
naval supremacy belongs, since for the present, accordi

CONCLUSION

o the Washington agreements, they possess ten units
f naval power as against the six or seven assigned
o the rest of the world. To this condition, which
belongs to the international order of things, there is to
be added another, of an internal or inter-imperial order
—namely, that to be strong the Empire must retain
ts cohesion : if any important part were to detach itself
from the whole against the will of the others the breach
might be fatal. To keep its cohesion, therefore, the
Empire must be strong ; and by that doctrine British
policy is always inspired, even in its proposals for general
disarmament.

APPENDIX

THE BRITISH EMPIRE

—	Area in Sq. Miles	Population	Chief Exports
EUROPE			
United Kingdom .	121,400	47,230,000	
Gibraltar . .	2	16,000	
Malta . .	120	225,000	
Total	121,522	47,471,000	
ASIA			
India . . .	1,802,000	315,156,000	Jute, cotton, rice, hides, tea, cotton goods, oil seeds, wheat, wool
Cyprus . .	3,600	311,000	Carobs, potatoes, wheat, wine, raisins, cattle, barley, tobacco
Aden, Perim, Socotra . .	10,400	60,000	Coffee, gum, hides
Ceylon . .	25,000	4,686,000	Tea, rubber, copra, coconut-oil
Straits Settlements	1,600	846,000	Tin, rubber, spices
Federated Malay States . .	50,000	1,280,000	Rubber, tin
Other Malay States		930,000	Rubber, tin
Borneo . .	77,086	840,000	Rubber, tobacco, timber
Hong Kong .	400	561,000	
Wei-hai-wei .	285	150,000	Ground-nuts, cotton, sugar
Total	1,970,371	324,820,000	
AFRICA			
Ascension . .	34	250	
St Helena . .	47	3,650	
Nigeria . .	330,000	16,750,000	Almonds, palm-oil, tin, ground-nuts

THE BRITISH EMPIRE—*continued*

—	Area in Sq. Miles	Population	Chief Exports
AFRICA—*continued*			
Gold Coast . .	80,000	1,500,000	Cocoa, gold and gold dust, cola-nuts
Sierra Leone .	32,000	1,404,000	Almonds, palm-oil, cola-nuts
Gambia . .	4,000	208,000	Ground-nuts
Mauritius . .	800	385,000	Sugar
Seychelles . .	156	25,000	Coconuts
Somaliland . .	68,000	300,000	Hides, gum
Kenya Colony .	250,000	2,807,000	Cotton, coffee
Uganda . .	110,000	3,318,000	Cotton, coffee
Zanzibar . .	1,019	200,000	Cloves, copra
Nyassaland . .	40,000	1,218,000	Tobacco, cotton
Union of South Africa . .	473,000	6,000,000	Gold, wool, diamonds, hides, mohair, maize, coal
Rhodesia . .	440,000	1,699,000	Gold, copper, seeds
Swaziland . .	6,712	100,000	Tin
Basutoland . .	11,000	406,000	Cattle, wool
Bechuanaland .	275,000	125,000	Cattle
Egypt . . .	350,000	12,751,000	Cotton
Sudan . . .	1,000,000	3,400,000	Gum, seeds, cattle
Total	3,471,768	52,599,900	
AMERICA			
Canada . .	3,745,000	8,360,000	Wheat, flour, timber paper pulp, bacon cattle, cheese
Newfoundland .	163,000	259,000	Fish
Honduras . .	8,500	42,000	Timber, gum
Guiana . .	90,000	311,000	Sugar
Bermuda . .	20	22,000	Vegetables
Jamaica . .	4,200	891,000	Sugar, coffee, bananas, timber
Turk's and Caicos Is. . . .	224	5,600	
Cayman Is. . .	89	5,400	
Barbados . .	170	192,000	Sugar
Windward Is. .	500	180,000	Cocoa, sugar, cotton
Leeward Is. . .	700	128,000	Sugar
Trinidad and Tobago . .	2,000	381,000	Cocoa, sugar, oil
Falkland Is. and South Georgia .	7,500	3,250	Wool, whale product
Total	4,021,903	10,780,250	

APPENDIX

THE BRITISH EMPIRE—*continued*

—	Area in Sq. Miles	Population	Chief Exports
AUSTRALASIA			
Australia . .	2,974,000	5,141,000	Wool, wheat, flour, hides, meat
British New Guinea	90,000	200,000	Copra, rubber
New Zealand .	105,000	1,200,000	Wool, butter, cheese, meat, hides
Fiji Is. . .	7,700	163,000	Sugar, copra
Tonga, Solomon Is., etc. . . .	11,460	205,000	Copra
Total	3,188,160	6,909,000	
FORMER GERMAN COLONIES			
Tanganyika . .	380,000	7,660,000	Sisal, cotton
South-west Africa	320,000	150,000	Diamonds
Togoland . .	33,700	1,032,000	Almonds, palm-oil
Cameroon . .	32,800	500,000(?)	Almonds, palm-oil, rubber, cocoa
New Guinea .	70,000	500,000(?)	Copra
Bismarck Archipelago . .	15,800	190,000	Copra
Samoa . . .	1,260	41,000	
Total	853,560	10,073,000	

BIBLIOGRAPHY

THE bibliography of the British Empire is enormous, and all that we can hope to do here is to indicate the most important works that we have consulted. Some of them, moreover, also contain bibliographies.

In the footnote references to our bibliography we have referred to the works by the name of the author and the number on the following list.

1. ANSON, Sir W. R.: *Law and Custom of the Constitution* (Oxford University Press, 1907–8, 2 vols., 8vo, 430 and 688 pp.).

2. ASHLEY, Sir W. J., edited by: *British Dominions: their Present Commercial and Industrial Conditions* (Longmans, 1911, 8vo, xxviii+276 pp.).

3. ASHLEY, Sir W. J.: *The Tariff Problem* (King, 1911, 8vo, 269 pp.).

4. ASQUITH, H. H.: *Trade and the Empire* (Methuen, 1903, 8vo, 96 pp.).

5. AVALLE, E.: *Notices sur les colonies anglaises* (Paris, Berger-Levrault, 1883, 8vo, viii+696 pp.).

6. BALTZER, F.: *Die Kolonialbahnen* (Berlin, 1916, 8vo, 462 pp.).

7. BÉRARD, VICTOR: *L'Angleterre et l'impérialisme* (Paris, Colin, 1901, 8vo, 381 pp.).

8. BESANT, Sir W.: *The Rise of the Empire* (H. Marshall, 1897, 8vo, xiv+125 pp.).

9. BOWMAN, ISAIAH: *The New World* (London, Harrap; Yonkers-on-Hudson, World Book Co.; 1921, 8vo, viii+632 pp.).

10. BRIGHT, Sir C.: *Imperial Telegraphic Communication* (King, 1911, 8vo, xxiv+212 pp.).

11. "The British Empire Series," vol. v, *General* (London, Kegan Paul; New York, Funk and Wagnalls; 1902, 8vo, xx+682 pp.).

12. "The Oxford Survey of the British Empire," vol. v, *General Survey* (Oxford University Press, 1914, 8vo, viii+386 pp.).

13. BRUCE, Sir C.: *The True Temper of Empire* (Macmillan, 1912, 8vo, vi+211 pp.).

14. BRUCE, Sir C.: *The Broad Stone of Empire: Problems of Crown Colony Administration* (Macmillan, 1910, 2 vols., 8vo, xxxiv+512 and viii+556 pp.).

15. CALDECOTT, A.: *English Colonization and Empire* (Murray, 1897, 8vo, viii+277 pp.).

16. CARTON DE WIART, E.: *Les grandes compagnies coloniales anglaises du XIXe siècle* (Paris, Perrin, 1899, 8vo, xix+280 pp. (bibliography)).

17. CHAILLEY, J.: *L'Inde britannique: société indigène; politique indigène; les idées directrices* (Paris, Colin, 1910, 8vo, xvi+513 pp.).

18. CHIROL, Sir VALENTINE: *India, Old and New* (Macmillan, 1921, 8vo, x+319 pp.).

19. CHIROL, Sir VALENTINE: *The Egyptian Problem* (Macmillan, 1920, 8vo, xii+331 pp.).

20. COLOMB, J.: "Britannic Confederation," in *Scottish Geographical Magazine*, May 1891, pp. 233–47.

21. *Report of Commission to investigate the Natural Resources and Economic Potentialities of Canada, Australia, New Zealand, South Africa, and Newfoundland and their Trade, etc.* (H.M. Stationery Office, Cd. 7210, 1914).

22. CROMER, Lord: *Modern Egypt* (Macmillan, 1908, 2 vols. 8vo, 612 and 612 pp.).

22a. CUNNINGHAM, W.: *The Growth of English Industry and Commerce* (London, Cambridge University Press; New York, Macmillan Co.; 1890 and 1892, 2 vols., 8vo, 626 and 771 pp. (bibliography)).

23. CUNNINGHAM, J. CLINTON: *Products of the Empire* (Oxford University Press, 1921, 8vo, 299 pp.).

24. CURTIS, L.: *Dyarchy* (Oxford University Press, 1920, 8vo, xlvi+606 pp.).

BIBLIOGRAPHY

5. CURTIS, L., edited by : *Commonwealth of Nations* (Macmillan, 1918, 8vo, xxiv+710 pp.).

6. DEMANGEON, A. : " Problèmes britanniques," in *Annales de géographie*, vol. xxxi, 1922, 8vo, pp. 15-36.

7. DIGBY, W. : " *Prosperous* " *British India* (T. Fisher Unwin, 1901, 8vo, xlvii+661 pp.).

8. DILKE, Sir C. W. : *Greater Britain : a Record of Travel in English-speaking Countries* (Macmillan, 1894, 8vo, x+633 pp.).

9. DRAGE, G. : *Imperial Organization of Trade* (London, Murray ; New York, Dutton ; 1911, 8vo, xviii+374 pp.).

10. DUVAL, J. : *Histoire de l'émigration européenne, asiatique et africaine au XIXe siècle* (Paris, Guillemin, 1862, 8vo, xvii+496 pp.).

11. EGERTON, H. E. : *Federations and Unions within the British Empire* (Oxford University Press, 1911, 8vo, 302 pp.).

12. EGERTON, H. E. : *The Origin and Growth of the English Colonies* (Oxford University Press, 1903, 8vo, 223 pp. (bibliography)).

13. Report of the Special Mission to Egypt (Milner Report), (H.M. Stationery Office, 1921, 8vo, 27 pp.).

14. *The Empire and the Century : a Series of Essays on Imperial Problems* (Murray, 1905, 8vo, 895 pp.).

15. FISHER, F. B. : *India's Silent Revolutions* (Macmillan, 1920, 8vo, 192 pp.).

16. FLETCHER, C. B. : *The New Pacific : British Policy and German Aims* (Macmillan, 1917, 8vo, xxxiii+325 pp.).

17. FLETCHER, C. B. : *The Problems of the Pacific* (London, Heinemann ; New York, Holt ; 1919, 8vo, xxix+254 pp.).

18. FROUDE, J. A. : *Oceana, or England and her Colonies* (London, Longmans ; New York, Scribner ; 1886, 8vo, xi+396 pp.).

19. GILCHRIST, R. N. : *Indian Nationality* (Longmans, 1920, 8vo, 246 pp.).

20. GRICE, J. W. : *The Resources of the Empire* (Allen and Unwin, 1917, 8vo, 64 pp.).

THE BRITISH EMPIRE

41. HALL, H. D.: *The British Commonwealth of Nation* (Methuen, 1920, 8vo, xviii+393 pp. (bibliography)).

42. HIGHAM, C. S. S.: *History of the British Empir* (Longmans, 1921, 8vo, x+276 pp. (bibliography)).

43. HYNDMAN, H. M.: *The Awakening of Asia* (London, Cassell New York, Boni and Liveright; 1919, 8vo, viii+291 pp.)

44. JOHNSON, S. C.: *A History of Emigration from the Unite Kingdom to North America, 1763–1912* (School o Economics Thesis, University of London, 1913, 8vo xvi+387 pp.).

45. KEITH, A. B.: *War Government of the British Dominion* (Oxford University Press, 1921, 8vo, xvi+354 pp (bibliography)).

46. LAJPAT RAI: *England's Debt to India: a Historical Nar ration of Britain's Fiscal Policy in India* (New York B. W. Huebsch, 1917, 8vo, xxx+364 pp.).

47. LEROY-BEAULIEU, PIERRE: *Les nouvelles sociétés anglo saxonnes* (Paris, Colin, 1901, 8vo, xx+487 pp.).

47a. LEROY-BEAULIEU, PIERRE: *De la colonisation chez le peuples modernes* (Paris, Colin, 1902, 2 vols., 12mo).

48. LUCAS, Sir C.: " The Place-names of the Empire," in *Scot tish Geographical Magazine,* December 1917, pp. 529–40

49. LUCAS, Sir C.: *The British Empire* (Macmillan, 1918 8vo, 250 pp.).

50. LUCAS, Sir C.: *Introduction to a Historical Geography o the British Colonies* (Oxford University Press, 1887 12mo, xii+142 pp.).

51. LUCAS, Sir C.: *Historical Geography of the British Colonie* (Oxford University Press, 12 vols., 8vo, 1886–1916).

52. LUGARD, Sir F. D.: *The Dual Mandate in British Tropica Africa* (Blackwood, 1922, 8vo, xxi+643 pp.).

53. LYALL, Sir A.: *The Rise and Expansion of the British Dominion in India* (Murray, 1898, 12mo, xvi+288 pp.)

54. MONDAINI, G.: *La colonisation anglaise,* translated int French by G. Hervo (Paris, Bossard, 1920, 2 vols., 8vo 500 and 458 pp. (bibliography)).

55. POLLARD, A. F.: *The British Empire: its Past, it Present, and its Future* (published by the League o Empire, 1909, 8vo, xxxii+864 pp.).

288

BIBLIOGRAPHY

6. PULSFORD, E.: *Commerce and Empire, 1914 and After* (King, 1917, 8vo, x+248 pp.).

7. SARGENT, A. J.: *Seaways of the Empire* (Black, 1918, 8vo, xii+171 pp.).

8. SARKAR, J.: *Economics of British India* (Longmans, 1917, 8vo, viii+376 pp.).

9. SCOTT, E.: *A Short History of Australia* (Oxford University Press, 1916, 8vo, xx+363 pp.).

0. SEELEY, Sir J. R.: *The Growth of British Policy* (London, Cambridge University Press; New York, Macmillan Co.; 1895, 2 vols., 8vo, xxiv+436 and 403 pp.).

1. SIEGFRIED, A.: *Le Canada: les deux races* (Paris, Colin, 1906, 12mo, 415 pp.).

2. SIEGFRIED, A.: *La démocratie en Nouvelle-Zélande* (Paris, Colin, 1904, 8vo, 360 pp.).

3. SMITH, C. A. M.: *The British in China and Far Eastern Trade* (London, Constable; New York, Dutton; 1920, 8vo, vii+295 pp.).

4. STODDARD, LOTHROP: *The New World of Islam* (London, Chapman and Hall; New York, Scribner; 1921, 8vo, vii+306 pp.).

5. STRACHEY, Sir JOHN: *India* (London, Kegan Paul; New York, Scribner; 1888, 8vo, 399 pp.).

6. WEBSTER, R. G.: *The Awakening of an Empire* (Murray, 1917, 8vo, xxvi+326 pp.).

7. WEDGWOOD, J. C.: *The Future of the Indo-British Commonwealth* (Theosophical Publishing House (Asian Library), 1921, 8vo, xvii+251 pp.).

8. WILLIAMSON, J. A.: *A Short History of British Expansion* (Macmillan, 1922, 8vo, xxv+647 pp.).

9. ZIMMERMANN, A.: *Die Kolonialpolitik Grossbritanniens* (Berlin, Mittler, 8vo): vol. i, *Von den Anfängen bis zum Abfall der Vereinigten Staaten* (1898, xv+479 pp.), vol. ii, *Vom Abfall der Vereinigten Staaten zur Gegenwart* (1899, xiv+407 pp.) (bibliography).

0. ZIMMERMANN, MAURICE: "La colonisation européenne dans le monde," in *Revue de géographie*, vol. ii, 1908, 8vo, pp. 629–89.

T

THE BRITISH EMPIRE

There are certain periodical publications, devoted exclu sively or especially to colonial questions, which are necessar for reference. Such are, in English, *United Empire*, th Journal of the Royal Colonial Institute, *The Round Table* a quarterly review of the politics of the British Common wealth, and the *Journal of the Royal Statistical Society*, an in French *L'Afrique française*, *L'Asie française*, *Bulleti économique de l'Indo-Chine*, and *Bulletin de statistique et d législation comparée*.

There also exist some statistical publications which ai very useful, particularly on economic questions : *Statistic Tables relating to British Self-governing Dominions, Crow Colonies, Possessions, and Protectorates* ; *Statistical Abstra for the same* ; and *Statistical Abstract for the British Empir* These are obtainable from H.M. Stationery Office or fro Messrs P. S. King and Son.

INDEX

ABEOKUTA, 109
Accra, 264, 265
Aden, 55, 95, 99, 100, 128
Advisory Medical Committee for
Tropical Africa, 120
Afghanistan, 54, 57, 58
Africa, partition of, 49; tropical,
135, 136
Africa, British East, 51, 52, 93,
135, 136, 212, 259
Africa, German East, 87
Africa, German South-west, 86, 87,
226
Africa, West, 93, 109, 117, 135, 136,
206, 218, 264, 265
Africa, South, 29, 82, 92, 138, 140,
181, 188, 260; extension of, 51,
85-88; emigration to, 70, 74, 81;
communications with, 100, 218;
railways of, 108; irrigation in,
110-111; government of, 172;
federation of, 174, 176; her
part in the Great War, 189,
191; trade of, 199 ff.; nationalism
of, 224-225; imperialism of, 226;
native problem in, 227-230, 265
African Company, 38
Ahmed Khan, Sir Syed, 270
Ahmedabad, 271
Alaska, 216
Alberta, 149
Alexandria, 99, 266
Algoa Bay, 81
Aligarh, 270
Amboyna, 45
Amritsar, 251, 273
Anglo-Persian Oil Company, 60, 61
Antigua, 42, 133
Antilles—see Indies, West
Antwerp, 22, 28
Arakan, 54
Archangel, 33
area, statistics of, 89, 90, 244;
and see Appendix
Armada, Spanish, 36

Ascension I., 96, 98
Asiatic Trading and Land Act, 229
Asiento Treaty, 27, 44
Assam, 54
Assiut barrage, 114
Aswan barrage, 114
Atlantic Ocean, centre of traffic in
medieval times, 16
Auckland, 93, 234
Australasia, 73 ff., 79 ff., 84, 85, 89,
142, 172, 174, 187, 230 ff.
Australia, 84-85, 93, 140, 163, 168,
181, 187, 230 ff., 276; emigra-
tion to, 68, 70, 71, 73-75, 78-
81; communications with, 98,
100, 218; railways of, 107;
irrigation of, 110, 111; land
system of, 142, 145 ff.; govern-
ment of, 173 ff.; her part in the
Great War, 188 ff.; trade of,
199 ff., 240
Azores, 97

BACON, LORD, 65
Baffin, William, 33
Bagdad, 34, 37, 60 ff., 99
Bahrein Is., 60
Balfour, Lord, of Burleigh, 207
Baltic Sea, 16, 19
Banjuwangi, 100
Banks, colonial, 117, 130
Bantus, 265
Barbados, 42, 66, 119, 133 ff.
Bassorah, 61, 62
Basutoland, 86
Basutos, 227
Batavia, 100
Bathurst, 264
Bechuanaland, 86
Beira, 87, 108
Bell I., 216
Beluchistan, 57, 59
Bender-Bushire, 99
Bengal, 53, 117, 246, 248, 254, 256
Bermudas, 42, 96, 98, 206, 264

INDEX

INDEX

INDEX

INDEX

THE BRITISH EMPIRE
THROUGHOUT THE WORLD
ON MERCATOR'S PROJECTION

Steamship distances are given in Nautical Miles
Principal Railways shown thus ———